Creation, Character,
and Wisdom

Creation, Character, *and* Wisdom

Rethinking the Roots of Environmental Ethics

Dave Bland
and
Sean Patrick Webb

WIPF *&* STOCK · Eugene, Oregon

CREATION, CHARACTER, AND WISDOM
Rethinking the Roots of Environmental Ethics

Wipf & Stock
An Imprint of Wipf and Stock Publishers
199 W. 8th Ave., Suite 3
Eugene, OR 97401

www.wipfandstock.com

PAPERBACK ISBN: 978-1-4982-3730-7
HARDCOVER ISBN: 978-1-4982-3732-1
EBOOK ISBN: 978-1-4982-3731-4

Manufactured in the U.S.A.

To our fathers

Contents

Acknowledgments | IX

Introduction | 1

1 Creation, Humans, and Wisdom | 10

2 Mysticism and Wonder | 35

3 Wisdom and the Character of Creation | 61

4 Creation as Character | 92

5 Creation, Justice, and Food | 119

6 Justice for All Creation | 143

Conclusion | 172

Bibliography | 181

Acknowledgments

DAVE: I WANT TO express appreciation to the administration at Harding University for allowing me a sabbatical to complete the majority of work on this project during the spring of 2015. I am also blessed to work with a faculty who is most encouraging and supportive of projects like this. I am most indebted to my father who raised a family, ran a small farm, and gave me abundant opportunities to enjoy the outdoors, all the while being totally blind. He inspired me to love and care for God's creation.

Sean Patrick: I am indebted to the Department of History at Texas Tech University which has granted me sufficient grace and latitude from my other research and teaching commitments to pursue this project. Specifically, thanks are due to Mark Stoll who initially indoctrinated me into a field in which I had no previous experience, to Patricia Pelley and Zach Brittsan whose longsuffering and encouragement in my diffuse early academic wanderings have permitted this kind of interdisciplinary endeavor, and to Carie Eugene Whittaker, Joshua Tracy, and Cari Babitzke who were early readers and merciless critics of these chapters in their infancy. My coauthor, Dave Bland, requires particular mention for taking me—very much his junior in wisdom and experience—under his wing and treating me with a collegiality and respect which I have by no means earned. Finally, I owe an inestimable debt of gratitude to Ashley Webb who for the last eleven years has played every roll asked of her: wife, coach, teacher, cheerleader, confessor, and tireless research assistant. Whatever I may accomplish must ultimately be credited to her influence.

We both want to express gratitude to Caleb Dillinger for his invaluable assistance in the editing process, which enabled us to meet our deadline and produce a better and more reader-friendly product. We would also like to thank the libraries of the Harding School of Theology and Texas Tech University for their assistance in gathering the necessary resources.

Introduction

We must rethink and refeel our nature and destiny.

—LYNN WHITE

THE HISTORY OF MODERN Christian environmentalism began in dramatic fashion in 1967 when UCLA professor Lynn White pointed the finger of blame at Christians for the entire ecological crisis. White, a self-confessed "churchman," weighed his own religion in the balance and found it wanting. He reasoned that, "by destroying pagan animism, Christianity made it possible to exploit nature in a mood of indifference to the feelings of natural objects."[1] Christianity's unprecedented focus on the human being as unique and central made possible for the first time the disinterested subjugation, exploitation, and destruction of the non-human natural world. The solution, so White declared, could only be to reject the then axiomatic view in Christianity that creation existed apart from and for humanity.

White's essay was not so much a warning shot as a broadside, and Christian thinkers responded accordingly with sometimes cogent, sometimes frantic defenses of Christianity. Many Christians agreed with White's analysis, arguing that an internal reformation in Christian thought was needed. Others assumed that he had misdiagnosed the problem. Some turned to ecumenical action as the solution. Others doubled down on their apocalyptic prediction that human intervention in the environment was irrelevant. Some married ecological activism to feminism; others put their faith in synods, conferences, and committees of ecclesiastical men to draft responses. Of course, Christian environmental thought had existed for centuries before. White himself wrote favorably of Francis of Assisi, who, though lacking an environmental crisis and thus not an environmentalist

---

1. White, "Historical Roots," 1205.

1

in the modern sense, nevertheless had a uniquely rich view of God's creation. In truth, from the moment that human industry began to degrade and denude the environment, there were prophetic Christian voices to denounce environmental degradation.[2] Still, White's article was published at a moment when the environmental crisis loomed large in the American mind. Within a few years Americans celebrated (or bemoaned) the founding of the Environmental Protection Agency and, *en masse*, participated in the first Earth Day. It could not have been more obvious to American Christians, in the pulpit and in the pew, that they could no longer afford to ignore their lack of a unified vision of the environment. At this decisive moment, White's was the article that launched a thousand rebuttals.

Christian environmentalism never coalesced around a single vision, a fact which is true now no less than in 1967. Christians today who want to step into the myriad hotly debated environmental issues—anthropogenic global warming, organic produce, renewable energy, the tragically low annual birth rates of pandas—find themselves buffeted on every side by equally ignoble impulses. On the one hand political correctness demands a certain level of eco-consciousness that is governed more by the facile fashions of our culture than by any careful consideration of environmental ethics. Reusable grocery bags, hybrid and electric cars, USDA certified organic groceries, and a host of other branded and manufactured "green" commodities mark their user off as a member of an educated, sophisticated, progressive elite who have the luxury of investing in a kind of political clout that comes with speaking and thinking just the right way about the environment. To critique these trends, even from a place of genuine environmental concern is to become an outsider.

Even as political correctness pulls Christians toward a fashionable environmentalism, economic self-interest, a kind of personal profit motive, works to create an entirely different form of environmental thinking. The average American Christian is arguably the most affluent in the world. Certainly we have come a long way from early Christianity, derided by the Romans as the religion of the poor and women. This affluence has come, unsurprisingly, with new expectations about what constitutes luxury and wealth and just how much control we deserve to have over our treasures on earth. The most basic and radical suggestion of environmentalism, hinted

---

2. In fact, most of the modern American environmentalist movement traces itself to just a handful of self-consciously Presbyterian forefathers. See Stoll, *Protestantism, Capitalism, and Nature in America.*

at even by White, that perhaps convenience, technology, and civilizational improvement do not justify unethical behaviors toward the environment, could never be heard over the din of the SUV engine of headlong American progress. That is why, so often, public debates about environmentalism devolve into shouting matches between those who think that the dunes sagebrush lizard cannot possibly stand in the way of the oil drilling that is needed to fill our cars and fund our public schools and those who think that the highest imperative is saving the dunes sagebrush lizard because they heard somewhere that extinction of lizard subspecies is bad.

In general, the level of environmental discourse among Americans, and among American Christians more specifically, leaves a lot to be desired. In our best moments though, Christians have returned to the Bible to find answers, and, in the roughly half a century since Lynn White opened the flood gates of Christian environmentalism, have devised myriad scripturally-grounded responses to the present environmental crisis. Yet new problems have arisen with the way that Christians have approached Scripture in search of answers, and it is precisely two of these problems that this book tries to address.

When new problems arise that challenge our faith, particularly in the public and dramatic fashion that environmentalism has challenged Christianity, the immediate and natural impulse has been to look for the quickest and most direct answers to the problem. Enter Genesis 1:28–29. For Lynn White, the problem began with a creation narrative that stressed human dominion over the non-human world, and so many rushed to respond either by embracing the call to subdue and rule the earth or by contesting the meaning of the Hebrew or by shifting the focus to the stewardship of Genesis 2:15. There is a certain undeniable logic to this. Nowhere in the Bible is the relationship between God and the non-human world (and humanity and the non-human world) addressed with such thoroughness and single-minded focus as in the first two chapters of Genesis. But very quickly and for the vast majority of Christians, the theology of creation and the roots of environmental ethics were textually quarantined to a few introductory pages in what is undeniably one of the fullest, richest, most diverse religious texts the world has ever seen.

Certainly scholars and laymen alike have looked to other verses, often as they appeal to distinct streams within environmental thought. Those who champion the eco-justice position—that God's demand for justice must include all of creation as the object and collaborator in seeking justice—turn to the Law and the Gospels for clear statements about commitment to the poor and disposition toward the land. Many who take an eschatological approach to the problem—recognizing that God has promised the redemption of nature as well as humanity—creatively turn to a handful of texts in the prophets, especially Isaiah, Micah, and Daniel, and to Revelation. Many looking for a New Testament corollary to the force and immediacy of Genesis 1–2 have found useful passages in Romans 1 and 8. Others turn to the rebukes of Jeremiah to see how God responds when the Israelites fail to be good stewards of the land. The levitical injunction to observe a year of jubilee appears constantly in debates.

What is missing in all of the above is the Wisdom Literature. In fact, a quick look at the Scripture index of Robert Booth Fowler's history of Protestant environmentalism reveals that Wisdom Literature is all but absent, with the exception of a few references to the so-called "Creation Psalms" artificially wrested from their context and segregated for analysis. The same is true of Calvin Beisner's history of evangelical environmentalism, which gives dozens of citations from Genesis and yet only a handful collectively from Job, Psalms, Proverbs, Ecclesiastes, and Song of Solomon.[3] The fault is not with these historians, of course. The sapiential literature of the Bible has played a muted role in Christian debates about environmental ethics.[4] And why not? A thorny collection of notoriously difficult, seemingly inconsistent texts hardly lends itself to the same ready incorporation into environmental theology that Genesis does. Fifty years of vigorous debate has shown that Christians are perfectly capable of constructing theologies of creation and then disagreeing over the many features of those theologies all without incorporating Wisdom Literature. Do we really need to complicate things even more?

We do; for a number of reasons. The first and most obvious of which is that the sages have a lot to say about God, creation, and ethics, despite the neglect by many environmental thinkers. Unlike the rest of the Old Testament that relies on the mighty acts of God in history as its theological base, the sages do not. Instead they rely on the fundamental theology of creation. Consider Job confronted with the creative masterwork of the

3. Fowler, *Greening of Protestant Thought*; Beisner, *Where Garden Meets Wilderness*.

4. Scholarship recognizes Job, Proverbs, and Ecclesiastes as making up the main core of Wisdom Literature. Some psalms are recognized as wisdom psalms. In addition, in some circles the Song of Songs is classified as a wisdom book. We will reference the Song of Songs in some portions of this book and a few of the psalms. Our main focus will be on the three core books.

Leviathan (Job 41). Consider not only the many "creation psalms" but also the equally important non-creation psalms—and see the restorative power of nature that forms the metaphorical assumption behind the familiar refrain "he makes me lie down in green pastures; he leads me beside still waters; he restores my soul" (Ps 23:2–3). Consider the instructive position of the ant, who in the Proverbs represents nature at its most imitable, a paragon of virtuous wisdom to be emulated (Prov 6:6). Then consider the words of the Teacher who looks at the same creation—the daily circuit of the sun, the blowing winds, the never-full sea—and draws a much more dour conclusion (Eccl 1:5–8). The Teacher then counters that by offering an earth-based alternative of enjoying the simple gifts of God in working, eating, and drinking (5:18–20). Consider the lover and the beloved of the Song of Solomon whose awe at each other is most readily and beautifully couched in metaphors of awe at nature. Finally, in studying the corpus of Wisdom Literature, Christians learn that creation has much to teach us about the virtues that form character. Can so rich a resource, so steeped with allusions of God as creator, creation as good, and humans as inextricably intertwined as creature, really be fruitfully excluded from the discussion of environmental ethics?

It is not enough though to simply point out that the Wisdom Literature represents an untapped resource for environmental ethics (though certainly it does). If debates about Christian environmental ethics already have a canon-within-a-canon—and each specific environmental position its own favorite handful of texts—it would complicate rather than solve the problem to make Wisdom Literature just one more canon within that canon-within-a-canon. The truth is that the human disposition toward the environment does not lend itself to the kind of easy and direct solutions that we often wish it did. The problem arises in part from the fact that the question "can Christians be environmentalists" appears at first blush to be an ethical question on the order of "can Christians be Gentiles." For the latter question, we can turn to Acts, join Peter on the roof en route to baptize Cornelius, and be bludgeoned, as he was, three times with the answer. The former question is more difficult because the relationship between God, humanity, and non-human creation extends beyond any particular ethical question. Unsurprisingly, its scope stretches out to include everything that we can know and say about God, humanity, and non-human creation. As such it demands a more holistic approach than has thus far been attempted. Susan Power Bratton rightly observed that "environmental commentators who restrict their reading to Genesis often miss the complex interweaving of the Old Testament concept of creation with other themes. . . . Since the theme of creation in the Old Testament is not independent of other themes, current Christian attitudes about creation cannot be independent of other related issues such as salvation."[5] Or, as we will see, the theology of creation is intertwined with themes of justice, righteousness, worship, sin, family, and economics.

Thus, because creation is not an isolated theme but one intricately woven into the tapestry of Scripture, it cannot be treated in isolation, either thematically or textually. A comprehensive textual approach is needed. This book, however, does not presume to undertake so monumental a task. Instead, we propose to take the first step by redirecting attention to the too often neglected creation theology of the sages. The marginalization of the Wisdom Literature from the broader environmental discussion has been nearly complete, and so what follows will be an attempt both to find those obvious texts which ought never to have been excluded from the environmental discussion and to take seriously the totality of the subject at hand by taking creation theology in the Wisdom Literature and bringing it to bear on apparently unrelated themes. The point is not to suggest the final word on Christian environmental ethics nor even, strictly speaking, to simply offer one more voice to the cacophonous chorus of Christian environmentalist perspectives. Instead, the hope is to provide the building blocks for and to promote the crafting of increasingly integrated environmental theologies until, one day, the question is no longer "can Christians be environmentalists" but "how could we have ever asked that question to begin with."

Debates over various creation-themed passages in the Bible has created problems for Christian environmental ethics in another way. As is so often the case within churches in general, the tendency of Christians in negotiating internal theological disputes is to become insular in their thinking. In a world in which ostensibly secular voices take up an increasing share of American cultural space, Christians cannot afford to neglect and ignore alternative voices. Even if Christians can convince the world that Lynn White was wrong and that the Bible is not the problem, if all we ever do is negotiate with one another over its meaning, it will be everywhere apparent that it is also not the solution. For Christian ethics to function in our present world, environmental or otherwise, they need to be able to present at times a productive complement and when necessary a coherent

5. Bratton, "Christian Ecotheology," 59, 70.

alternative to the many decidedly non-Christians ways of approaching nature that are vying for cultural currency in the public marketplace of ideas. To engage the authoritative voice of respectable outsiders is quite in keeping with the practice of the Israelite sages who called on others outside their faith community to offer fresh perspective. For example, there are the thirty sayings of the Egyptian sage Amenemope that the Israelite sages incorporate into their material in Proverbs 22:17—24:22. Israelite sages, however, did not accept the Egyptian sage's words without theological critique. Israelite sages are quite open to learning from, adapting, and critiquing the ideas of outsiders, which remains an important lead to follow.

Not unlike the various Christian varieties of environmentalism, many of which have their secular counterparts, environmental thought in America lacks cohesion on an even more basic level than Christian environmentalism—which, with remarkably few exceptions, at least accepts to some degree the authority of Scripture for Christian ethics. It is therefore difficult to imagine, in the absence of a single secular perspective on environmentalism and without the almost utopian holistic Christian perspective imagined above, that any interaction between the two could be very productive. Yet it is necessary for two reasons. First and foremost, neither the environmental crises of our times nor the measures being implemented in response to them will wait for Christians or non-Christians to get their stories straight. Waiting for a perfect solution will only let our problems get beyond solving. Second, the dialogue itself is productive. It would be wrong to assume that a Christian of sufficient piety and intelligence could be locked in a room with the Bible and emerge later with all the necessary wisdom to tackle the environmental crisis. It is not enough to recognize that justice and creation are intertwined themes in Scripture if we are unwilling to turn to the social sciences to find out what injustices are being perpetrated in our times. It is not enough to acknowledge that God's creation is supremely mutable and responsive to human behavior if we are unwilling to inquire of the physical sciences just how our present behavior may be changing the world. It is in the interaction between the world of Scripture and the world at large that we formulate both the right questions and the right answers.

What follows will attempt to do just that, within its admittedly limited scope. Based on the examination of Wisdom Literature and its role in conditioning Christian environmental ethics, disciplines outside of or on the fringes of Christian thinking will be considered for what they can offer to the formulation of Christian environmental ethics. How can history, political science, or heterodox viewpoints help Christians to focus on the right issues for our time and circumstance? At the same time, the Wisdom Literature will be used as a lens to critique these other traditions. If Christianity is to offer complements and alternatives to other contemporary ethical systems, it must stake out a distinctive ground from which to be a prophetic presence to the world. The wisdom of the sages is by no means the only ground on which Christians can stand, but their particular ethical focus offers, in some ways, a clearer and more direct voice than is immediately available elsewhere. We come to realize that the answer to the environmental crisis of the day does not lie necessarily or primarily in discovering new technologies but in the process of transforming the character of human beings.

The chapters that follow are organized into couplets roughly corresponding to the two purposes of the book described above: the first inviting Wisdom Literature to address some theme of environmental ethics, the second taking that theme and considering it in a broader context. Chapter 1 investigates the relationship God intends for humans to have with creation and probes whether or not this relationship explains humanity's distinct place in God's scheme of creation. Sapiential literature does cast human beings as distinct from the rest of creation, and part of that distinction is the wonder and awe that humanity has been made to feel at the created world. The following chapter takes up this theme of awe by exploring the way creation and particularly wonder at the natural world has figured into Christian mysticism historically. Wonder before God is the quintessential disposition of the Christian mystic, and historically the suprarational (i.e., nonscientific) consideration of nature has played an important role in generating that sense of wonder before God. Though mysticism is not outside the realm of Christian thought, most mystics past and present have hovered at the edges of Christian orthodoxy, giving them a unique perspective on God's creation.

The next set of chapters focuses on the theme of character. Chapter 3 notes that God created the world by wisdom according to the sages and that, as such, the world operates efficiently because it has virtuous character qualities embedded in it. By observing and submitting to the order of creation humans learn how to live wisely and responsibly. In turn humans also learn how to better care for creation. If, however, Christians are really to understand the importance of creation as a teacher of virtue, they must first overcome their tendency to view creation as merely an object in the human story. Using a mix of fairytales, biblical stories, and environmental history, the fourth chapter establishes the importance of seeing creation as having some divinely granted agency in its own right. Only if we understand that God intended creation to work for human benefit in a nonutilitarian way (i.e., apart from human use of natural resources) can we grasp the imperative of conserving creation.

Finally, chapters 5 and 6 turn to the question of justice. Whereas the prophets ground the practice of justice in the mighty acts of God, wisdom grounds justice in the theology of creation. God is creator who imbued creation with justice. Those who observe creation learn to practice social justice in the daily routine of life. Because justice is rooted in the theology of creation, environmental behaviors have implications for social justice. Not only are acts of environmental destruction expressions of injustice in their own right, but they often result in the kinds of deprivations that are the more conventional concerns of Christian social justice thought. Using observations of the environmental justice movement, chapter 6 explores the double victimization that occurs because environmental disasters produced by humans disproportionately affect the disenfranchised in society.

In what follows, the method and subject are of just as much importance as the conclusions drawn. Christian environmental ethics demands a broader engagement with Scripture and, at the same time, a broader engagement with environmental thinking beyond the confines of the church. The environmental crisis of our times is multifaceted and the Christian response cannot afford to be anything less. It demands that we engage not only every Scripture but all of Scripture and that we be prepared to give an account to an expectant world for why we stand where we stand on one of the most pressing and divisive issues of our time.

Chapter One

Creation, Humans, and Wisdom

Introduction

A VIBRANT RELATIONSHIP BETWEEN humans and creation that generates healthy interdependence is difficult to describe and even more difficult to live out. Biblical wisdom enables us to better understand and define that relationship and empowers both humans and non-humans to fulfill their God-given purpose in this world. This chapter attempts to bring clarity to that relationship.

One of the problems we face in understanding this relationship, however, is that we have lost a sense of place. We have limited stake in our physical surroundings or our interpersonal relationships. As a result we possess little understanding of who we are and what we are to become; we have lost our bearings and evolved into a society of displaced persons. In the words of Norman Wirzba, many people in the postmodern era live in "non-places," spaces where constant mobility, "impersonal shopping," and "uniform housing," among other causes, prevent us from developing deep relationships with others.[1] As a result we do not know how to act or interact with the world around us.

Many would have us accept these "non-places" as the natural habitat of the postmodern human. Some time ago Pico Iyer on TED Talks drew the conclusions that because our modern day mobility prevents it, people cannot find their sense of place in a particular physical location.[2] Instead, he suggested that home has less to do with a piece of soil than a piece of

1. Wirzba, *Food and Faith*, 40.
2. Iyer, "Where Is Home?"

soul. Home is what you carry around inside you. The speaker related how he found his home when he got away from all his technical devices and learned to sit in silence at a monastery for several days. His decision to fast from his mobile devices for an allotted period of time is certainly laudable, as is the effort to leave behind the frenetic busyness of life for a while. But finding a sense of place cannot come exclusively from within a person, at least not according to the teachings of the sages. Human beings are situated spatially in a material world; our inability to locate ourselves in it cannot be resolved by pretending like physical places do not matter.

There are, of course, errors at the opposite extreme. On Sunday morning, May 18, 1980, Mount St. Helens erupted in the state of Washington. Scientists had been closely monitoring the activity of the volcano for many months prior to that. As the activity began to increase, officials warned residents on and near the mountain to evacuate. Finally authorities issued a mandatory evacuation for everyone within a "red zone" area that had been established. One man, Harry R. Truman, who owned Spirit Lake Lodge just to the north of the mountain refused to leave. He had lived on the mountain for fifty-two years and remained defiant in his refusal saying, "I buried my wife and my daughter and my dog here; I love this country. . . . I won't go! It will take an Act of God and the Congress to move me out."[3] When the mountain erupted, Truman, along with his lodge and sixteen cats, was buried beneath 150 feet of ash, rock, and lava. Thirty years later a reporter for the *Oregonian* reminisced about Truman's stubbornness: "He could have evacuated the lodge, moving to town . . . displaced but alive. Or would he be? He was eighty-three years old and alive. Why would he want to be eighty-four and anywhere else?"[4] Truman's whole identity was tied to the land.[5]

While a sense of place cannot be derived exclusively from within a person, neither does it necessarily come from living in the same physical location for a long time. Most of us are not Harry R. Truman; we live highly transient lives with little connection to one particular place for any length of time. That, however, does not mean we cannot develop a clear understanding of who we are and how we are to live. Our transience calls us to work more intentionally at grounding ourselves in our physical surroundings

3. Cooke, "Letter from America."
4. Michael Lloyd, "Harry R. Truman, Folk Hero."
5. For a video tribute to Harry Truman, see go to: https://youtu.be/7yBS_bFZbMo.

however long we remain in a particular location. Norman Wirzba may be on the right track:

> Though my "house" is a space that can be located on a map, my "home" is a place that is defined not by numbers, streets, latitude or longitude, but by the affections and responsibilities that are always being worked out there. Houses matter. But what people crave is a home, a place of welcome, nurture, and support. Homes are precious because they hold the memories of all the life-giving relationships that have circulated through them. What we love about a house is the fact that it has become a home for us.[6]

According to the biblical sages we gain our bearings, our character, primarily from the relationships around us. These relationships are all inclusive: one's relationship with God, with other humans, and with the non-human world. The most neglected of these, especially among Christians, is the non-human world of creation. That is what this chapter explores. As Wirzba puts it, "A human life is unimaginable without particular relations to soil, microorganisms, plants, insects, animals, mothers, teachers, and companions."[7]

Our relationship with creation has seldom been a topic of discussion in the churches. Usually sermons and Bible classes make only passing references to praising God for the beautiful world in which we live. More recently, because of the present environmental crisis, at least some biblical scholars have demonstrated a keen sense of urgency in exploring the role of creation in God's divine plan. Still not a lot of the conversation has migrated into the church. We have been primarily concerned with the spiritual well-being of humans as if the well-being of one part of creation had no effect on another. Most hold to the belief that creation is a neutral non-value entity. Christianity is about what is spiritual; the physical is at best peripheral.[8] We are coming to see more clearly, however, that Christianity should be much more holistic—equal parts spiritual and physical or, better still, both and neither, a liminal faith that moves freely between the

6. Wirzba, *Food and Faith*, 214.

7. Ibid., 38.

8. There is, of course, a real risk that people will carry their understanding of the world too far in the other direction, though this is decidedly more common outside Christian circles. It is nevertheless critical to resist the scientific mindset of our day that says, for example, that reversing environmental degradation is primarily a matter of public health and survival. We must understand that the environmental crisis is a crisis not only of our physical well-being but of our spiritual well-being as well.

immaterial divinity that created and the material creation with which we are so intimately intertwined. At the very least, as Wendell Berry rightly contends, Christianity is not "earthly enough," because a valid spiritual life must have "a material result."[9] The physical influences the spiritual and the spiritual the physical. In striking the appropriate balance, the biblical sages prove to be an invaluable guide.

The Language We Use

Our culture and Christians in particular remain confused about their relationship with the created world. People describe that relationship differently. From an agricultural perspective, Whitney Sanford correctly concludes that the language and metaphors we use about food and agriculture shapes the way we interact with creation.[10] Industrial agriculture uses mechanistic language to describe the relationship. The land is passive. The farmer uses the latest technology to master the land and feed the world. If the world is a machine then it can be manipulated and its use is primarily instrumental. Our mindset becomes one of control, ownership, and profit.[11] As Berry puts it, "If we work with machines the world will appear to us as a machine, but if we work with living creatures the world will appear to us as a living creature."[12] On another occasion he describes the problem this way, "We are killing our world on the theory that it was never alive but is only an accidental concatenation of materials and mechanical processes."[13]

Not everyone buys into this mechanistic approach to the world. Others describe their relationship as one of "loving nature." Yet Sanford maintains that simply loving nature is not adequate.[14] Homeowners appeal to their love for nature to explain why they build in the middle of beautiful forests without considering the negative side effects for both the homeowner and the forest. Love, stripped of any theological content, is reduced to a very

---

9. Berry, *Gift of the Good Land*, 167.

10. Sanford, "Ethics," 284.

11. Wirzba, *Food and Faith*, 7.

12. Berry, *Way of Ignorance*, 95. Precisely this contrast between treating the world as a machine and understanding the agency of God's living creation will be taken up at greater length in ch. 4.

13. Ibid., 62.

14. Sanford, "Ethics," 286.

destructive aesthetic appreciation. This is a "love" without wisdom, the character of which can be seen in the results.

Some contemporary philosophies cling to the metaphor of Mother Earth. A number of nature religions and cultural groups adopt a perspective of creation that deifies creation, either explicitly or by implication. New Age thought, Wicca, and other novel religious movements have appropriated the language of many Native American spiritualities and some East Asian religions to elevate nature to divine status.[15] Often proponents of these worldviews have felt called to resist using any type of scientific discovery, even if it may contribute to the long-term sustainability of creation. Salvation comes only when humanity bends to the inscrutable will of the world. Science and human agency are the problem. Yet, whether we see ourselves as "masters, members, citizens," or some other metaphor, the language and stories we use to talk about creation affect the way we interact with it.[16]

The Language of Scripture

Genesis' Language

As Christians, Scripture informs our language about creation. Its language and stories are central to understanding the relationship between humans and the environment. In exploring that relationship scholars and writers have almost exclusively focused on Genesis 1 and 2. Though it is necessary to move beyond them, the initial chapters in Genesis do provide a theological foundation for insight into the nature of creation and the relationship God intended humans to have with it. The narrative centers on God and how God brought animate and inanimate, human and non-human beings into existence. It describes a God who deeply invests in, interacts with, and cares for the created world.

Much of the conversation on Genesis revolves around the meaning of "dominion" in 1:26 and 28. God's command to "let them have dominion," generates polarizing responses among contemporary readers. As N. T. Wright paints the scenario, some react with relief knowing that someone's in charge, everything will be under control. Others respond in revolt and anger believing this means oppression and abuse.[17] Norman Habel believes

15. Gushee, "Environmental Ethics," 255.

16. Ibid., 284.

17. Wright, *After You Believe*, 73.

the idea of dominion mentioned in the first account of creation promotes abuse.[18] Habel argues that the two creation accounts originate from two different traditions, with the first tradition firmly communicating that human's rule (Gen 1:26–28).[19] This vision of dominion opens the way for humans to misuse creation. Many individuals, businesses, and corporations have lived by the principle that because humans rule over creation, creation was made for humans to use in order to advance their own status and well-being. In essence, as Christopher J. Preston describes it, "capitalism made the creation of wealth through the transformation of natural resources into its own end."[20] There can be no denying that such abuses have occurred, but it should be clear that "dominion" does not mean domination. That is not the way God created the world. God created the world not by sword but by the word, not by destroying one element to create another but by the power of separation (Gen 1:6, 9–10, 14–15).[21] In turn God expects humans not to dominate but to serve and care for creation.

Genesis 2:15 speaks of humanity "serving" and "keeping" creation, an important bulwark against self-serving interpretations of "dominion." God gives humans the responsibility to protect creation from elements that pose a threat to its well-being. The word translated "to keep" can be translated "to observe." Humans are to observe the garden and learn from it just as they are to observe and keep the Torah.

Wisdom's Language

Critical though Genesis is for understanding our relationship with and responsibility toward creation, other more marginalized voices must also contribute. Wisdom Literature offers an important perspective on the relationship between humans and creation. One of the reasons is that a theology of creation is foundational to understanding the message of this genre. While it is true that the biblical writers seldom take up creation as a subject of its own, it is an integral part of the biblical infrastructure. Creation theology is woven all through Scripture in such a way that if the theme or

18. Habel, *Season of Creation*, 145–46.

19. Habel believes the second account of creation maintains that humans serve and preserve (Gen 2:15). He asserts these two traditions should not be harmonized but must remain in conflict with one another, 145–46. See also Habel, "Geophany," 25–37.

20. Preston, *Saving Creation*, 74.

21. Brown, *Seven Pillars*, 44, 70.

theology of creation were removed the whole of Scripture would collapse. This is especially true for the theology of Wisdom Literature. Whereas the Torah and the Prophets base much of their theology on all the mighty acts of God in history, wisdom's theology is fundamentally founded on creation. Job, Proverbs, and Ecclesiastes hardly mention the Exodus, or the covenant, or the crossing of the Red Sea, or the conquest of the land, or the temple. Rather Wisdom Literature returns repeatedly to God as Creator and builds its theology on this premise.

Job 38–41 and the Relationship between Humans and Creation

As a sophomore in college I took a zoology class.[22] The class went on weekly field trips throughout the state of Arkansas looking for various species of animals. Each student was required to collect and identify 150 different species of animals from microscopic hydra in ponds, to trilobite fossils, to scorpions and tarantulas, to snakes and salamanders, and lizards and frogs. During that semester I was fascinated with what I encountered. I loved chipping away at a bank of limestone rock and discovering to my delight a brachiopod (a plant fossil), or on rare occasions someone would unearth a trilobite (a fossil in the arthropod family). I recall picking up a rock on one occasion and seeing three scorpions flattened out beneath quickly scurrying off to safety. These all were exciting discoveries, and I was awestruck by some of the "critters" (the technical term we used to talk about our finds) I had heard about but had never before seen. I gained a whole new appreciation for God's animal kingdom though I was only exposed to a sliver of the 1.8 million species. Yet as amazing as this experience was, it pales in the face of the field trip on which God took Job.

In the book of Job, God provides Job with a whole new understanding of his place in the world. Having suffered severely for no apparent reason, Job demands justice from God. But justice, at least as Job imagines it, never comes. When God finally answers Job it is in two whirlwind speeches which together constitute the longest sustained reflection on creation in the Bible (Job 38–41). The first speech describes every aspect of creation in methodical order. God initially gives Job instruction in astronomy and oceanography (38:4–21). Job witnesses the expanse of creation including the ocean, sun, light, and darkness. From there God gives Job a meteorological lesson

22. The reference is to Dave Bland.

as God speaks of snow and rain and ice and clouds and stars and lightning (38:22–38). As God proceeds through the catalog of creation, it becomes apparent that no part of the earth is God-forsaken. God makes rain fall on the waste and desolate parts of the earth even though no humans dwell there (38:26–27). Not only does God send rain on the just and the unjust but also on fertile and infertile land. Then Job gets a hands-on zoology lecture being exposed to mountain goats, deer, lion, wild donkeys, raptors, and a war horse (38:39–40:2). Job reverses the Genesis account of creation. Whereas God brought the animals to Adam to be named, God brings Job to the animals to learn about their mysteriously wild habits and habitats. Ultimately the tour ends up in "Jurassic Park" with two exotic beasts, Behemoth (40:15–24) and Leviathan, to whom a whole chapter is devoted (41:1–34). Some scholars speculate that Behemoth and Leviathan may be identified with the hippopotamus (or a water buffalo) and the crocodile respectively. Whatever the case may be, these are real but far from ordinary animals. Listening to how the Creator God describes these two monsters—the epitome of what it means to be wild and beyond human control—provides insight into how humans are to relate to non-human creatures.[23]

These creatures represent creation on steroids, and there is a sense of mystery and overwhelming amazement in beholding it. So fearsome and so wondrous is the Leviathan that the Creator taunts Job with a divinely wicked humor, telling him, in essence, poke it once and see how that works out for you (Job 41:8). God proudly displays this creation, like a mother doting over her daughter's achievements. The Leviathan and Behemoth, like every creature, have a role to play in the grand scheme of creation and, at the same time, each is a "world unto itself" within creation.[24]

We learn from this tour, among other things, that God does not micromanage, does not dominate creation. This is no well-managed zoo, no peaceable kingdom with the lamb snuggling up to the wolf. Creation is a beautiful, awesome chaos, an alien and messy world that God loves and allows to run its own course. If God does not presume to dominate it, neither should humans. Unsurprisingly the environment set before Job is no place for people. Just as no adults dwell in the cartoon world of "Peanuts," no

23. Brown, *Wisdom's Wonder*, 116. For the interpretations in the paragraphs that follow we are indebted to William Brown's work on this section in Job in both *Wisdom's Wonder* and his earlier work, *Seven Wonders*.

24. Brown, *Wisdom's Wonder*, 116.

people live in God's wilderness. Job is in "no-man's land."[25] So much for the belief that "man is the measure of all things."

Many urbanites can only relate to animals as pets imagining no natural state of existence other than peace and harmony existing between animals and humans. Job's cosmic tour turns this romantic notion on its head. To claim that domesticated animals were the original state of all creatures to which we must return is not true. Humans will never be able to domesticate creation. A portion of God's kingdom will always remain a wild kingdom.[26] The wildness that resides in creation is not bad in and of itself. God sends rain on "the waste and desolate land" (Job 38:27). In addition to the wild kingdom described in Job, the psalmist speaks of the "wild goats" in the mountains and the lions roaring for their prey (Ps 104:18–21). The wilderness becomes corrupted through human sin. There is, however, an important place for wildness and wilderness in God's creation and God affirms that in his whirlwind speech to Job.[27]

Even though no other humans are seen in this account of creation, they still play a role. It is significant that Job is the only one God invites on the tour, because Job, as a human, is the only creature with the ability to see the whole of creation, possess some level of appreciation for it, and express wonder at what God creates and continues to sustain. There is one brief reference to humans when Job enters the Jurassic Park part of the tour. As God describes the first exotic beast, God says, "Look at Behemoth, which I made just as I made you" (40:15a).[28]

Here Wisdom Literature substantially expands on the perspectives offered by Genesis. The stress in the Genesis creation account is on the peculiarity of humans, who alone are made in the image of the divine. This has seemed to endorse and sustain centuries of anthropocentric dispositions towards God's non-human creation. Yet when the sages recall creation, the stress is on the commonality of all God's creatures. When humans do appear in Job's grand tour it is by virtue of their common place before God, the Creator. Of all things Job and the monster possess some similar

---

25. Brown, *Seven Pillars*, 125.

26. This of course runs counter to the belief some hold that Isaiah's vision of the peaceable kingdom (Isa 11:6–9), with the wolf and lamb living in harmony, is the ideal and exclusive vision of the future. The ideal vision for the future, however, appears to be more complex than that.

27. For further development of this see Rolston, "Loving Nature."

28. All Scripture references are taken from the *New Revised Standard Version* unless otherwise indicated.

characteristics! God made Job out of the same earth material from which Behemoth was made. Job's character is mirrored in the character of the animal world. As we will come to see humans do play an important role in God's creation, but it must be as a part of that creation.

As we take the tour with Job we learn that all creatures have a place, a specific environment in which they live regardless of how wild or dangerous they might be. Within defined boundaries God gives all these animals and beasts freedom to fulfill their purpose, utterly without regard for the wishes and designs of humans. Even with the chaos and messiness that is a part of creation, there is still a sense of order that is ultimately only comprehensible to the God who created it. Every animal has a beauty and a sense of place in God's kingdom and brings joy to the Creator even if it all remains a mystery to humans. Job moves from being dumbstruck to embracing a sense of comfort and a desire to trust the designs of the Designer God even though he still does not understand them.

For readers who take the tour with Job, certain virtues rise to the surface. As a result of disciplined attentiveness to the world God has led him through, Job develops a profound sense of humility and gratitude.[29] These qualities, as we will see in a later chapter, contribute to the way in which we care for the earth. Through disciplined attentiveness and the sense of awe and wonder it produced, Job allows creation to develop virtues in him that he has lacked (Job 42:3).

Proverbs and the Relationship between God, Humans, and Creation

The book of Proverbs also provides an important perspective on the relationship between humans and the environment. To better understand this, however, we first must observe how God interacts with both the human and non-human world. The belief is that the way God interacts with humans in many ways parallels the way the Creator interacts with the non-human world. So how does God relate to human beings?

As mentioned earlier, in the book of Proverbs the sages record no mighty acts of God in history, no spectacular interventions, no storms or floods or pillars of fire for which God takes direct responsibility. Instead the sages show God working in a much more subtle and elusive way, placing human action at the forefront of the book of Proverbs. When they behave

29. Bouma-Prediger, *For the Beauty of the Earth*, 97.

in accordance with wisdom, the sages hold a high view of what humans can accomplish.[30] Humans use their minds to plan and set goals and their skills to carry them out. Because God gives humans free will and the power to choose the path they desire to follow whether the path of wisdom or folly, the sages take a no holds barred approach to persuade youth to choose to follow the path Woman Wisdom leads (Prov 1–10). The sage believes that individuals who live responsibly can achieve much success. At the same time those who are wise know their own limits. The perspective of wisdom believes in the all-pervasive presence of God, not through miraculous interventions but in the daily routine of life, in the decisions humans make. This becomes especially clear in Proverbs 16:1–9. Here human limitations are clearly shown as God sets boundaries to the plans they make. In the realm of the mind where individuals believe they exercise the most control, God establishes a presence.

> The plans of the mind belong to mortals,
>> but the answer of the tongue is from the LORD. (v. 1)
> The human mind plans the way,
>> but the LORD directs the steps. (v. 9)

While remaining a mystery and without impeding human freedom, God works through the thought processes to bring about the divine will. Such an arena for the Lord's activity appears insignificant in the grand scheme of things, but if the search for wisdom is partially an activity of the mind, then it is in the minds of human beings that God is most directly active.

Similarly God works in subtle and elusive ways in the world of creation. As we will explore in more detail in a later chapter, God created the world by wisdom. This means that every aspect of creation is infused with God's presence and with limitations (Prov 8:27–29). As with humans, God's presence in no way impedes the freedom of the created order within the boundaries set. As seen in Job's tour with God, God gives the wild kingdom plenty of reins. Yet by the wisdom instilled in the creation of the world, God remains actively involved with the inhabitants and the habitat of the earth.

God continually works in the subtleties of the constantly changing developments taking place in creation as plants and animals adapt to their environment. God is an encouraging presence, a catalyst, creating new possibilities in the order of creation. God coaxes and shapes and nurtures

---

30. Bland, *Proverbs and the Formation of Character*.

for health and diversity like a parent coaxing a child to maturity.[31] Holmes Rolston describes the relationship succinctly: "God did not compel anything but without God opening the doors and presenting the good options the possibility of progress would have been slight."[32]

Human Interaction with Creation

God's behavior toward and interaction with the whole of creation, both human and non-human, ought to inform human interaction with creation. Since humans are created in the image of God, since we are image bearers of the Divine, then our relationship with creation should mirror God's relationship. How, then, does God's behavior inform the way humans interact with creation?

Keeping Contact with Creation

First, God is intimately acquainted with the created world. God is involved in the smallest details of its inner workings. To be aware of the world around us, to engage, to interact with, and to celebrate creation is the first order of business for humans. The lack of familiarity with creation lies behind much of the folly of some of the characters described in Proverbs. The gang, for example, in the opening poem has little, if any, relationship with creation (1:8–19). The gang lives a greedy and unscrupulous life. Its members wreak havoc wherever they go and unleash chaos on whomever they contact. The gang maintains no connection with the land or with creation. It is immersed in the life of urban blight. The gang members have no knowledge of any other life. They are totally ignorant of who they are and the consequences of what they are doing. They have completely lost their sense of place.

The gang does not know how to "consider the lilies of the field" or observe "the birds of the air." The very first proverb quoted in the book uses an example from nature to warn the son about the gang's destructive lifestyle, "For in vain is the net baited while the bird is looking on" (1:17). A bird closely watching fowlers bait a trap has enough sense to avoid it. But the gang members, who are completely blinded by their desire for instant

31. Preston, 203, 208, 214.
32. Ibid., 215.

wealth, cannot see the trap they themselves are setting. They "set an am-bush—for their own lives!" (1:18). They are more ignorant than the bird! At least the bird had enough sense to see obvious dangers and avoid them. In contrast, gang members have neither the simple wisdom embedded in creation nor the prudence to learn from this teacher. They are not even worthy of being called birdbrains. Completely out of touch with creation, they suffer from "nature deficit disorder."[33]

Consider now how the gang stands in contrast with the wise woman in the closing poem of Proverbs (31:10–31). The woman is intimately in touch with the land. Seven times the sage references her hands and the work she does with them, implying the close connection she maintains with the earth. Her hands are at work in providing food for her family. Her hands work with wool and flax and "with the fruit of her hands she plants a vineyard" (31:16). She uses the local knowledge of the land and community to farm; she learns from creation. While the gang ventured far away from the land, the woman remains close. The woman has a clear sense of her identity.

Beyond the gang and the wise woman, the book of Proverbs offers still more contrasting character studies. A similar contrast exists between Woman Folly described several times in chapters 5 through 7 (5:1–14; 6:20–35; 7:6–27) and Woman Wisdom, the quality of wisdom God uses to create the world (3:19–20; 8:22–31). Woman Folly maintains no con-nection with creation. She is housebound, only venturing away from the threshold of the door just far enough and long enough to capture her next victim using all the deceptive tricks of the trade. Like a Venus flytrap (5:8; 6:26), she is a predator with a single-minded purpose of seducing weak and vulnerable victims into her maw with the promise of sweet, forbidden nectar (7:10–15).

Woman Wisdom in contrast pervades creation and rejoices in the cre-ated world (8:30–31). Woman Folly of chapter 7 imports her "bed coverings" (7:16–17) from Egypt, "the height of ancient conspicuous consumption."[34] Using the same term and having followed the path of Woman Wisdom, the wise woman in chapter 31 weaves with her own hands her "bed coverings" (31:22). While the wise woman continues to derive her livelihood from the earth, so that her fate is intimately bound up with the fate of all creation,

33. Rolston, *New Environmental Ethics*, 48.

34. Davis, "Preserving Virtues," 196.

Woman Folly has lost connection with creation and as a result lost sight of the moral boundaries. She is a "stranger" to the world.[35]

These contrasting scenarios exist together in Proverbs. On the one hand, the characters that lack contact with creation lose perspective on life and as a result plunge themselves and, even worse, others around them into a world of despair, deceit, and destruction. On the other hand, the characters that remain close to the earth develop a broader and deeper understanding of the world and of their responsibility to creation and the human community. They model God's investment in the world. They have a sense of place.

Job's interaction with creation in his wild kingdom tour with God provides Job with a whole new sense of place in the world. Throughout the book Job berates God, accusing God of practicing gross injustices against him (9:17–24). Job's relentless harangue is almost blasphemous. Job imagines different scenarios where some mediator would finally stand up for him and convince God of Job's innocence (9:30–33; 16:18–22; 19:23–29). Finally God appears to Job and reveals to him sights and wonders of creation Job had never seen or ever before imagined. God gave Job a rigorous shock and awe therapy session.

Job is in the midst of intense suffering and pain, a man filled with rage and bitterness and God responds by taking him deep into the world of creation. It worked. Job came out a completely different person but still without knowing why he was suffering. Job's encounter with creation changed his whole worldview. Why? There is something about a serious encounter with creation that changed Job and also changes us. Such encounters do not take away the difficulties of life, the suffering, the losses, or the disappointments. Rather such encounters provide new perspective, produce power to endure, and furnish the ability to at least manage the messes of life.

The first stanza of Thomas Moore's (1779–1852) classic hymn "Come Ye Disconsolate" (1816) may describe Job's state of being:

> Come, ye disconsolate, where'er ye languish,
> Come to the mercy seat, fervently kneel.
> Here bring your wounded hearts, here tell your anguish;
> Earth has no sorrow that heaven cannot heal.[36]

---

35. The Hebrew word for Wisdom Folly can be translated "stranger" or "foreigner."
36. See http://www.hymntime.com/tch/htm/c/y/d/cydiscon.htm.

The nineteenth-century naturalist John Muir (1838–1914) changed one word in the last line of this stanza and in doing so may have very well summed up Job's encounter with creation, "Earth has no sorrow that earth cannot heal."[37]

Caring for Creation

So the first insight gained from God's relationship and interaction with creation is that God is intimately involved with and proud of what he created. Therefore we too should have intimate and consistent encounters with the natural world. The second insight gained is that even though God is intimately involved in the order, development, and sustaining of creation, God does not intrude or impose on the freedom of creation. God does not conquer, dominate, or lord over creation. Every part of creation is given the freedom to do what God made it to do. Knowing well the needs of creation, God can continually sustain and provide for it. God expects the same kind of relationship between humans and creation.

Consider for example, Proverbs 12:10, "The righteous know the needs of [literally 'the soul of'] their animals, but the mercy of the wicked is cruel." A righteous farmer not only takes care of animals, the farmer knows the "soul" of the animal. In other words, because of the farmer's attentiveness the farmer has an intuitive understanding of how the livestock feel and what are their needs. The farmer treats livestock as sentient creatures. The same phrase also occurs in Exodus 23:9, "You shall not oppress a stranger, since you yourselves know the feelings of [literally 'the soul of'] a stranger, for you also were strangers in the land of Egypt." The Israelites show compassion to sojourners because they themselves have been sojourners. When the sages characterize the righteous as those who know the soul of God's creatures, it is simple to infer that this knowledge is based on their common nature. As with Job standing before the Behemoth, the righteous look at God's creation and see themselves.

As such, the righteous care for the most defenseless of God's creation (cf. Deut 22:6–7; 25:4). The righteous are those who treat all of God's creation with respect. In contrast, a wicked farmer practices a "cruel mercy," (Prov 12:10) an odd description to say the least. In other words, even at best the kindest acts of the wicked farmer are still cruel. The wicked make it a practice to exploit creation; they use livestock solely for gain.

37. *John Muir in His Own Words*, 24.

Proverbs 14:4 speaks in a similar vein: "Where there are no oxen, the manger is clean, but abundant crops come by the strength of the ox."[38] The proverb chastises the lazy farmer who bemoans having to care for his livestock. If he had no oxen, he would not have to worry about cleaning out the cribs, but he also would have no grain. After all, it is the oxen and not the farmer who do the heavy work of plowing the fields. The comparatively easy work of providing a clean and safe space for the livestock is a small price to pay. The proverb indirectly asserts the value of other animals in the scheme of God's creation. Like the oxen that plow fields, the animals that populate God's creation contribute to the maintenance of an incomprehensible order of which humans are only a small part.

I have seen both sides of the spectrum when it comes to an awareness of the needs of livestock.[39] As a teenager, I worked for a large dairy farm adjacent to my parents' farm. Then again in college I worked at another dairy just outside a small town in Arkansas. The dairy I worked for as a teenager milked 150 Holstein cows twice a day, morning and evening. I helped in milking cows on the weekends and saw some of the full-time milkers beat them mercilessly as they came through the stalls; it was a "cruel mercy." Done ostensibly in the name of efficiency, it seemed obvious to me that the behavior was mostly born out of anger and frustration. They had little if any compassion for the animals. They did not know the traits or needs of the cows. For the milkers it was just a job, nothing more. The animals' welfare held no interest.

In contrast, as a farmer my dad knew quite well the needs of his livestock. He never laid a hand on them except when they became stubborn and needed coaxing along, and, even then, nothing would ever rise to the level of abuse. During the summer Dad always provided them with plenty of shade, food, and water. During the cold Colorado winters, he chopped ice in the canal so they would have easy access. The corrals were regularly cleaned. The livestock always had shelter and a dry place to lie down. They were provided with plenty of fresh straw for bedding. The animals were not pets; they were livestock providing the family with meat, milk and cream, eggs and some extra money from the sale of the beef from a few steers and the wool from a few sheep. Dad was well acquainted with each of the animals on the farm. He knew their needs.

---

38. English Standard Version.
39. Reflections from Dave Bland.

The farm consisted of a variety of livestock including a half-dozen steers, chickens, turkeys, pigs, usually between twenty and forty head of sheep, and a couple of Guernsey milk cows named Frisky and Jolly. Daily chores were assigned to both my brother and me. We were called on to carry water to the hogs and the beef cows. Like the lazy farmer in Proverbs, however, the chores were done with reluctance. One of my jobs was to milk at least one of the cows. Milking is hard work, much harder than the average city kid going to a farm on a school field trip realizes. You have to squat down onto a two-legged stool near the rear of the cow, fending off her nasty tail that seems constantly to be hitting you in the face. All the while, you are desperately blowing the flies off your own face while simultaneously holding onto the udder to continue the milking process. All this, however, takes a back seat to staying constantly on guard against the very real possibility of getting kicked when the cow becomes impatient with the process or when her udder is a little sore. Though I often forgot it when I was younger, patience toward the animal is an essential quality to a successful outcome. After all, the milk cow is the one doing the real work, and I was only there to see her across the finish line. (Just as "abundant crops come by the strength of the ox," abundant milk comes from the strength of the cow.) More than just patience, the milking part takes strong hands and wrists and after twenty or thirty minutes your hands can barely squeeze anymore. Finally, on occasion when the milk bucket is almost full and the cow decides to make a sudden move that ends up kicking over the bucket, there is that long dreaded walk to the house to report to Dad that there will be no milk tonight.

I often did my chores only begrudgingly, always looking for ways to cut corners, but to no avail because of the oversight and wisdom of a father who was not only concerned about the proper care of the livestock but also the training of his son. It was a lesson in learning to serve and protect creation regardless of the discomfort. A quote from Berry sums up the situation well, "To farm well requires an elaborate courtesy toward all creatures, animate and inanimate. It is sympathy that most appropriately enlarges the context of human work."[40] Long before Berry, the sages had already tapped into the same wisdom: "Know well the condition of your flocks and give attention to your herds" (Prov 27:23).

---

40. Berry, *Way of Ignorance*, 100. Berry concludes that a farmer is "a dispenser of the 'Mysteries of God,'" 99.

The Healing Power of Creation

Knowing well the needs of the non-human world and maintaining close contact with it not only enables animals to live up to their God-created potential, it brings a deep sense of satisfaction to human beings as well. Listen to another farmer who reflects on his experience as a youth growing up farming with his grandfather in Kentucky around 1947:

> When you see that you're making other things feel good, it gives you a good feeling, too.
>
> The feeling inside sort of just happens, and you can't say this did it or that did it. It's the many little things. It doesn't seem that taking sweat-soaked harnesses off tired, hot horses would be something that would make you notice. Opening a barn door for the sheep standing out in a cold rain, or throwing a few grains of corn to the chickens are small things, but these little things begin to add up in you, and you can begin to understand that you're important. You may not be real important like people who do great things that you read about in the newspaper, but you begin to feel that you're important to all the life around you. Nobody else knows or cares too much about what you do, but if you get a good feeling inside about what you do, then it doesn't matter if nobody else knows. I do think about myself a lot when I'm alone way back on the place bringing in the cows or sitting on a mowing machine all day. But when I start thinking about how our animals and crops and fields and woods and gardens sort of all fit together, then I get that good feeling inside and don't worry much about what will happen to me.[41]

This Kentucky farmer understands a critical dimension of the relationship between humans and the non-human world and that is the close contact necessary for the relationship to thrive, not just for farmers and ranchers but for people from all walks of life. When that contact is lost, the care and respect will also be lost which opens the door for misuse of land and animals, either directly by those who work with them or, as is more common today, indirectly by those of us who do nothing when we witness misuse and abuse. A basic familiarity with and an appreciation for the world of creation not only benefits farmers and ranchers, it benefits all humans. Most importantly for our purposes, keeping in touch with creation, learning to

41. Ibid., 100–101.

serve and protect it, influences the moral decisions we make and ultimately shapes character.

One does not have to live on a farm or go to a farm, however, to connect with creation. Contact with the outdoors can come in many different ways. It can come in simple everyday activities of yard work or working in vegetable or flower gardens. It can come in taking up regular outdoor activities available to all of us like bike riding, walking, spending time in a local park or on a green-way, and, for the more adventurous, activities like hiking, canoeing, kayaking, or fishing. Communities across the country are becoming more aware of the value of creating green-ways along rivers or through nearby wetland or wooded areas. The benefits go far beyond physical health to include mental, spiritual, and moral well-being.

Most importantly, such outdoor experiences generate a wonder and appreciation for God's creation. For most of us, we do not need a Leviathan to make us speechless; the rare sight of a wild rabbit in a patch of dewy grass in our otherwise concrete landscape is and should be enough to leave us transfixed. In a sermon titled "Earth Has No Sorrow That Earth Cannot Heal," Karen Pidcock-Lester tells of Nien Chang, imprisoned during China's Cultural Revolution for refusing to worship a Chinese god.[42] After being tortured, Chang remembers a brief encounter with creation when the guards returned her to her cell. She watched a small spider slowly and meticulously weave silken threads produced from its body back and forth between two rusty bars. The web was an architectural feat of beauty and wonder and that little bit of beauty gave her strength, confidence, and hope in God.

A healthy spiritual and emotional state involves staying close to nature. The question remains, however, how close do we get and at what point does it become counterproductive, invasive, and even destructive of the physical realm? That is the question to which we now turn.

Between Control and Neglect

God sets boundaries for creation but within those boundaries God allows it much freedom. One of the conundrums regarding the relationship between humans and the environment is to what degree should humans intervene in the course of nature. The degree of involvement is complex and hotly contested. Do we let nature run its course? After all nature knows best and

42. Pidcock-Lester, "Earth Has No Sorrow," 130–31.

should be allowed to regulate itself. Or do we actively manage nature? If we do then to what degree do we intervene?

All landscapes need periodic pulses of natural disturbances to keep them vibrant. They need fires, flooding, drought, windstorms, grazing, and even insect infestation. None of these were actually disasters until humans came along. It was when these phenomena adversely affected humans that the natural disturbances became disasters. When do humans step in and attempt to defer the damages?

Take the case of forest fires. The debate rages on regarding the level of intervention. A major change in the way fires were fought occurred in the Northwest during the summer of 1910. Nearly three million acres of forest burned and eighty-five people died.[43] After the fire, the newly formed Forest Service Department—just five years old at the time—took on as their reason for existence the fighting of forest fires to ensure this kind of disaster never happened again. They believed that nature could be controlled. Fire was a beast fire fighters could hunt down and conquer.[44] From 1910 on through the 1960s, "the Forest Service decided that every wildfire in the country should be put out by the morning after it was reported."[45] Because the Forest Service regularly intervened and prevented fires from running their course, an abundance of undergrowth built up over the decades. Add to this the drought conditions of the past couple of decades, and the result is that fires have become bigger and hotter.

The Forest Service came to the conclusion that fire suppression is the wrong policy for the environment. Enter the Yellowstone fire of 1988. A lightning strike ignited a small fire in the National Park. The fire grew bigger and bigger but park officials chose not to intervene. It grew to the point where it burned 1.2 million acres, a third of the park. One newspaper heading read: "If you want to see the world's largest charcoal grill, just visit Yellowstone."[46] The Forest Service was sharply criticized for following the mantra of letting nature regulate itself and believing that the best management is no management. But knowing when to intervene is not a simple matter. What now complicates matters even more is the growing "wildland-urban interface."[47] With people building homes in the mountains and

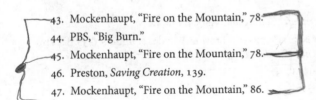
43. Mockenhaupt, "Fire on the Mountain," 78.
44. PBS, "Big Burn."
45. Mockenhaupt, "Fire on the Mountain," 78.
46. Preston, *Saving Creation*, 139.
47. Mockenhaupt, "Fire on the Mountain," 86.

forested areas, firefighters cannot let fires burn the way they need to. Their priority now has shifted to protecting the increasing number of homes surrounded by forests.

Fire is just one example of the complexity of the interface between humans and the environment. The complexity extends to every aspect of creation: flora, fauna, water, soil, and air. Creation is dynamic, ever changing, and unpredictable not unlike humans, who were also crafted by the same Creator to be masterpieces of complexity. As such, complexity will always be part of the interrelationship between human and non-human creation. No easy answers exist. Biologist Evan Eisenberg's rule of thumb, that we should "manage nature so as to minimize the need to manage nature," shows how even the most axiomatic solutions to the problem ultimately resolve themselves in paradox.[48] Accepting this paradox, and with it the limits of human power and knowledge, provide a more workable, and more biblical, approach to creation. We must start by no longer placing all our hopes in unraveling the complex interrelationship between the human and non-human world with scientific precision and instead approach nature with a very different disposition.

The Wonder of It All

Holmes Rolston and William Brown,[49] among others, have raised awareness of an underlying virtue essential to a healthy relationship between humans and creation. It is the virtue of wonder. Brown concludes that the abuse and degradation of creation originates in part from a "crisis of wonder, of wonder about God's good creation."[50] Wonder propels us forward into faith in God and leads to the beginning of wisdom.[51]

In closely observing raptors and reptiles and ships on high seas not understanding how they propel themselves without apparent effort through air, land, and water, all the sage in Proverbs can conclude is that these "things are too wonderful for me" (Prov 30:18–19). Wonder is what Job expressed after his whirlwind tour with God. He confesses, "Therefore I have uttered what I did not understand, things too wonderful for me,

48. Quoted in Davis, *Scripture, Culture, and Agriculture*, 32.

49. Rolston, "Caring for Nature," 277–302. Brown, "Wonder of It All," 33–38. See also his most recent book, *Wisdom's Wonder* (2014).

50. Brown, "Wonder of It All," 37.

51. Ibid., 34.

which I did not know" (42:3). Contrary to some thinking, the rapid-fire questions God hurls at Job are not designed to put Job down. Rather they are an invitation to Job and to us as readers to share in the delight God takes in the created order. God wants Job to experience the same enthusiasm and zeal he possesses for the amazing and wild animal world.

The posture of wonder is part of the quality of what it means to fear the Lord. All the wisdom books describe the sage as one who fears the Lord and calls on others who seek wisdom to begin with the fear of the Lord (Job 1:1; 28:28; Prov 1:7; 31:30; Eccl 5:7; 7:18; 8:12–13; 12:13). The fear, reverence, and awe before the Lord lead individuals to see the world through fresh eyes. Fearing God and enjoying the world God made leads one to experience amazement and wonder (Eccl 8:10–15). Through a deepening relationship with God, investing in the world God created, and learning to appreciate its depths and mysteries, we cultivate the virtue of wonder. When we understand creation as dynamic and alive, not static or passive, we realize we can never master or understand it. It will always remain a mystery. And as long as mystery remains, we can marvel at it and celebrate its beauty.

The Limits to Human Understanding

The mystery of creation has motivated people for centuries to explore new territories. It was one of the motivations for the Lewis and Clark expedition across this continent to the Pacific Ocean (1803–1806). It was what inspired Charles Darwin to make a five-year trip on the Beagle traveling from England across the Atlantic, along the coast of South America, across the Pacific Ocean to Australia, then to Africa and finally back home to England collecting rare specimens along the way (1831–1836). It is what moved centuries of explorers to press farther and farther southward, looking for the mythic frozen continent, *Terra Australis*, and, when found, what inspired Ernest Shackleton to arrange an expedition to attempt the first land crossing of Antarctica (1914–1917). It is what calls humans now to explore the ocean's depths and the galaxies of outer space.

Our curiosity also gets us in trouble when we believe we know more than we do about the world. The world of creation continues to humble us as it did Job. A couple examples from history reveal how overconfident we often have been in our knowledge of creation. On July 8, 1879, George De Long set sail out of the San Francisco Harbor on a ship called the Jeannette to explore a passageway to the North Pole.[52] De Long and his crew of thirty-three men planned their trip around the existence of an Open Polar Sea. Scientists in the late nineteenth century accepted as a veritable certainty that there was a warm undercurrent that kept the water at the North Pole free of ice. A ring of ice surrounded the Pole but once a ship broke through that ring it entered warm ocean water, the Open Polar Sea. The North Pole was an oasis in a desert of ice, a polar utopia. De Long and his crew prepared for the expedition secure in the belief that such an oasis existed. In addition, it was commonly believed that icebergs contained fresh water and would provide an unlimited supply for the crew. They came to discover that neither of these "certainties" was true, and their gross miscalculation ultimately resulted in the death of thirty-one of the thirty-three crew members, including De Long. Nature is always full of surprises, sometimes costly surprises.

During the late 1920s and early thirties the Federal Bureau of Soils announced that "the soil is the one indestructible, immutable asset that the nation possesses. It is the one resource that cannot be exhausted, that cannot be used up."[53] It was also believed that plowing up fields of sod would stir up the atmosphere and cause it to rain.[54] Both beliefs proved terribly unfounded and led to costly mistakes. Farmers plowed up millions of acres of land on the Great Plains, sparking one of the most disastrous environmental crises this country has ever experienced. Nearly a decade of consistent drought in some areas of the Great Plains, a period known today as the "Dirty Thirties," led to the displacement of nearly half a million Americans and untold damage to the environment.

Today the myth of a warm polar sea or the immutability of soil seem foolish to us. But they should serve as a warning against our hubris. Scientific research will continue to reveal new knowledge and provide new insights about the world that will benefit both humans and non-humans. There remains, however, much about creation and weather, flora and fauna, oceans and mountains that we will never understand. We must learn to respect those mysteries and to embrace their existence, not only because our hubris often leads to unintended consequences but because when we convince ourselves that we have figured creation out, we lose the sense of awe and wonder that the sages have before creation. The greatest problem

52. Sides, *Kingdom of Ice*.
53. Egan, *Worst Hard Time*, 51, 126.
54. Ibid., 23.

with a purely scientific approach to the world is not that we sometimes draw bad conclusions; it is that it always assumes an incorrect posture. To act in the world as if we have mastered it, understood it, reflects a spiritual defect. Our fundamental stance must be one of recognized ignorance rather than knowledge, because, like the God who created it, creation will always be more unknown to us than known. Instead of focusing on erasing all mystery from the world we must embrace creation's mysteries and celebrate that which we "do not know" (Eccl 11:1–6). In order to be fully human before God, we seek out all means to foster the sense of wonder generated both from understanding and from accepting our own limitations.

Conclusion

In vicariously taking the cosmic tour with Job, we come to a deeper appreciation of and learn a great deal about the character of creation. We see that God does not interact with creation in a rigid mechanical way, but sets boundaries within which the cosmos is given free reign. It is a wild and messy reign, but in the midst of it Job can do nothing except respond in awe. That does not mean, however, that humans must keep their distance from creation. The sages in Proverbs instruct just the opposite.[55] It is absolutely necessary for humans to interact with the physical world in a close and respectful way if we are to keep immediate and relevant in our lives the experiences the sages describe for Job. If there is no regular engagement in that world, humans lose sense of their place in that chaotic order that is creation. They lose perspective on life. They lose character.

Reclaiming that perspective, that sense of place, involves first and foremost recovering Job's perspective of awe. For all the sages, the common denominator in their relationship with creation is the sense of wonder. Wonder is that virtue that acts as a bond to connect humans to non-human creation, and all of creation back to God. But wonder also acts as an important restraint in keeping humans from exploiting creation. Wonder keeps in constant check the arrogance that is born out of the illusion of control that science and technology have given us in almost every aspect

---

55. A similar relationship is found in Exodus when Moses approaches the burning bush (Exod 3). God calls Moses to take off his shoes because he is on holy ground. The holiness of God, however, does not result in Moses keeping his distance from God. Rather it brings him into an intimate relationship with God as Moses engages God in one of the longest conversations recorded between a human and the Divine found in Scripture (Exod 3–6).

of our lives. When we stand in awe before creation realizing we can never completely understand nor control it, we come to respect the wildness of creation. Only then can we begin to find ways to responsibly interact with the world God created.

Chapter Two

Mysticism and Wonder

Who is this that looks forth like the dawn,
fair as the moon, bright as the sun,
terrible as an army with banners?

—SONG OF SOLOMON 6:10

SONG OF SOLOMON SITS uncomfortably at the murky margins of Wisdom Literature and, if we are being entirely candid, at the edges of the biblical canon as a whole. While referencing neither covenant nor law, which are the themes of much of the rest of the Hebrew Bible, the Song of Solomon also distinguishes itself from Job, Psalms, Proverbs, and Ecclesiastes by neither mentioning nor musing on the nature or pursuit of wisdom. Instead, for eight chapters the bride and bridegroom, lover and beloved serenade each other with semi-erotic testimonies to their blossoming love. Unsurprisingly, the book has inspired centuries of intense debate about how it might be interpreted, with the typical resolution involving sanitizing the apparent sexuality of the text. Just as often, however, the Song of Solomon has been pointedly and puritanically ignored, deemed by quiet consent to be that part of Scripture not talked about in polite company.

Nevertheless—and whatever else may be said about the Song of Solomon—it is clear that the author imbibes deeply of the same respect and awe for creation that pervades the rest of the sapiential literature. In fact, in ways significantly more overt even than Proverbs, the author places the fruits of God's creative impulse at the center of the story. Consider just a brief selection of the efforts of the bridegroom to woo his would-be bride:

How beautiful you are, my love, how very beautiful!
Your eyes are doves behind your veil.
Your hair is like a flock of goats,
　moving down the slopes of Gilead.

Your teeth are like a flock of shorn ewes
　that have come up from the washing,
　all of which bear twins,
　and not one among them is bereaved.

Your two breasts are like two fawns, twins of a gazelle,
　that feed among the lilies.

Your lips distill nectar, my bride; honey and milk are under your tongue;
　the scent of your garments is like the scent of Lebanon.
A garden locked is my sister, my bride,
　a garden locked, a fountain sealed.
Your channel is an orchard of pomegranates
　with all choicest fruits, henna with nard,
　nard and saffron, calamus and cinnamon,
　with all trees of frankincense, myrrh and aloes,
　with all chief spices. (4:1–2, 5, 11–14)

The bride answers in kind, at times echoing his praise exactly: the bride-groom's eyes are like milky doves, his cheeks like spices, his lips like "lilies distilling liquid myrrh," his arms like gold, his body like sapphire-encrusted ivory, his hair like a raven, his arms like alabaster, his appearance like the cedars of Lebanon (5:11–15).

Many of the comparisons strike our modern sensibilities as more than a little unusual. (With good reason, Hallmark does not make a Valentine's Day card that says, "You're beautiful like a flock of goats running downhill, like sheep that have just had a bath and a haircut.") Yet what is abundantly clear is that the lover and beloved both hold up God's creation as the bench-mark for awe-inspiring, poetry-producing, dumbfounding beauty. Every-thing from precious gems to herd animals, running water to gardens full of exotic fruits and spices evokes for these swooning lovers an almost ineffable wonder—the only kind of wonder, in fact, that can accurately describe their ecstatic experience of each other's love. While seeming to talk only and entirely of each other, the bride and her bridegroom rhapsodize their way through creation, inviting the reader to experience the awesomeness of their love through the awesomeness of God's diverse and magnificent creation.

In truth, this aesthetic tour of God's creation mirrors very closely the tour that God arranges for Job. As discussed in the previous chapter, God offers Job a grand tour of creation, from the most miniscule to the most magnificent of the divine works, and in the process Job is forced to learn important lessons, to become both wiser and more virtuous for having attended to creation. While Job's grand tour seems to suggest just how small he is in the grand scheme of God's world—though this is only one of the lessons that Job desperately needs to learn from creation—the same tour in Song of Solomon proposes just the opposite, that all the greatness and beauty of creation is available to humanity. As they teach distinct but complementary lessons, these catalogs of God's creative work provoke the same basic disposition, one shared throughout the sapiential literature: wonder.

Yet, as already suggested, the modern world has a peculiar deficit of wonder. After all, at some point in humanity's not-so-distant past we crossed an invisible threshold: science has taught us so much about the mechanics of the world that there is now too much for any one person to know. The problem is no longer that the world is too mysterious to understand (as it was for our forebearers); instead, the world is too known to understand, at least without a team of specialists in a thousand different overlapping fields of physics, chemistry, biology, geology, and so on. Whether or not science has really laid bare, in any meaningful sense, the character of God's creation, all of us can now look off at the sunrise or at blooming flowers or at golden autumn leaves and know with confidence that, even if we cannot understand how it all works, someone out there can catalog, dissect, and enumerate it for us.

There is no amount of knowledge, however, that absolves Christians of their basic obligation to stand before God's creation with awe both at it and at the Creator whom it reflects. It would be foolish to assume, for example, that had he read Stephen Hawking's *Brief History of Time* the bridegroom would have changed even a single word of his psalm in praise of his bride. The elegy is not based in his ignorance but in God's greatness. The bridegroom's sense of wonder at creation, his apparently instinctive understanding that God's work alone is the standard for everything awe-inspiring and beautiful in the world, can and must be reclaimed regardless of the progress of science. Fortunately, Christians have a vast historical library of resources, largely untapped, written by men and women who understood how to revel in their awe at God and the magnificent world of creation. These spiritual successors to the sages offer a treasury of inspiration and reflection for Christians hoping to reestablish an environmental ethics—and more basically a relationship with God through creation—that understands that wonder is the default stance of humanity toward the non-human world. They are the Christian mystics.

The Roots of Christian Mysticism

Mysticism, not unlike the Song of Solomon, is notoriously difficult to pin down. So, unsurprisingly, like the Song of Solomon it provokes a certain amount of anxiety among those unfamiliar with it. Images of Romani fortune tellers, clad in flowing clothes and golden bangles, peering into a crystal ball mingle with more domestic images of bored suburbanites of an earlier generation gathered around a flickering candle with a medium who rattles the table while she channels the spirits of the dead. Mysticism signals to many of us an association with magic or the occult. Even those with some little knowledge of the mystical traditions of the world think of the whirling dervishes or Buddhist ascetics in mountain monasteries and can see no link between mysticism and the biblical truths of Christianity.

The problem is not limited to those uninitiated to the study of mystical theology. Historian Andrew Louth wrestles with the question of whether or not there can be any such thing as a "Christian mystical theology," admitting that "there are many—particularly Protestants—who say not."[1] Even if mysticism is admitted as a possibility for Christians, it is normally isolated from the bulk of church life, as something unessential, relegated to a few of exceptional (or exceptionally odd) religious temperament. Catholics and Protestants are particularly prone to this view, drinking deeply as Western European traditions did of the modern revolution in rational and scientific thought. The Orthodox Church stands largely alone among major Christian bodies in continuing institutionally to embrace mystical expressions of Christianity, leading Orthodox theologian Vladimir Lossky to lament that "one frequently hears expressed the view which would see in mysticism . . . an exception to the common rule, a privilege vouchsafed to a few souls who enjoy direct experience of the truth, others, meanwhile, having to rest content to a more or less blind submission to dogmas imposed from

1. Louth, *Origins of the Christian Mystical Tradition*, xiv.

without."[2] Thomas Merton, famed Catholic author and Trappist monk, announces the same problem from within the "Western" tradition, noting that Christians too often behave "as if mysticism were for saintly women and theological study were for practical but, alas, unsaintly men."[3]

Yet for all the stigma accumulated to "mysticism," for both the uninformed and the experts, a proper definition of the term and a biblical context for its exploration allows mystical theology to occupy an important, even an essential, place in Christian practice—even among the most doggedly rational Protestant communions. Lossky offers a valuable starting point in this quest for a definition, suggesting that the simplest way to understand mysticism is as the logical and necessary experiential counterpoint to the rational pursuit of theology—always reminding Christians that theology is not a gnostic practice in which accurate propositional knowledge of God is an end in itself and always itself being kept in check by a theology which interprets, rejects, or confirms religious experiences which might otherwise be meaningless or even deceptive.[4] Louth offers much the same direction, coupling mystical experience and revealed knowledge, when he defines mysticism as the "context for direct apprehensions of the God who has revealed himself in Christ and dwells in us through the Holy Spirit."[5] Yet he gives a more complete and, for our purposes, more revealing answer to his own question, "Can there, indeed, be such a thing as Christian mystical theology":

> The phenomenon seems persistent, however impossible. . . . But it can be characterized as a search for and experience of immediacy with God. The mystic is not content to know *about* God, he longs for union with God. "Union with God" can mean different things, from literal identity, where the mystic loses all sense of himself and is absorbed into God, to the union that is experienced as the consummation of love, in which the lover and the beloved remain intensely aware both of themselves and of the other. . . . Yet the search for God, or the ultimate, for His own sake, and an unwillingness to be satisfied with anything less than Him; the search for

2. Lossky, *Mystical Theology*, 8.

3. Merton, *New Seeds of Contemplation* 254–55. Like Lossky, Merton argued that this sort of thinking impoverished, even crippled, both theology and spirituality, doctrine and mysticism.

4. Lossky, *Mystical Theology*, 7–9.

5. Louth, *Origins*, xi.

immediacy with this object of the soul's longing: this would seem to be the heart of mysticism.[6]

The depiction of mysticism as the courtship of a lover and beloved and the intense sense of longing in which nothing less than the object of desire will satisfy evokes, perhaps deliberately, the language of the Song of Solomon. This hardly surprises, as the desire to know the fullness of God and the divine wisdom by which all things are created, ordered, and sustained form the core of all the sapiential literature in Scripture.

Moreover, just as creation stands at the heart of the sages' sense of wonder in this experience of God, so too does the natural world occupy a central place in the history of Christian mysticism. Understanding the relationship between creation and the mystical quest to experience the divine offers new ways to engage Scripture with a rich, though often neglected, tradition of Christian thought and provides new avenues for enriching not only contemporary spirituality—which, like the sages and mystics, ought to be intimately concerned with experiencing the immediacy of God—but also Christian environmental ethics. What follows are brief sketches of a variety of Christian mystical thinkers and traditions—two medieval and one modern; one each from Catholic, Orthodox, and Protestant Christianity—which suggest the richness and depth of Christian mystical thought about the environment, and particularly the importance of establishing the correct spiritual posture before God's creation.

The Peaceful, Playful God of Meister Eckhart

Born in the mid-thirteenth century, Eckhart von Hochheim—later and more commonly known as Meister Eckhart—already had a tremendous wealth of mystical teaching on which he could and did build. Yet, like many of those mystics who came before and just as many since, Eckhart struggled to strike balance between the supposedly immutable doctrinal truths espoused by the church and the very real imperative to experience God directly and personally. Like Thomas Aquinas, who lived a generation before, Eckhart would twice hold the honored chair of theology at Paris, an immense honor for any theologian at the time. Yet he would also be the first master of theology to be brought before the Inquisition and threatened with execution at the stake. The source of this mixed legacy is, in many

6. Ibid., xiv-xv.

ways, also the key to understanding the way Eckhart's distinct mysticism allowed for a critical reevaluation of God's creation.

Much of Eckhart's trouble stemmed from his tendency to devalue language, a tendency which has a profound effect on how he approaches creation. Disagreements about the adequacy of language for speaking about God raged in the thirteenth and fourteenth centuries, occupying the attention of many of the greatest theological minds of the period. Scholastics, Thomas Aquinas preeminent among them, had concluded that there was a genuine analogy between words as they applied to God and those same words as applied to creatures. The result was a positive affirmation of language as a means for expressing truth. Eckhart, drawing from a much older Christian tradition typified by Pseudo-Dionysius, countered that language had value only insofar as propositions about God must be made in order for them to be negated and that the ineffable distance between God and creatures corresponded to the ineffable distance between language and the realities it tried to describe. Words, at their best, corresponded to the abstractions contained within them rather than to any external reality, making words fundamentally incapable of representing truth about a reality as absolute as deity.

The purpose, for Eckhart, in this depreciation of language was to separate himself from the rationalistic theological optimism of Thomas Aquinas and the theologians who followed in his tremendous wake. Eckhart carefully, and prudently, avoided any direct challenge to Thomas but nevertheless subtly undermined Thomist thought at every turn. Even when Eckhart stole entire passages from Thomas, the imitation was more subversion than flattery.[7] In truth, Eckhart departed from Thomas and other scholastics on many key propositions about the accessibility of God to the human mind: he denied that God could be experienced in theophanies, that the multiplicity of divine attributes was rooted in the divine essence, that there was a common sense solution to the disjunction between the order of things and the order of the mind, and that, when reasoning from analogy, positive qualities genuinely inhere in both God and creatures. In each case, by undermining the efficacy of language, Eckhart undermines

---

7. For example, in an effort to "clarify" the thought of Pseudo-Dionysius, Eckhart pulls an argument verbatim from Thomas. Yet, as the context shows, the application of Thomas in this manner actually does more to modify the thought of Thomas than Pseudo-Dionysius, with whom Eckhart is generally more inclined to agree anyway. See Tobin, *Meister Eckhart*, 70–71. Another example is offered in Hollywood, "Preaching as Social Practice," 85.

the optimism of scholastics who believe reason and the senses can cooper-
ate to attain knowledge of and access to God, with whatever degree of pious
equivocation the scholastics attached to their claims. Eckhart believed, in
the words of Frank Tobin, that attempts to describe God "transcend the
state of complete impotence only to an infinitesimal degree" because this
inexpressibility of God tended toward a realization of the incomprehensibility of God, something Eckhart's scholastic contemporaries failed to
respect.[8]

It is important to note that, while Eckhart the mystic rejected all efforts
to grasp God with words, Eckhart the preacher never took the inadequacies
of language as a cue to stop talking, or even more specifically to stop talking
about God. Just the opposite. For Eckhart, the recognition that his language
could never ascend to the level of scientific precision freed him to embrace
rhetorical and poetic modes of preaching that broke with scholastic convention. Because language would never be able to bear the burden scholastics expected it to, Eckhart shed the chains of conscientious accuracy and
allowed himself freer forms for directing his listeners toward the truth.[9]
In an important way, by recognizing the narrow boundaries of language,
Eckhart allowed himself, and implicitly invites others, to transgress those
boundaries with impunity, breaking dramatically with conventional modes
of speaking about God.[10]

Having removed the inexpressible, incomprehensible God to the inac-
cessible high heavens through his critique of language, Eckhart makes a
powerful and paradoxical theological move: this same God is immediately

---

8. Tobin, *Meister Eckhart*, 84.

9. Cf. Hollywood, "Preaching," 89.

10. Precisely this transgression proved Eckhart's downfall. In his opposition to liter-
alism, Eckhart had, as usual, subverted Thomas who believed that all senses of a biblical
text must proceed from the literal sense. Eckhart agreed with Thomas that there was a
single literal meaning, but reinterpreted this affirmation to conclude that all meanings,
insofar as they were true, were the literal sense of the text because God had literally
intended all of them. The precedence of intent to meaning became the central issue at
Eckhart's heresy trial, where he swore that he could not have taught anything heretical
because he had not intended to teach anything heretical. His inquisitors countered that
they could only respond to "the literal meaning" of his teaching, not his intent. In essence, Eckhart argued that he could not have said anything incorrect about God because
he knew he could not say anything about God at all. His judges, with a wealth of controversial homilies in front of them, simply could not understand. They were, in essence,
speaking two different languages: the one the precise language of scholastics, the other
the fluid expression of the mystic. See Duclow, *Masters of Learned Ignorance*, 171–72;
and Tobin, *Meister Eckhart*, 14.

present in creation. The paradox flows naturally out of Eckhart's thought. Following the logic of his devaluation of human language and, consequently, human knowledge, he arrives at the inevitable conclusion that creatures are nothing and God alone is being. Here again Eckhart contradicts Thomas, who argued that creatures could be properly said to possess being. Eckhart rejects this possibility but does not therefore consign creature to nonexistence. The obvious fact that creatures exist suggested to Eckhart that they too must, in some sense, have being. Yet, because only God is being, Eckhart is forced to conclude that, insofar as creatures have being, they are manifestations of God. The result is a truly radical language about the nature of God's creation:

> Now I shall say something I have never said before. God enjoys himself. In the same enjoyment in which God enjoys himself, he enjoys all creatures. With the same enjoyment with which God enjoys himself, he enjoys all creatures, not as creatures, but he enjoys the creatures as God. In the same enjoyment in which God enjoys himself, he enjoys all things. . . . God becomes God where all creatures express God: there he becomes "God."[11]

Creatures can contribute nothing to their own existence, so every aspect of them which exists is not the creature but God.[12] It is unsurprising then that Eckhart should see the discovery of God in creation as the first step toward the soul's encounter with the divine.[13]

In part, this view of the presence of God in creation broke with contemporary scholasticism simply because the scholastics lacked the vocabulary and the thought forms necessary to express the kind of paradox Eckhart envisioned here. Eckhart had already gone so far beyond scholastics in envisioning the transcendence of God that he bordered on agnosticism. At the same time, he now proposed so radical a view of the immanence of God

11. Eckhart, Sermon 3, in Fox, *Passion for Creation*, 76–77.

12. Tobin, "Mysticism and Meister Eckhart," 18–20; Linge, "Mysticism, Poverty, and Reason," 471–72. Linge represents an older scholarship which sees a tension between the early Eckhart who argued that creatures were being and God was not and the later Eckhart who centered his theology on the assertion *esse est Deus*. A recognition of Eckhart's views on the inadequacy and therefore fluidity of language, discussed above, has gone a long way toward reconciling these apparently contradictory stances and allowing for the above synthesis.

13. Fox, *Passion for Creation*, 10; Albrecht Classen stresses that this contemplation is of all beings in their spiritual rather than material manifestations, though the substantial non-dualist impulses in Eckhart's thought make such a distinction more theoretical than real. See Classen, "Meister Eckhart's Philosophy," 12.

in creation that it bordered on pantheism. Language was so inadequate that it expressed truth about God only in a way so infinitesimally minute as to approach nonexistence. Meanwhile, God inhered so thoroughly in creation that the distinction between them could be seen only in the fact that unity implies a nonexistent multiplicity. The structured, rational question and answer disputations of the scholastics simply did not possess the necessary finesse to convey this paradox to the soul, not the way Eckhart's poetic, mystical preaching did.[14]

Yet more important than whether or not Eckhart was a pantheist or an agnostic, a saint or a heretic and more important than the role of creation in the encounter with the divine (discussed below at great length with a different group of mystics) is the way in which Eckhart's reinterpretation of God in nature moves creation out of the periphery and into the center of human spirituality.[15] Liberated from concern over doctrinal clarity by his devaluation of language, Eckhart was free to give poetic voice to the bond between Creator and creation, expressing with affective force the beauty of a relationship characterized by love and peace and joy. When he declares that "God enjoys himself, he enjoys all creatures," Eckhart implicitly invites all of us to partake in that joy. In Job 40–41, the God Eckhart imagines giddily lays out his toys before a dumbfounded Job and says, "Look at this! Isn't it incredible." When the creative, joyful God of Eckhart's sermons sees the bride's desire for her beloved and her coy invitation that they should "go out early to the vineyards, and see whether the vines have budded, whether the grape blossoms have opened and the pomegranates are in bloom" (Song 7:12) so that she might give him her love, God delights that humanity is taking its rightful place wrapped literally and rhetorically in the awesome fecundity of divine creativity.

---

14. Fox, *Passion for Creation*, 29; Tobin, "Mysticism," 19.

15. Thomas had an important place for creation in his thinking, but it was as a means for the central actors rather than as a primary arena for divine presence and action. For Thomas and those who followed, God created and sustained creation but did not inhere in it the way Eckhart suggested. Creation was a means by which the reason, after collecting empirical data, could begin its rational ascent toward the divine, the prime example of this being Thomas's famous cosmological arguments for the existence of God. For Eckhart, however, creation did not merely serve as a launching point, directing the mind to its source. It contained its source by virtue of its existence and therefore required no scholastic journey to reach God. In Eckhart, creation becomes itself a "grace," a term which Thomas would never apply to it. See Fox, *Passion for Creation*, 30; and Tobin, "Mysticism," 19.

For God, creation is a source of abounding joy and, as bearers of the divine image, we are encouraged to look to it for joy as well. In his commentary on Eckhart's sermon, theologian Matthew Fox explains,

> Creatures, the words of God, are not only good but divine.
>
> But whether we experience the creatures as they are divine depends on us. We can be puny-minded and timid in our vision. . . . The outer person enjoys the loaf of bread, a glass of wine, and a slice of meat merely as bread, wine, and meat. This way lies boredom and, one might imagine, obesity. The inner person also enjoys bread, wine, and meat but . . . nourishes a sense of gratitude and even wonder at the gift that the ecstasies of creation bless us with. But there is still a third way to experience the gifts of creation. . . . In this tasting, the finiteness of human pleasure is overcome and the grace-filled satisfaction of divine beauty is imbibed. This beauty, the taster knows, will never die.[16]

In every encounter with creation, whether it be scaling majestic heights or sitting down to even the most spare meal, we are invited to share in the immeasurable and enduring joy which God radiates for creation.

More than merely joy, however, God looks to creation as an object and source of both peace and love. Eckhart preaches, "If I were asked to give valid information concerning what the creator's aims were when he created all creatures, I would say: 'Repose.' . . . Moreover, God loves himself in all creatures. Just as he is seeking love for himself in all creatures, he is seeking also his own repose in them."[17] Significantly, Eckhart takes as the text for this sermon, a wisdom text from the apocryphal book of Sirach:[18]

> I [Wisdom] came forth from the mouth of the Most High,
>   and covered the earth like a mist.
> I dwelt in the highest heavens,
>   and my throne was in a pillar of cloud.
> Alone I compassed the vault of heaven
>   and traversed the depths of the abyss.
> Over waves of the sea, over all the earth,
>   and over every people and nation I have held sway.

16. Fox, *Passion for Creation*, 81.

17. Meister Eckhart, Sermon 27, in Fox, *Passion for Creation*, 380.

18. Eckhart only specifically cites the first half of Sir 24:7, but like most preachers before and after him, the selected text serves a mnemonic to focus listeners' minds onto what would have been a familiar text.

Among all these I sought a resting place;
in whose territory should I abide? (24:3–7)

While the author of the book of Sirach goes on to detail how wisdom was made to find its rest specifically with Israel, Meister Eckhart sees in this passage a more fundamental statement about the relationship of God (through wisdom) to creation. It is in creation that God the Creator looks to find a resting place, and wisdom pervades the created order for precisely this reason. Eckhart goes so far as to fundamentally reinterpret the basic creation story: quite contrary to the hubris of many modern Christians who tend to see all of creation as culminating in the sixth day with the creation of all-important, world-defining, world-ruling (and world-destroying) humanity, Eckhart argues that creation climaxes on the seventh day, divine rest.

Yet, just as with the primordial Sabbath described at the start of Genesis 2, the search for divine repose in creation which Eckhart draws from wisdom literature is not due to any exhaustion or necessity in God; it is a cue to humans who bear the divine image that they should find their rest by filling themselves with the masterpiece of God's creative handiwork. To the extent to which humanity can produce the outpouring of love and joy for nature which God models and to the extent to which they can find their rest in God's world—this world, and not only in the hope of a world to come—humanity mirrors their Creator's behaviors and priorities. To phrase it in terms a mystic like Eckhart would understand, when we wonder at creation we become like God.

Another group of mystics, living during roughly the same period as Eckhart, would find themselves similarly challenged by elements within the church. Like Eckhart, these thinkers would be forced to defend their teachings before those who believed that mysticism threatened the doctrinal purity of the church and, in doing so, espoused a mystical theology in which creation played a distinctive and critical role. Unlike Eckhart, they would prevail and set Greek-speaking Christianity on a very different historical path than Catholics and later Protestants.

Hesychasm and Mystical Knowledge of Creation

Hesychasm, a word utterly without meaning for most Protestants and Catholics, represents the zenith of theologically-sound mysticism among Orthodox Christians. Though the term hesychast, meaning "quietude," originally referred to any monk, by the late thirteenth century hesychasm emerged as a more defined movement typically marked as beginning with Nicephorus the Hesychast (fl. 1270). The thirteenth through fifteenth centuries were an especially tumultuous time for Greek-speaking Christians. At the beginning of the thirteenth century, Catholic Crusaders—ostensibly coming to aid the Orthodox in holding back the Turkish Muslim Sultanate of Rum—sacked Constantinople, pillaged Byzantine land, and set up the Latin Empire (1204–1261). The Orthodox would regain control of Byzantine land from Catholic hands only to be forced by the end of the fourteenth century to submit to the suzerainty of the Ottoman Emperor. In 1453, the last vestiges of the Eastern Roman Empire would fall to the Ottomans, and Greek-speaking Christians would be left for the first time in over a millennium without a political body to augment the unity offered by the church. In this context, the now mature mystical spirituality of the hesychast played a crucial role in redefining Orthodox dogma and spirituality for a new age. At the forefront of this effort was a succession of fourteenth-century hesychast teachers and students who left an indelible imprint on Christian mysticism: Gregory of Sinai, Gregory Palamas, and Nicolas Cabasilas.

In the midst of this political turmoil and a simultaneous Byzantine renaissance that historian Jaroslav Pelikan appropriately called the "last flowering of Byzantine Orthodoxy,"[19] the hesychasts occupied themselves primarily with epistemological debates—arguments over the nature of knowledge, what could be known and how it could be known—that were raging across Europe and western Asia at the time. Though debates of this sort seem the sole province of philosophers and theologians, concerns over the appropriate activity and aims of the mind became important for the hesychasts precisely because they had real spiritual import. In particular the hesychasts were concerned about the philosophy being advanced by Byzantine humanists[20] and, more pressingly, by Barlaam the Calabrian. As a result of his radically agnostic theology in which God was totally unknowable,[21] Barlaam maintained that the only appropriate activity for the mind was the rational exploration of creation. He established a sharp distinction between theological and secular sciences and insisted that the latter remained the

19. Pelikan, *Spirit of Eastern Christendom (600–1700)*.

20. On the humanists, see Meyendorff, *Study of Gregory Palamas*, 116: "An abyss, which the humanists made no claim to cross, yawned between intellectual activity and the religious life, between philosophy and theology."

21. Barlaam argued that God is totally unknowable in an effort to introduce a note of dogmatic relativism into union negotiations between Orthodox and Catholics.

only appropriate rational field of thought.[22] Without following his lead too precisely, other opponents of the hesychasts—Gregory Akindynos, Nicphoros Gregoras, and much of Byzantine humanism—partook of Barlaam's preference for the study of natural phenomena.[23] Sounding centuries ahead of their modern counterparts, Barlaam and the humanists essentially declared that science should be left to the scientists, religion to the priests, and never the twain shall meet—as though studying God and studying creation had nothing at all to do with one another.

Steeped in a mystical tradition in which God was knowable and wonder at creation was central, the hesychasts balked at the idea of a divorce of creation from Creator—both with regard to the study of nature and with regard to the accessibility of God to created humanity. Part of the problem, for the hesychasts, was the supreme hubris of Barlaam and the humanists who believed that they could, independently through their reason grasp the truth of God's creation as it existed. Like modern industrialists, they approached the natural world as if it was something to be understood rather than something to strike us with awe precisely because of our ignorance of it.

For the hesychasts, like the sages, to study creation rationally as an end in itself was to miss the point entirely. Quite frankly, it was impossible. Each of the three great hesychasts in turn reminded his readers that even in their most rational moments, what humans perceived in creation was not the essence of the thing itself but only an impression of a small part. To look at creation was to see an image of it, filtered through human imagination, rather than to truly understand it. Only God who created and sustained the world could ever truly look on it and understand.[24] So resolute was Gregory Palamas in his skepticism of a purely empirical knowledge of creation that he consciously refused to make a point of dogma out of anything within the realm of physical science, leaving room for continually changing research and observation. Whereas many modern Protestants have taken rigidly dogmatic stands on such scientific issues as evolution and, for our purposes more significantly, anthropogenic climate change, Gregory understood that

22. Meyendorff, *Study of Gregory Palamas*, 116.

23. Sinkewicz, *Saint Gregory Palamas*, 5–8.

24. The full expression of this theology about the imagination and its role in perceiving creation is scattered throughout the writings of the hesychasts, but see for examples *Capita 150*, 15–17, 28; Gregory Palamas, *Triads*, I.2.1–2; *On Commandments and Doctrines*, 1, 62, 69, 72, 118, 173; Gregory of Sinai, *On Stillness: Fifteen Texts*, in *Philokalia*, vol. 4, 3; Gregory of Sinai, *On Prayer: Seven Texts*, in *Philokalia*, vol. 4, 7; *Life in Christ*, VI.7, 10–11; *Commentary*, 21.

intellectual humility required us to constantly reevaluate what we think we know about the way God has made and continues to operate in creation. He even dared to make corrections to the scientific knowledge of such canonized luminaries as Gregory of Nyssa.[25]

While the opponents of the hesychasts allowed a theological agnosticism to sideline any possibility of knowing God, the hesychasts themselves were not spiritual escapists just because they believed God's creation could never be fully known. In fact knowledge and contemplation of God's creation was absolutely essential to their spirituality, not because it can be known but because our ignorance-induced wonder at God's creation points toward the source of both that creation and a genuine knowledge of the truth. For the hesychasts, even if knowledge of creation were possible with any clarity it would still not be proper in itself as an end for knowledge. An accurate perception of reality would yield "images of intellections or the rational demonstration of facts" but not thereby any kind of "real wisdom and contemplation" or "undivided and unified knowledge."[26] Such knowledge cannot come from creation, only from the Creator. Insofar as creation directs the knower inevitably to knowledge of God, even if—or precisely because—we cannot ever fully understand and experience it as God does, Christians must seek an intimacy with nature as a prerequisite for intimacy with God.

Gregory of Sinai confirms this in an uncharacteristically positive passage regarding empirical knowledge drawn from the senses:

> The physical senses and the soul's powers have an equal and similar, not to say identical, mode of operation, especially when they are in a healthy state; for then the soul's powers live and act through the senses, and the life-giving Spirit sustains them both. . . . When there is no satanic battle between them, making them reject the rule of the intellect and of the Spirit, the senses clearly perceive sensory things, the soul's powers intelligible things; for when they are united through the spirit and constitute a single whole, they know directly and essentially the nature of divine and human things. They contemplate with clarity the *logoi*, or inward essences of these things, and distinctively perceive, so far as is possible, the single source of all things, the Holy Trinity.[27]

---

25. *Triads* II.2.30. See also Meyendorff, *Study of Gregory Palamas*, 148–49.

26. *On Commandments and Doctrines*, 2–3.

27. Ibid., 98.

Notably, even if the senses are able to "perceive sensory things" so clearly that they "know directly and essentially" creation, this serves only to direct the thinker to its ultimate goal: "the single source of all things, the Holy Trinity." This was because "in created things you will perceive the outward expression of the archetypes that characterize them."[28] All the *logoi* in created things point to "the divine Logos, the substantive Wisdom of God the Father."[29]

That creatures operated thus was not incidental, not merely a by-product of creation having God as its source and origin. Through divine wisdom, God created with this end in mind, namely that humanity should through a study of creatures be directed to knowledge of the Creator, even if knowledge of the divine could not properly be derived from creation. Everything which may be discovered in the physical sciences and the intellectual pursuits of philosophy had this as part of its created purpose. So Nicholas Cabasilas mused, "What was the reason that He created heaven and earth . . . ? Does He not teach us the whole philosophy which derives therefrom in order that He may turn us to Himself?"[30]

The combination of the unreliability of sensory knowledge and the necessity of singular focus of the mind on God as the proper object of knowledge led hesychasts in a curious circle of mystical reasoning: to contemplate creation truly was to contemplate God, but since only God can truly know creation, to know creation humanity must first know God. Thus, Gregory of Sinai concluded, matter-of-factly, that "a right view of created things depends upon a truly spiritual knowledge of visible and invisible realities."[31] Thus, those who purported to have knowledge of creation as

---

28. Ibid., 134.

29. Ibid; Nicholas Cabasilas, *Life in Christ*, II.19; and, to a greater extent, Gregory Palamas. Meyendorff, *Study of Gregory Palamas*, 118–119, would also seize on this idea of the *logoi*, a concept which originated with the Stoics but was transmitted to Palamas by the Greek Fathers, especially Justin Martyr. The divine *logoi* were imprints of God on creation by which all humanity might, through the purest use of observation and reason, come to some knowledge of God. The presence of these *logoi* necessitated that any proper knowledge of created beings would lead ultimately to knowledge of God. This had been part of God's purpose in constructing creation the way it was, namely so that it might lead Adam to fuller knowledge of the divine. From the moment of his creation, the first man had before him a mirror of divine reality by which to apprehend truth.

30. *Life in Christ*, VI.8.

31. *On Commandments and Doctrines*, 25; this truly spiritual knowledge, he will immediately clarify, is a proper knowledge of God, with the invisible reality being the Trinity and the visible reality being the incarnation (26).

their primary aim apart from knowledge of God—such as Barlaam or the Byzantine humanists, who radically divorced science from theology,[32] or modern environmentalists who believe that the problems of and solutions to the environmental crisis must be entirely secular—deceived themselves because accurate knowledge of creation was only attainable by focusing the mind on God. Gregory Palamas expressed a similar sentiment: "Where can we learn anything certain and free from deceit . . . about the world as a whole, about our own selves? Is it not from the teaching of the Spirit?"[33]

Writing long before humanity would quarantine itself conceptually from the rest of creation, pretending in our self-deceit that we are not "created" or "natural" like the rest of non-human creation or nature, all three hesychasts understood that principle among those truths of creation which could not be known apart from knowledge of God was the nature and status of humanity before its creator. Gregory Palamas insisted that to know God was to also know the image of God in humanity, on which humanity's purposes were predicated.[34] Gregory of Sinai similarly argued that without this correct perception of the human as God created it, people could not understand their own depravity.[35] Nicholas Cabasilas, most of all, saw in the incarnation the fullest and truest revelation of human nature as God intended it. To find salvation, one must first understand how far humanity had fallen. To understand depravity, one must first understand the person in a pristine state. To know the perfect human was to know God Incarnate. "Our reason we have received in order that we may know Christ . . . since He Himself is the Archetype for those who are created."[36] Knowledge of God permitted knowledge of self which, like all knowledge of created reality, prompted greater desire for knowledge of God.

Thus knowledge of creation and knowledge of God represented a harmonious interplay of revelation where creation both revealed God and was revealed in truth by God. Knowledge of God, therefore, was the crux of the epistemological endeavor.

> In other words, [the true philosopher] interprets what is intelligible and invisible in terms of what is sensible and visible, and the visible sense-world in terms of the invisible and suprasensory

32 See Meyendorff, *Study of Gregory Palamas*, 116.

33. *Capita 150*, 21.

34. Ibid., 26.

35. *On Commandments and Doctrines*, 50.

36. *Life in Christ*, 12.

world, conscious that what is visible is an image of what is invisible and that what is invisible is the archetype of what is visible. He knows that things possessing form and figure are brought into being by what is formless and without figure, and that each manifests the other spiritually. . . . In this way the visible world becomes our teacher and the invisible world is shown to be an eternal divine dwelling-place manifestly brought into being for our sake.[37]

Summarizing this view, Gregory of Sinai wrote, "A true philosopher is one who perceives in created things their spiritual Cause, or who knows created things through knowing their Cause."[38]

Thus contemplation of the creation all around us stood at the locus of genuine spirituality for these fourteenth-century thinkers. The experience of God, particularly the direct sense of God's immediacy in the created world (especially in our own lives as part of this created world) began by looking beyond ourselves to the vast expanses of God's creative handiwork. Critically, as with the sages, the disposition of the hesychasts to creation was not scientific curiosity and certainly not exploitative pragmatism. Instead, gripped with acute awareness of their own ignorance, these mystics stood before creation in wonder and contemplated the true God who alone has created and understands our world.

Contemporary Mysticism and the Environment

Though the terrain of Christian mysticism is substantially more familiar to church historians than to ministers, mysticism is far from an antiquated relic of Christianity's past. The past century has produced a wealth of new mystical thought and with it a continued focus on the importance of creation as an object of contemplation and wonder. This is particularly true in the Orthodox tradition, which, as mentioned, never separated its dogmatic from its mystical theology. As such, the most developed and theologically rigorous mysticism continues to come from an apparently endless wellspring of Orthodox theologians, among them Vladimir Lossky (already quoted from above), Dumitru Staniloae, John Meyendorff, John Romanides, Georges A. Barrios, and Christos Yannaras.

These are joined by many Orthodox thinkers of a less theological vein, like Romanian novelist Petru Dumitriu who, very much in the spirit of his

37. *On Commandments and Doctrines*, 127.
38. Ibid.

more familiar contemporary Elie Wiesel, writes of experiencing the immediacy of God in darker tones, in the doubt and turmoil of the atrocities peculiar to our modern world. He begins what he calls his "Conversation with a Nonexistent Interlocutor" with the paradox he believes is essential to faith in the modern world: "How can one love God when he obviously does not exist?"[39] Growing up in one of the most tumultuous times in European, and specifically Romanian history, Dumitriu was forced to flee his homeland to escape communist rule. During World War II and the communist aftermath in Eastern Europe, the confusion and disorientation of the immanence of evil, the perceived absence of God, and the impotence of humanity to understand or cope with either affected Dumitriu deeply, not only in the way he interacts with God but, in related ways, how he looks at a world that is laid bare by science but nevertheless alien: "for nothing is simple, and the universe is mathematicable, but incomprehensible."[40] Yet having admitted his sense of isolation and abandonment and having confessed that the experience of evil disproves the existence of God, Dumitriu turns to that same incomprehensible creation to find the joy which reminds him not only of the existence but of the intimacy of his Creator:

> It is enough to take one deep breath in a field after rain. It is enough to breathe, while you wipe your hands or your brow, after laying a hedge, to breathe in its smell of honey. It is enough to go outside on a winter's day, and take a deep breath, when it is very cold and the air is as dry as crystal. It is enough to breathe, to begin to rediscover good.[41]

Having found once again a simple hope which triumphs over even the most impenetrable despair, Dumitriu invites readers to join in mystical prayer, not only with each other but with all of creation.

> It is enough to swim in the sea or in a limpid river, with broad, slow movements, face plunged into the emerald water fused with sun, eyes open on the depths shot with radiant light. We can sense the joy of dolphins who dance round the bows of a ship, or enter into the slumber, the dream-life, of the swarms of translucid [sic] jellyfish, pale blue in the intenser blue of the waves. . . . We can see with our own eyes the love of life in animal and vegetable species as long as they have enough sun and water, and we feel

39. Dumitriu, *To the Unknown God*, 12.
40. Ibid., 45.
41. Ibid., 71.

the same sort of joy, essentially the same, though displayed on a human scale, which extends from sheer animal spirits to the joy of contemplative communion in prayer. And we are not alone.[42]

Neither are the Orthodox alone in their continued embrace of mysticism. Modern mystics emerge even among Protestants, where mysticism has been most deliberately and thoroughly marginalized from a discussion of Christian spirituality. As these Christian thinkers turn again and again to creation as the object of their awe and one of many sources of intimacy with the divine, modern mystics must grapple much more directly with the contemporary environmental crisis. Thus it is in their writings that we can see most clearly potential ways to link new directions in environmental ethics with old observations about the centrality of nature to the mystical experience of God.

Preeminent among these contemporary Protestant mystics is David James Duncan, whose fiction and nonfiction has been at the forefront of the fusion between environmentalism and Christian mysticism since the 1980s, when his novel *The River Why* became a best seller. Born a fifth-generation Seventh Day Adventist, Duncan very quickly realized that the doctrinal and ethical confines of what he unsympathetically terms "fundamentalist Christianity" could never lead him to anything like an authentic faith. In fact, he admits that from the first time he "heard a trout stream give a sermon"[43] he felt himself called down a mystical path unknown to or unacknowledged by typical American churches:

> Intense spiritual feelings were frequent visitors during my boyhood, but they did not come from churchgoing or from bargaining with God through prayer. The connection I felt to the Creator came, unmediated, from Creation itself. The spontaneous gratitude I felt for birds and birdsong, tree-covered or snowcapped mountains, rivers and their trout, moon and starlight, summer winds on wilderness lakes, the same lakes silenced by winter snows, spring resurrections after autumn's mass deaths—the intimacy, intricacy, and interwovenness of these things—became the spiritual instructors of my boyhood. In even the smallest suburban wilds I felt linked to powers and mysteries I could sincerely imagine calling the Presence of God. . . . Following intuition and love with all the sincerity and attentiveness I could muster, I consciously chose a life spent in the company of rivers, wilderness, Wisdom literature,

42. Ibid., 72.

43. Duncan, *God Laughs & Plays*, 5.

like-minded friends, and quiet contemplation. And as it turned out, this life—though dirt-poor in church pews—has enriched me with a sense of the holy, and left me far more grateful than I'll ever be able to say.[44]

Like sages and mystics for millennia before him, Duncan found in nature a sermon at once more compelling and more incomprehensible than anything he had or ever would hear from a pulpit. Like his forbearers, he felt most comfortable describing his relationship with it in terms of wonder.

When asked one winter to give a talk at a Christian college about his personal faith and churchgoing experience, Duncan worried about finding an appropriate way to express his unorthodox religious inclinations to a decidedly orthodox group of religious students.[45] Ultimately, he organized his speech around three words, the first of which was "wonder." Yet, in the speech, he struggles to define the term. Duncan describes the wonder he feels at creation as something like grace, particularly in that wonder is not something we seize but something which seizes us. We can resist wonder, we can dodge it—much in the same way that we can refuse God's grace—through cynicism or rationalism or arrogance (especially of an environmental sort), but if, in contrast, we seek wonder we must wait patiently on it to take hold of us. From there, however, Duncan finally grasps a means to define the character of wonder: it is something familiar suddenly filled with mystery, something closed suddenly becoming open, something terrible made bearable through patient consideration.

It is this wonder which stands at the heart of the Christian spiritual experience. In seeking God, wonder stands at the intersection of the desire to know and the inescapable fact of our own ignorance, so that in admitting this paradox wonder becomes "unknowing experienced as pleasure." Yet the centrality of wonder does not cease there, because wonder is then key to producing the kind of love that comes from experiencing God. In fact, wonder, for Duncan, is the key component of that love, as he suggests that "maybe love is just wonder aimed at a beloved."[46] Admittedly, this tentative definition of love falls far short of embracing everything that might be said about the biblical concept, but Duncan nevertheless locates wonder appropriately at the heart of our loving, grateful encounter with our Creator. The

44. Ibid., xiv.

45. The speech, "Wonder; Yogi; Gladly," with introduction can be found in Duncan, *God Laughs & Plays*, 5–16.

46. Duncan, *God Laughs & Plays*, 8.

wonder which we offer to God begins, for Duncan as for other mystics, in a wonder experienced when lost in creation.

Duncan manages to experience this wonder even in those features of creation which strike us as mundane. If the sages confuse us in Song of Solomon with their aesthetic appreciation of goats and nard, nothing in the Wisdom Literature compares to the panegyric offered by Duncan in praise of aquatic flies. Duncan describes—in prose too long to reproduce and too poetic to replicate—the many wonders of aquatic insects which he has encountered as a fly fisher: from the caddis fly who "knows, without even having to attend school, how to build itself a mobile home out of bits of river gravel" and sink that home to the bottom of the river. From there swarms of flies emerge in what Duncan can only surmise is the "insect world's rendition of the Baptist notion of 'Rapture,'" emerging from the confines of their material homes and the perilous waters to float weight-lessly into the heavens.[47]

Mayflies deserve even greater praise, as Duncan describes how "such a speck can figure out how to grow . . . not one but three delicate tails, and not two but four gossamer wings, and a suit of armor, the exoskeleton, which it sheds not once but as many as a hundred times as it grows: more miracles!" Mayflies are not, Duncan knows, all the same either, as within this one overlooked and seemingly insignificant corner of God's creation an infinite variety of shapes, sizes, and colors can be found. They are beautiful and wonderful and, he is quick to remind, entirely harmless. Adult mayflies do not even have mouths like other aquatic insects that are prone to bite or sting humans. The mouths are used to swim underwater as nymphs, but when they reach maturity, mayflies' mouths are sealed shut, causing them to "commence a fast that will last the rest of their lives." Like the caddis fly, they ascend into their own version of heaven in which Duncan observes them "hovering like angels—in order to mate like rabbits!"[48] It would be easy to chalk up Duncan's appellation of mayflies as "sexy spiritual beings"[49] to a kind of mystic's madness before creation until we remember the paral-lel semi-erotic tones with which the lover and beloved in Song of Solomon talk about rivers, gardens, spices, and herd animals. In every hyperbolic contour, the wonder that Duncan experiences before mayflies mirrors the wonder of the sages before God's creation.

47. Ibid., 134.
48. Ibid., 135.
49. Ibid., 136.

Duncan's is by no means a wonder-for-wonder's-sake either. As already noted, he believes strongly that wonder produces both knowledge and love of God. At the same time, he also insists that this wonder is the root of a rigorous environmental ethic. Like most environmentalists, Duncan bemoans the state of our collective response to the environmental crisis, and he is quick to single out corporate malfeasance and political apathy, double-talk, and profit motive as the most egregious offenders. Duncan is particularly concerned about the fate of Pacific salmon in the Snake and Columbia River systems in his native Pacific Northwest. As Duncan sees it, a small minority of dams are threatening the fish with extinction and the refusal of national political actors to accept this threatens to unravel the entire ecosystem of which salmon are the heart and soul.[50] Yet it is important to note that Duncan's Christian mysticism places important checks on his environmentalist activities, creating the framework for engagement with the environmental crisis and allowing him to think critically about the application of environmental ethics.

The above praise of aquatic flies, for example, actually occurred in the context of criticizing the American environmentalist movement not praising it and certainly not speaking on its behalf. Like the protagonist in his *The River Why*, Duncan is an avid fly fisher which often sets him at odds with many environmental activists groups, among whom Duncan believes lurk "some of the most highly principled, one-pointed, *humorless* people on earth."[51] It was in giving a talk to one such organization that Duncan encountered a woman who equated his love of catch and release fishing to animal torture. At first, Duncan tried explaining the scientific importance that many fishers and hunters play in the preservation of ecosystems and the importance of taking joy in the natural world as a way to heighten its immediacy for us, and thus the urgency of its protection. Failing to convince her, Duncan launched into his sermon on the angelic mayfly as a way to illustrate the hypocrisy of the environmental bias toward megafauna—the fact that, in spite of protestations about a general concern for nature, most of the attention and funding for environmental protection goes to pandas and whales—and, more importantly, to explain that humans must protect nature as participants in it rather than observers of it. The

---

50. One of many possible examples of Duncan's concern over these issues can be seen in the speech he gave to the Pacific Writers' Connection entitled "No Great Things . . ." and included in *God Laughs & Plays*, 105–28.

51. *God Laughs & Plays*, 131.

predatory impulse of humanity, within its proper and natural bounds, is no more immoral than the trout's predatory impulse to consume the equally magnificent mayfly.[52]

In essence, Duncan argues that by allowing humans to live as they were created to live and to engage nature as they were designed to engage it, by being the vehicle through which humanity rediscovers the wonder of God's world, the trout participate in their own preservation by silently reminding humanity of its duties to the created world. It is no small stretch to imagine that Duncan's mysticism leads him down a path in which the members of PETA[53] as much as the heads of Exxon or BP would be enriched by a weekend fishing the Snake River.

Conclusion

Notably, however, David James Duncan's mysticism also directs him away from the confines of conventional Christianity. Though he continues to speak in highly Christian terms about God and a specific reverence for Jesus and his biblical teachings, these exist as much as artifacts of his Christian upbringing as they do dogmatic beliefs in the basic tenets of the Christian faith. He instead has embraced with equal vigor the sapiential literature of Buddhism and Hinduism, saying of the Christian claim to exclusivity that he can be "glad you're standing strong in the sunbeam named Christianity. But the existence of your beam does nothing to lessen the intensity or reality of the other beams."[54] What is left is a kind of pan-religious theistic mysticism, strongly flavored by the Jewish sages and Christian mystics but by no means unadulterated.

Duncan alerts us to the same problem which was introduced at the beginning of the chapter, the necessary interdependence of mysticism and theology, of the dynamic immediacy of personal experience and the cool stability of church life. Whereas he suggests that the rejection of mysticism has violently separated Christianity "from its own greatest spiritual and communal riches"[55] and may well be responsible for the denominationalism and secularism of the Western world, Duncan fails to see how his own

---

52. The complete interchange can be found in Duncan, *God Laughs & Plays*, 130–38.

53. People for the Ethical Treatment of Animals, an American animal rights advocacy organization.

54. Duncan, *God Laughs & Plays*, 186.

55. Ibid., 98.

rejection of theology and institutional Christianity have left him equally (if oppositely) impoverished. Vladimir Lossky explains:

> Outside the truth kept by the whole Church personal experience would be deprived of all certainty, of all objectivity. It would be a mingling of truth and of falsehood, of reality and of illusion: "mysticism" in the bad sense of the word. On the other hand, the teaching of the Church would have no hold on souls if it did not in some degree express an inner experience of truth, granted in different measure to each one of the faithful. There is, therefore, no Christian mysticism without theology; but above all, there is no theology without mysticism.[56]

For all the truth to be found in the purely mystical Christianity of Duncan—and, make no mistake, it is amply present—there is the ever-present specter of illusion lurking always right behind it.

Here the sages offer a way forward, because even in their most awe-struck moments theirs is never a wonder without knowledge. In fact, the opening refrain of the Proverbs testifies to the critical importance of instruction in the pursuit of wisdom, immediately precluding the purely individual wanderings that might lead us to believe our experiences are the sole measure of truth. Immediately the young seeker is warned, "Hear, my child, your father's instruction, and do not reject your mother's teaching" (1:8). Parents are but one source of guidance, and the sage's admit many others: wise friends, wise spouses, and wise teachers among them. Though they rarely speak of them directly, it would be foolish to assume that the sages do not also have their own religious background in mind when they talk about the importance of guidance. Certainly when they speak of God's creation, they do so in a full knowledge of the creation narratives. When they write of justice in that creation (the subject of the final two chapters of this book), they do so knowing the law and what it describes as just. When they write of the greatness of God, in both pleasure and wrath, they surely do so firmly in the knowledge of the mighty acts God performed on behalf of their ancestors, even if the flood, the Exodus, and the conquest of Canaan are not spoken of explicitly.

Mystics who have stayed close to their respective churches have often, as Lossky suggests, proved the greatest and most orthodox theologians, though there are certainly ample cases in which mystics have been shunned, excommunicated, or, like Duncan, gone into a kind of voluntary

56. Lossky, *Mystical Theology*, 9.

ecclesiastical exile. For every Meister Eckhart accused (perhaps unjustly) of heresy there is a Gregory of Nyssa remembered as one of the earliest and ablest defenders of the divinity of Jesus and the Holy Spirit. The desire for and pursuit of a personal experience of the immediacy of God through wonder at his creation—what we have been calling "mysticism"—need not necessarily lead to unorthodoxy and certainly not a pantheistic worship of nature.

What it must lead to, quite necessarily, is a more robust sense of the urgency of environmental protection. What the mystics demonstrate conclusively—building directly on what the sages clearly suggest—is that the survival and health of the vast and wonderful creation around us is essential not only to our physical health (a claim so obvious that it is appalling how regularly science needs to publicly defend it) but, much more importantly, to our spiritual health. If God's creation is the nearest and most accessible means by which we can experience wonder and, in so doing, begin our ascent to a fuller, richer experience of the fullness of God's divinity, love, and creative genius, then its preservation is an ethical imperative. After all, as Duncan reminds us, "it is *this* world . . . that God loved so much that He bequeathed it His Son,"[57] and by mirroring that love for the world we may begin a mystical return journey to its infinite divine source.

---

57. Duncan, *God Laughs & Plays*, xxvi.

Chapter Three

Wisdom and the Character of Creation

Introduction

THE 2011 DOCUMENTARY MOVIE *Buck* tells the story of Buck Brannaman, a man who travels the country holding clinics teaching people how to train horses. Buck's story served as the inspiration behind the 1998 Robert Redford movie *The Horse Whisperer*. As a boy Buck's father physically abused him and his older brother until, at the age of twelve, a football coach saw the scars on Buck's body and found a foster home for him. His foster parents treated him with respect, care, and loving discipline. This new home environment transformed Buck's view of the world and surprisingly changed how he trained horses, something Buck had always loved doing. Buck no longer trained horses in the traditional manner of "breaking" them but started taking a much more humane approach. His approach evolved into a philosophy which teaches that fine horsemanship is a way of life and informs how you treat your spouse, neighbors, strangers, and how you discipline your children. According to Buck, you do not shift out of one way of acting around people to another way of acting around horses.

In his clinics Buck explains that how a horse behaves says a lot about the horse's owner: "A horse is a mirror to your soul and sometimes you might not like what you see in the mirror. When you start handling horses your own personal issues start coming out."[1] He tells his students that if they observe their horses carefully they can learn much about themselves, their character, and how to relate to others.

---

1. *Buck* (2011).

In our increasingly urbanized world, fewer and fewer of us have any significant contact with horses, but the principles are by no means limited to the equestrian world. What is true for horses is true for all of creation, flora and fauna, habitat and inhabitants alike. Regular contact with some form of creation is essential to developing healthy relationships, a healthy character, and a healthy lifestyle. This chapter explores why, what, and how we can learn from the world around. The first half lays a foundation for that relationship while the second half, building off that foundation, describes more specifically what we learn from creation. For those who have eyes to see and ears to hear, creation is a teacher of vices to avoid and virtues to nurture.

The World Created By Wisdom

In creating the world, God breathed into it wisdom, therefore creation possesses value separate and apart from its use to humans. Wisdom fills creation with intrinsic worth. One text in particular reveals this core quality, Proverbs 8:22–31:

> The LORD created me [Wisdom] at the beginning of his work,
>> the first of his acts of long ago.
> Ages ago I was set up,
>> at the first, before the beginning of the earth.
> When there were no depths I was brought forth,
>> when there were no springs abounding with water.
> Before the mountains had been shaped,
>> before the hills, I was brought forth—
> when he had not yet made earth and fields,
>> or the world's first bits of soil.
> When he established the heavens, I was there,
>> when he drew a circle on the face of the deep,
> when he made firm the skies above,
>> when he established the fountains of the deep,
> when he assigned to the sea its limit,
>> so that the waters might not transgress his command,
> when he marked out the foundations of the earth,
>> then I was beside him, like a master worker;

and I was daily his delight,

   rejoicing before him always,

rejoicing in his inhabited world

   and delighting in the human race.

Wisdom proclaims that she was created first *before* God created the heavens and the earth, before the mountains and hills and streams. Wisdom announces that she was also with Yahweh *during* the creation process: "I was there," "I was beside him" (vv. 27, 30). God used wisdom to create, shape, and form the cosmos. Finally, wisdom describes her delight as a "master worker," skilled in building and rejoicing in the results that ended with the creation of both non-humans and humans (vv. 30–31). Wisdom existed before creation, was beside God as the world was created, and became God's building partner. Under God's tutelage Wisdom became a skilled craftsman; she gained expertise in developing and building in the cosmos. It is no surprise then that immediately following Proverbs chapter 8 Wisdom is found building her earthly home (9:1–6; see also 24:3–4).[2]

Wisdom is the bond between God and creation as well as the tie that binds humans to creation. One cannot talk about creation without talking about wisdom; the two are fused together. It is necessary, however, to broaden our perspective and explore further the dynamics of how wisdom and creation interact with their surroundings.

The Nature of Creation: Stability and Flexibility

Wisdom rejoices in her relationship with God, with creation, and with other human beings as the following verses describe:

Then I was beside him, like a master worker;

and I was daily his delight,

rejoicing before him always,

rejoicing in his inhabited world

and delighting in the human race. (8:30–31)

God created the bond between wisdom, creation, and humans, empowering them with an element of independence from God. Creation

---

2. It is significant then that the wisdom books define the quality of wisdom, when embraced by humans, as the skill or expertise in "building" or creating a successful life and negotiating its complexities. See Bland, *Proverbs, Ecclesiastes, Song of Songs*, 29.

possesses endemic qualities enabling it to make adjustments to other forces of nature. For example, while creation contains certain predictable traits, it can also be quite unpredictable. On the one hand, the seasons of the year come and go with regularity (see Gen 8:22). Mountains and hills and rivers and oceans and land formations remain relatively unchanged for thousands of years. Wildlife exhibit predictable behavior patterns and live in specific habitat. Bird migrations occur in routine cycles. Creation displays an established orderliness.

On the other hand, creation is not always predictable. Even though the seasons of the year display a predictable pattern, within those seasons there is much that remains capricious. As the Teacher in Ecclesiastes repeatedly says of nature, "you do not know" what is going to happen. The weather is quite unstable:

> Divide your means seven ways, or even eight,
> for *you do not know* what disaster may happen on earth.
> When clouds are full,
> they empty rain on the earth;
> whether a tree falls to the south or to the north,
> in the place where the tree falls, there it will lie.
> Whoever observes the wind will not sow;
> and whoever regards the clouds will not reap.
> Just as *you do not know* how the breath comes to the bones in the mother's womb, so *you do not know* the work of God, who makes everything.
> In the morning sow your seed, and at evening do not let your hands be idle; for *you do not know* which will prosper, this or that, or whether both alike will be good.[3] (Eccl 11:1–6)

The Teacher emphasizes the uncertainty of the world. Humans cannot always know where disaster will happen or which way a tree will fall or what direction the wind will blow or where it will rain or whether or not the crops will grow. Creation displays spontaneity with a sudden cloudburst or thunderstorm or earthquake or tornado. Sometimes snow and rain come at inappropriate times (Prov 26:1). God established boundaries for the surging waves of the ocean (Job 38:8–11) and set limits on the power of Behemoth and Leviathan (Job 40:15—41:34). But within those boundaries and limits creation displays an unpredictable wildness. By wisdom God gives

---

3. Emphasis added.

creation litheness. Stability operates in tension with spontaneity to create opportunities for nature's productive powers to work their effects.

The routine and reliable rhythms of creation are vital to the sages who rely on, learn from, and instruct others based on that order. According to them, the one who is wise will live in sync with the patterns of creation. A problem arises, however, when one puts too much stock in nature's predictability. The sages have been accused of possessing an unbending view of the order of the cosmos, of believing the cosmos operated by a rigid system.[4] This belief naturally carries over into the human realm, which supposedly reflects this same predictable quality. Automatically programmed to reward the pious and punish the perverse, human society, it was believed, operates on a strict system of rewards and punishments; a certain type of character automatically produces certain consequences.

Certainly it is true that some wisdom teaching appears to reflect this worldview (e.g., Prov 26:27). Many of the proverbs in Proverbs 10–15 appear to operate on a strict system that believes specific acts will produce specific consequences or certain types of character will automatically generate certain consequences. On a closer examination, however, the sages did not hold to a rigid view of order. While the sages did believe that consequences result from certain choices made, they also lead readers into more complex scenarios as they progress through the book of Proverbs. As the reader enters Proverbs chapters 16–29 rigidity and predictability are supplemented with ever more flexibility and complexity. For example, one finds ambiguity regarding the value of wealth as the better-than proverbs attest to (Prov 16:8, 16, 19; 17:1; 19:22; 22:1). Even more importantly, plans do not always work out, and humans are limited in their understanding of the world (Prov 16:1–9; 21:30–31; 27:1). Wisdom ensures neither wealth nor security, because in the human and non-human worlds unpredictability, flexibility, and spontaneity remain ever-present qualities.

The tension between stability and spontaneity means that creation does not run like a precision clock operated by some great clockmaker and wisdom is not creation's blueprint. Instead, creation is a vibrant, living reality, and wisdom must be understood as its genetic makeup. In fact, one of the reasons the sages personify wisdom in the form of a human (see Prov

---

4. Job and his three friends believe the cosmos operates out of a rigid set of rules. Even though Job believes he has done nothing wrong, he with his friends still holds to the belief that the righteous prosper and the wicked suffer. Job on one occasion says, "Ask the animals, and they will teach you; the birds of the air, and they will tell you. . . . Who among all these does not know that the hand of the Lord has done this?" (Job 12:7-9).

1–10) is to express its versatile nature. Like the complex personality of a human, wisdom expresses a full range of complexity, unpredictability, and incomprehensibility. None of which should suggest that wisdom manifests in creation through random acts, no matter how unpredictable nature seems to be. The choice by the sages of a human personality to describe the quality of wisdom brings out its relational dimension, giving form to the simultaneous experience of stability and spontaneity. The world, created and sustained by wisdom, is a social process that is constantly changing and moving.

Still, the sages did believe in an orderly universe, just not an order that functioned like an automaton; it was not fate producing. They expended tremendous energy uncovering certain patterns and discovering the physical and moral order, but they also understood that living in harmony with the order of the universe may not always bring wealth and fortune. It would, however, generate character qualities conducive to healthy relationships with others and with creation, just as neglecting that order would result in the deformation of character. In this the sages resemble, at least superficially, the countless primordial nature religions around the world that sought truth and happiness by tapping into the secret order of nature. What distinguishes sapiential thought, however, was that this knowledge of the natural world could never be an end in itself. The sages respected creation for what it revealed about the Creator God and the divine wisdom by which creation was accomplished. Precisely what was revealed and to what extent humans could access that revelation, however, requires considerations beyond acknowledging the tension between stability and spontaneity that wisdom brings to the created order.

Wisdom and Natural Moral Order

The relationship between revelation and creation has long been shackled to the controversial notions of general revelation and natural law. During the Protestant Reformation, those who broke with the Roman Catholic Church rejected general revelation in favor of *sola scriptura*.[5] This partly reflected the more dire view of sin held by many Protestants which believed that the capacity for human reason had become so corrupted that, even if God had in fact revealed the divine nature or cosmic truths in creation, fallen

---

5. General revelation holds that God is known through observing creation and human reason.

humanity could not be counted on to grasp them. It also radically simplified the grounds for Protestant doctrine; the Bible, at least in theory, was not open to interpretation in quite so broad a way as creation.

As the centuries progressed, the Enlightenment popularized a notion of natural revelation and natural law in which revelation in creation complemented and then eventually replaced the special revelation of Scripture. Forward-thinking theologians and deists increasingly depicted God as a benevolent clockmaker who had built the machinery of the world and set it in motion to operate on universal, static, and rationally accessible physical and moral laws. Building on and taking to one extreme the long Christian tradition of looking for the Creator in creation, these thinkers allowed science to supplant faith as the primary means for engaging both God and the world.

Contemporary Christians cannot help but realize that, on the one hand, *sola scriptura* has failed to produce a unified Christianity even without the complicating evidence of general revelation and, on the other hand, that science alone is an inadequate means to achieve knowledge of God (or even to pursue a morally upright course with regard to creation). It is necessary therefore to revisit once again the way in which creation reveals the Creator.

Moral Order in Creation

One premise of natural law has always been the belief in an objective moral order.[6] By breathing wisdom into the created world, God established boundaries and a general sense of right and wrong in the way the world operates. That sense of right and wrong is a natural part of the warp and woof of human and non-human life. It makes up the dynamic order of creation. This moral order of creation has direct bearing on humans. As has already been shown from Proverbs 8:22–31, there is clearly an interconnection between the cosmic realm and the human realm. Wisdom binds the two together (8:30–31). Therefore, what happens in the cosmic realm influences humans and what happens in the human realm affects the cosmos. This interdependence is displayed in one of the instruction poems in Proverbs.

> Under three things the earth trembles;
> under four it cannot bear up:

6. Bretzke, "Natural Law," 542.

> a slave when he becomes king,
>
> and a fool when glutted with food;
>
> an unloved woman when she gets a husband,
>
> and a maid when she succeeds her mistress. (Prov 30:21–23)

The realm of the cosmos is shaken when the human social realm is disturbed. The sages did not imagine literal earthquakes at these social reversals and neither should we. It is nevertheless significant to see the close connection between cosmos and social world in the imagination of the sages and their audience. It is reasonable to both that what happens in the realm of human interactions reverberates through the whole created order. God created the world with a sense of order. As God imposes an order on the cosmic realm, humans by wisdom are called to impose order on the social realm.

Discovering the Moral Order

Humans discover this natural moral order in different ways. One significant way is through careful attention, observation, and reflection.[7] The sapient understands the importance of observing the world from the smallest of creatures (e.g., an ant, Prov 6:6; or a bird, Prov 1:17) to the most powerful (e.g., a lion, Prov 30:29–31). Listen to how they describe the process of discovering insight from creation:

> I passed by the field of one who was lazy,
>
> by the vineyard of a stupid person;
>
> and see, it was all overgrown with thorns;
>
> the ground was covered with nettles,
>
> and its stone wall was broken down.
>
> Then I saw and considered it;
>
> I looked and received instruction.
>
> A little sleep, a little slumber,
>
> a little folding of the hands to rest,

---

7. Observation of nature is one source James Crenshaw, who has spent his life studying Wisdom Literature, identifies as important. Two other sources he mentions are (1) listening to the reports of others who claimed to have discovered valuable insight and (2) an immediate encounter with Deity. Crenshaw, "Acquisition of Knowledge," 245–52. As we saw with the mystics, this immediate encounter with Deity very often has the observation of nature as its prerequisite.

and poverty will come upon you like a robber,

and want, like an armed warrior. (Prov 24:30–34)

This wise individual happens upon a field one day as she is traveling along. She stops for a moment to observe. It is a field overgrown with thorns and thistles and the wall around it in disrepair. She reflects on her observations and receives valuable instruction or at least affirmation of a belief already held. Finally, she expresses the lesson learned in the rhetorical form of a proverb: "A little sleep, a little slumber, a little folding of the hands to rest, and poverty will come upon you like a robber, and want, like an armed warrior." Interestingly this same proverb is quoted on another occasion after a sage watches with intrigue the behavior of an ant (Prov 6:10–11).[8]

Discerning the natural law of creation not only involves observing the non-human realm but the human realm as well. The sages offer multiple examples of witnessing human interactions and learning from them. One classic example is the father observing the encounter between the strange woman and the vulnerable youth in Proverbs 7:6–23. Positive experiences are also observed and offered as instruction to youth (Prov 31:10–31). The parallel in methodologies is striking, as the sages make very few distinctions between how the wise look at and learn from creation and the behavior of humanity. Creation becomes, in essence, as wise a teacher as any sage or parent or circle of virtuous friends. Its wise students become participant-observers, integrated and active in the non-human world every bit as much as the human one. As such, they develop the skill of attentiveness but they do not simply observe.[9] They filter and rethink observations because of and through their faith in God, conserving and preserving them in memorable sayings along the way.[10]

8. A proverb is produced when observers discover a common thread of insight surfacing from among a number of different experiences. Thus a proverb is a short sentence based on the observation of a series of long and difficult experiences.

9. For a description of the methodology in doing participant observation, consult the following sources: Taylor and Bogdan, *Introduction to Qualitative Research Methods*, 15–75; Patton, *Qualitative Evaluation and Research Methods*, 199–219. For an excellent example of a study based on participant observation see Philipsen, "Speaking like a Man."

10. This is true of the sayings in Proverbs 22:17—24:22. Yahweh's sages have observed and learned from Egyptian wisdom, filtered it through their belief system, and incorporated it into their instruction. One observes creation and the world around and extracts the truths that God placed there. Scholars have long recognized that this section of Proverbs displays a very close affinity to the thirty sayings of the Egyptian sage

Prerequisites for Discovering Moral Order

Not just anyone, however, is able to glean insights into how the Creator expects humans to live responsibly in this world by observing creation, a fact which radically distinguishes the "natural law" observed by the sages from its more classical manifestations in Enlightenment theology. First, fundamental to the natural law of the sage, is that the "world has objective meaning because God made it through wisdom and God's wisdom shines through it."[11] This means that natural law for the sage is not purely a rational exercise of the mind but must include a faithful relationship with God most commonly described as "the fear of the Lord." Second, for the sage natural law does not come in the form of a codified set of rules but rather through understanding the dynamic order of creation and striving to align with that order in a way that reflects the image of God and serves to bring order in a specific social context whether it be family or a larger community. The order of creation is then less a feat of mechanical engineering, the laws of which may be discovered and replicated, than a complex dance that humanity is required to learn the steps to even as the song is playing.

Third, natural law from the perspective of wisdom enables nonbelievers to understand the fundamental moral order of the universe and live within that framework. At the same time the natural moral order enables believers to enter into a deeper relationship with God that leads to redemption. In other words, there is a general level of wisdom without which humans could not exist. The absence of this wisdom would result in total chaos. But then there is a more sacred wisdom by which those who fear the Lord operate.[12]

Fourth, Wisdom Literature is quite unpretentious about what one can learn from the natural moral order of the universe. One can learn the basics: that adultery leads to all kinds of destructive consequences including a loss of reputation (5:12–14; 6:33), personal loss (6:27–32; 7:21–3), and loss of physical well-being (Prov 5:11; 6:34–5). One can also know that robbery, murder, and greed are wrong (Prov 1:8–19). At the same time, wisdom is quite aware of the limitations of humans learning from the moral

---

Amenemope (ca. 1100 BCE). See, for example, Roland Murphy, *Proverbs*, 290–94. See also Fox, *Proverbs 10–31*, 756–62.

11. VanDrunen, "Wisdom and the Natural Moral Order," 162. Some of the following insights come from VanDrunen's essay.

12. VanDrunen, refers to these different levels as "common wisdom" and "sanctified wisdom." 162.

order of the universe. As much as a wise person plans and makes decisions, the Lord has the final say (Prov 16:1–3, 9). As much as we can learn from nature, there is much we do not know (Eccl 11:1–6). Many parts of nature are simply downright mystifying (Prov 30:18–19). The wise do not even know what the next day will bring (Prov 27:1). While much can be learned from the moral order of the universe, the wise know that much still remains hidden. Their encounter with creation, therefore, begins always in an awareness of their own ignorance rather than any epistemological hubris. Revelation through creation not only presumes faith to make it comprehensible, it also stops short of a complete knowledge of either God or the world created through divine wisdom.

In sum a theological framework is needed to responsibly interact with creation and appreciate its intrinsic value and moral order. This framework includes a reverence for God, an awareness of the dynamic order of creation, the ability of all humans to understand the fundamental ethics of the universe, and a humility regarding what one can learn. When individuals are attentive to creation, they learn something about the nature of God and how God works in the world. When we submit to the dynamic order of creation, we learn to live wisely and responsibly.

How We Learn from Creation

This theological foundation is a necessary prerequisite for learning from creation, but it is not itself the content of that knowledge. That God has filled creation with wisdom giving it intrinsic value makes up the core of its character, and we see that creation operates on the basis of a dynamic order holding in tension the qualities of stability and flexibility. Understanding this foundation now allows us to flesh out more specifically how we learn from creation, what we learn from it, and what we give in return.

The Art and Skill of Learning from Creation

The sages believed creation was a powerful and persuasive teacher of virtues.[13] They used examples and analogies from the natural world not just

---

13. This is also true of the one wisdom book in the New Testament, the book of James. James frequently uses analogies from nature to illuminate moral qualities and persuade his readers to embody those qualities in their lives, e.g., 1:6, 10–11, 18; 3:1–12; 3:18; 4:14; 5:7.

to impart information but as a persuasive strategy to move listeners to action. The gravitational pull for youth to live a selfish life was strong (Prov 1:8–19), so the teachers of wisdom used all means at their disposal to lure youth away from that appealing lifestyle. They became keen observers of their world thoughtfully processing those observations in a way that would best instruct youth on how to live morally responsible lives. By developing a certain perspective on life the sages tapped into this natural resource and discovered valuable insights to communicate via example and analogy. This perspective includes several characteristics.

First, and most fundamentally, it begins with one's relationship with God. The truly wise are those who fear the Lord. So being able to think and reflect analogously begins by believing that God is the Creator of the cosmos, and, by extension, that God and not humans are the center of that cosmos. The fear of the Lord means that individuals remove themselves from the center of life and live out the belief that God is the center of all things. It is through the fear of the Lord that people filter the experiences and observations of life. In other words, we do not approach experiences as a blank slate. We come to them with a set of beliefs, the most fundamental being a faith in the God who created the world. We come with a posture that embraces the fear of the Lord. But as the biblical sages say, the fear of the Lord is only the *beginning* of wisdom. We begin with the fear of the Lord but must move forward from that point.

Second, the ability to learn from creation comes not only from one's relationship with God but also from one's character. VanDrunen describes this dimension from the perspective of Proverbs:

> The person with deep moral knowledge is not someone with moral factoids floating in her head but the one who is the right kind of person, the person of character. Moral obligation objectively known through the natural order cannot ultimately be separated from the virtues subjectively possessed by the knower, an important issue that I do not have space to explore here. Moreover, building true moral knowledge in others, the kind that sinks in deep and makes one the kind of person who can navigate effectively through a messy world, requires more than communicating pieces of information. It requires persuasion. Proverbs does not simply make authoritative claims but winsomely persuades those prone to foolishness to follow a better course. For Proverbs, true moral knowledge involves not pieces of information but a perception

and appreciation of practical truths as part of a beautiful whole of a life well lived.[14]

The kind of character we bring to the observations we make shapes what we see. Someone who is driven by greed will come away from an experience with a different take on it than someone who is guided by gratitude and humility. As much as who we are shapes our experiences, our experiences also shape who we are, evoking the proverbial chicken-and-egg scenario. One's experiences influence character and one's character influences experiences. Determining which comes first is less important than making meaningful use of the process. Not a meaningless cycle, the process is most productive when observers are willing to assess their present character—and how it conditions their perceptions—and remain open to change as needed. A vicious character and sinful behavior form a self-reinforcing spiral of decline just as cultivated virtue and righteous behavior elevate. This is as true for the human relationship with creation as it is with any moral aspect of our lives.

Third, recognizing the connections between the human and non-human realm comes with an increased awareness and attentiveness to the world in which we live. Not only is an unexamined life not worth living, a life lived in an unexamined world is not worth living. Through disciplined practice and experience the sages increased their abilities to see more deeply into the world of creation around them. They develop a "knack for noticing."[15] The ability to be attentive to the world around is available to those willing to take the discipline, time, and patience to do so. For those who desire to increase their ability to serve others and effectively communicate with them, attentiveness is a gift but also a learned skill.

A couple of words of caution are necessary here. On the one hand, individuals can impose their theology onto their observations of creation. This is what Job and his friends do. They observe the created order and impose their strict theological belief that righteous people always prosper and wicked people always suffer onto their observations (e.g., Job 12:7–10). Rather than learning from creation, they force the order of creation to fit their traditional beliefs. On the other hand, the one who wisely attends to the dynamic order of creation does not force analogies out of observations but rather reflects on those observations and identifies insights that naturally arise. If we approach every experience and every observation

14. VanDrunen, "Wisdom and the Natural Moral Order," 160.

15. McKenzie, Novel Preaching, 11–26.

determined to pull out some life lesson, like pulling out the prize in a Cracker Jacks box, then we will miss the value of that moment. The true gift and skill of observation does not pander to our thirst for meaning by constructing artificial analogies. Rather it makes the most of the moment, reflects on it, mulls over it, and then if some insight naturally surfaces, one has identified a true lesson, which then has potential to become a powerful persuasive tool.

The Use of Examples and Analogies from Creation

The wise use two main forms to communicate instruction from creation: examples and analogies. We are not using these two terms in any technical sense at all but rather for the sake of better managing the material found in Wisdom Literature. "Examples" refers to more lengthy bodies of material that offer insights from creation, while "analogies" refers to brief rhetorical phrases that act as similes or metaphors, often embedded within the form of a proverb. Both of these forms stem from observing creation and both serve the purpose of instructing listeners about the virtuous life and persuading them to choose that path. Solomon, the wisest of the wise, gleaned much wisdom from learning the art of observing and used a plethora of examples and analogies from nature to pass on his wisdom to others (1 Kgs 4:29–34).

Examples from Creation

Wisdom frequently uses creation as an example of how to live a responsible and virtuous life. As Ellen Davis writes, the sages use nature "to illustrate the operation of the virtues. They look to the animal kingdom for models of behavior that humans should emulate or avoid; they look to the condition of the fertile soil to show the consequences of practicing or neglecting the virtues."[16] This is true in the case of Job and his friends. In response to his three friends, Job presents an argument from creation he knows they would not deny. And that is it is common knowledge that the beasts of the field, the birds of the air, and the fish of the sea all know what the three friends know. The friends are not revealing anything new. Job believes, as do the friends, that creation teaches important moral lessons, in particular

16. Davis, "Preserving Virtues," 187.

that when you sin punishment automatically follows. Though Job and the friends misread what nature teaches, they do bring up an important source for them to consider as they search for answers to Job's dilemma:

> But ask the animals, and they will teach you;
>> the birds of the air, and they will tell you;
>> ask the plants of the earth, and they will teach you;
>> and the fish of the sea will declare to you.
> Who among all these does not know
>> that the hand of the LORD has done this?
> In his hand is the life of every living thing
>> and the breath of every human being. (Job 12:7–10)

That Job and the friends misinterpret creation may indicate they were not as in touch with the natural world as they thought they were, not practicing the kind of attentiveness and observation described above as necessary for true knowledge. More likely the friends and Job stumbled for want of the proper theological framework for approaching creation; they lacked a relationship with Yahweh and a strong character, which together clouded their perception. Aware of its dangers and limitations, the wise nevertheless believed that humans have much to learn from nature. All of nature, animals, birds, plants, and fish, are teachers. At the end of the book of Job, God is much more persuasive than the friends in using creation to instruct Job (Job 38–41).

Psalm 1, a wisdom psalm, serves as another illustration of how the sages use creation as an example to instruct in right living. The psalmist teaches the reader about righteousness and wickedness by using two contrasting examples of a tree and chaff. The psalmist compares the righteous to trees:

> planted by streams of water,
> which yield their fruit in its season,
> and their leaves do not wither.
> In all that they do, they prosper. (Ps 1:3)

The psalmist points to a healthy tree and instructs, "Look how its roots go deep into the ground. It lives by sparkling streams; its leaves are full and provide shade; it produces fruit; it is prosperous." Then the contrasting example: "The wicked are not so, but are like chaff that the wind drives away" (1:4). Not much can be said about the wicked other than they are like a little flake of chaff that the wind blows wherever it wants. The tree is stable and secure. It does what it was made to do and that is it provides fruit, creates a home for wildlife, and gives shade. The chaff is directionless, momentary, and without purpose. The examples are crystal clear in their message: those who desire to live righteous lives will model themselves after the fruitful tree and not the aimless speck of chaff.

In metaphoric language replicating the imagery used in the Song of Songs, the sage teaches about faithfulness to one's spouse by using the example of streams and cosmic waters:

> Drink water from your own cistern,
>> flowing water from your own well.
> Should your springs be scattered abroad,
>> streams of water in the streets?
> Let them be for yourself alone,
>> and not for sharing with strangers.
> Let your fountain be blessed,
>> and rejoice in the wife of your youth,
>> a lovely deer, a graceful doe.
> May her breasts satisfy you at all times;
>> may you be intoxicated always by her love.
> Why should you be intoxicated, my son, by another woman
>> and embrace the bosom of an adulteress? (Prov 5:15–20)

Everyone knows that rivers should not flood into the streets of cities because God set limitations on where they are to flow (Prov 8:28–29; see also Acts 17:26). They must stay within the banks that God long ago created for them. When they break through those banks, they do not fulfill the purpose for which God created them. In the same way, when one engages in sexual intercourse beyond the boundaries of marriage, relationships are destroyed.

Many other instances are found throughout the pages of Wisdom Literature. For example, youth learn that going into the house of the strange woman is like an ox being led to a slaughterhouse or a bird rushing into a snare (Prov 7:6–23). One witnesses the consequences of living the life of a fool by observing the field of one who is lazy (Prov 24:30–34). By observing the demise of certain elements in nature, through images of a storm and birds and an almond tree and a grasshopper, youth learn to "remember your creator in the days of your youth" before they face the end of their life

(Eccl 12:1–7). One gains motivation for practicing generosity by realizing the risks farmers take in the face of nature's precarious weather patterns (Eccl 11:1–6). We learn about the virtues of enjoying the daily provisions God gives through eating and drinking (Eccl 2:24–26). We also learn of the brevity and vanity of life as we experience the redundant cycle of the sun, wind, rivers, and seasons of the year (Eccl 1:2–11).

Using examples from nature as a strategy for moral instruction is almost a lost art. One of the main reasons for this is the growing detachment between humans and nature. Another is our lack of attentiveness to the world around us. Creation, however, provides a rich repertoire of examples vital to moral instruction.

The Cache La Poudre River runs just a quarter of a mile from my parents' farm in Northern Colorado.[17] It is a fast flowing river fed primarily by snowmelt from the Rocky Mountains. I used to walk across the pasture to fish along its banks. Canoers, kayakers, and rafters frequently test their skills on its swift waters. At one point during the 1980s developers wanted to dam the river in order to provide water to ranchers on the eastern plains of Colorado during the dry summer months. The hydroelectric project would provide year-round power. Holmes Rolston believed, however, doing so would destroy the river's natural value.[18] Along with a group of supporters he contributed to making a successful argument for the intrinsic value of the river because it gives humans perspective on the transient nature of life. Nature represents stability; humans are always in flux. He maintained that the Poudre River would not only provide recreational but also geologic perspective to an increasingly urban people. "Wild and free rivers were an irreplaceable gift of nature to society."[19] In 1986 the river became the first in Colorado to gain a federal wild and scenic designation. One of the arguments for preserving the river was that nature possesses moral significance vital to the well-being of society. That well-being included among other things the ability to look at the high walls of the river canyon and marvel at the transience of human life.

In similar fashion, the psalmist looked to the star-filled sky and gained new perspective on the smallness of his life (Ps 8). In the New Testament's wisdom book, the book of James, the sage uses a whole litany of examples from creation including horses, forest fires, the "cycle of nature," fig trees,

17. Reflections by Dave Bland .

18. Preston, *Saving Creation*, 120–31.

19. Preston, *Saving Creation*, 130.

and salt water to persuade his readers to use their words in an ethically responsible way (3:1–12). Few people today reach moral conclusions based on observations from nature, let alone use those observations to instruct others. For the sages of Scripture, however, examples from creation were a fundamental source for instruction in the virtues that form a mature character.

Analogies from Creation

Not only did the wise use extended examples from creation to teach morals, they also referenced creation in brief analogic phrases embedded within the lines of their instructions. The sages were good at identifying connections between the non-human world and humans. The use of analogy is essential to the way the wise educate. It would take far too much space to treat this phenomenon exhaustively, but one section in Proverbs will suffice to illustrate the point. The rhetorical form of the sayings found in chapters 25–27 of Proverbs is referred to as comparative or analogic parallelism where the first line of the proverb uses an analogy from the natural or social realm to drive home the truth or clarify the meaning of the statement in the second line.[20] So for example the first line in Proverbs 27:17 puts forth the analogy, "Iron sharpens iron." Then the second line states the lesson gained from the analogy, "as one friend sharpens another."

The proverbs in chapters 25–27 are rich in references to natural and social phenomena. Here is a sampling of some analogies from the natural sphere. They are placed in categories based on the type of analogy used: food, weather, animals and birds, and objects.

Analogies from Food

If you have found honey, eat only enough for you, or else, having too much, you will vomit it. (25:16)

It is not good to eat much honey, or to seek honor on top of honor. (25:27)

The sated appetite spurns honey, but to a ravenous appetite even the bitter is sweet. (27:7)

---

20. There are exceptions to this pattern.

Crush a fool in a mortar with a pestle along with crushed grain, but the folly will not be driven out. (27:22)

Anyone who tends a fig tree will eat its fruit, and anyone who takes care of a master will be honored. (27:18)

Analogies from the Weather

Like the cold of snow in the time of harvest are faithful messengers to those who send them; they refresh the spirit of their masters. (25:13)

Like clouds and wind without rain is one who boasts of a gift never given. (25:14)

The north wind produces rain, and a backbiting tongue, angry looks. (25:23)

Like snow in summer or rain in harvest, so honor is not fitting for a fool. (26:1)

A continual dripping on a rainy day and a contentious wife are alike; to restrain her is to restrain the wind or to grasp oil in the right hand. (27:15–16)

Analogies from Animals and Birds

The lazy person says, "There is a lion in the road! There is a lion in the streets!" (26:13)

Like a dog that returns to its vomit is a fool who reverts to his folly. (26:11)

Like a sparrow in its flitting, like a swallow in its flying, an undeserved curse goes nowhere. (26:2)

Like a bird that strays from its nest is one who strays from home. (27:8)

Analogies from Various Objects

Like apples of gold in a setting of silver, is a word fitly spoken. (25:12)

Like a war club, a sword, or a sharp arrow is one who bears false witness against a neighbor. (25:18)

A whip for the horse, a bridle for the donkey, and a rod for the back of fools. (26:3)

For lack of wood the fire goes out, and where there is no whisperer, quarreling ceases. (26:20)

Whoever digs a pit will fall into it, and a stone will come back on the one who starts it rolling. (26:27)

A stone is heavy, and sand is weighty, but a fool's provocation is heavier than both. (27:3)

Iron sharpens iron, and one person sharpens the wits of another. (27:17)

Together, these represent only a small sample of analogies used from a small section in Proverbs. The sages use creation analogies in quite diverse ways sometimes as negative examples and sometimes as a positive. The analogies are used, for instance, to encourage the control of one's appetite, to emphasize showing honor to one in authority, to learn the importance of speaking a timely word, to refrain from boasting or backbiting, to illustrate the destruction of quarreling, to demonstrate foolish actions, or to underscore the value of healthy conflict. The analogies enable students to vividly visualize the moral lessons embodied in creation. They also allow students to experience vicariously through nature the consequences of a virtue practiced or ignored.

What We Learn from Creation

Learning from the Habitat

While we have long capitalized on the instrumental value of creation for humans (food, clothing, water, timber, oil, recreation, etc.), humanity has left almost completely untapped its intrinsic moral value. Through the disciplined practice of observation, creation has much to teach, and our neglect of those lessons has been pursued at our own peril. As we investigate the examples and analogies the sages use, some fundamental virtues rise to the surface.

One of the most basic character qualities we learn from creation is the virtue of discipline or self-control.[21] This virtue is not cultivated internally

---

21. James Crenshaw singles out "the virtues of self-control, restraint, eloquence, and honesty" as those on which the sages focused. Crenshaw, *Education in Ancient Israel*, 2.

and in isolation but through dynamic interaction with objective resources from without, particularly in relationship with family, community, and creation. In speaking about creation, Kevin Youngblood observes that the ultimate goal is for the individual to reflect the discipline of the larger "cosmic order that testifies to Yahweh's wisdom in creating a coherent universe."[22] An individual, a family, or a community that demonstrates self-restraint, reflects the order of creation.

Youngblood identifies similarities between the way the cosmos is created and the way a home is created by comparing the following two passages: Proverbs 3:19–20 and 24:3–4.[23]

> The LORD <u>by wisdom</u> founded the earth;
> <u>by understanding</u> he <u>established</u> the heavens;
> <u>by his knowledge</u> the deeps broke open,
> and the clouds drop down the dew. (3:19–20)

Now notice the underlined words in the description of wisdom building the cosmos (above) to wisdom building a home (below):

> <u>By wisdom</u> a house is built,
> and <u>by understanding</u> it is <u>established</u>;
> <u>by knowledge</u> the rooms are filled
> with all precious and pleasant riches. (24:3–4)

When a home is established by wisdom it imitates the way in which God created the cosmos.

Not only is wisdom to guide the way humans provide restraint and limitations to the larger social realm, wisdom is also employed to restrain an individual's emotions. Once again a parallel exists between what occurs in the world of creation and what occurs in the human world. God "assigned to the sea its limit, so that the waters might not transgress his command" (Prov 8:29). In the same way individuals must restrain their anger using the power of water as an analogy: "The beginning of strife is like letting out water; so stop before the quarrel breaks out" (Prov 17:14). The sages in Proverbs 5:15–20 also use the analogy of water overflowing into the city streets destroying homes and businesses as a description of the destructive power of uncontrolled lust. The Lord fixed certain boundaries in the cosmos for the sake of maintaining order and to enable the habitat

22. Youngblood, "Cosmic Boundaries," 140.

23. Ibid., 141.

to function at its maximum potential. Similarly when it comes to human emotions (anger, desire, pride, appetite, lust, etc.), crossing certain boundaries jeopardizes your well-being as well as the well-being of others. When emotions are kept within certain limits, it contributes to the social health of all. Therefore according to the sages, the skill to restrain self comes from without and not primarily from within. Individuals learn self-control from the family and community around them and from the cosmos in which they live.

Learning from the Inhabitants

Not only do habitats like water, wind, and soil serve as object lessons in self-discipline but so do the inhabitants, in particular animals. Walter Brueggemann perceptively writes that there is an element in which creaturely knowledge is not inferior to rational human thinking.[24] There are things we can learn from the non-human world, but often human hubris gets in the way of better understanding how we are to conduct ourselves. Sometimes the animal world knows better than we do and so a bird that avoids a trap is more prudent that foolish youth who blindly fall into it (Prov 1:17–18). The prophets observe that oxen, storks, turtledoves, swallows, and cranes are more aware of their responsibilities than are God's rebellious people (Isa 1:3; Jer 8:7). According to Jesus, we can learn from the birds of the air and the lilies of the field (Matt 6:25–30). The sage alerts young men to the dangers of sexual temptation by bringing to their attention the animal world: "Save yourself like a gazelle from the hunter, like a bird from the hand of the fowler" (Prov 6:5).

When Elihu gives Job his opinion on Job's situation, Elihu appeals to other oppressed people who do not cry out to God as Job does. Elihu goes further urging Job to learn from creation as Job faces injustices because, as he says, God "teaches us by the beasts of the field, Makes us wise by the birds of the heavens" (Job 35:11).[25]

---

24. Brueggemann, "Creatures Know," 8–12.

25. Translation by Marvin Pope in *Job*, 262. See also Clines, *Job 21–37*, 790, 800. *The Message* paraphrases the verse as follows: "When God sets out the entire creation as a science classroom, using birds and beasts to teach wisdom." The footnote in the NIV indicates that a few of the translators wanted to translate the verse as saying that God teaches humans through/by the beasts . . . through/by the birds.

Youngblood notes, "If a virtue is present in the instinctive behavior of an animal, it should be even more obvious in the intentional behavior of a human. Conversely, if a vice leads a senseless animal to disaster, it will lead a supposedly reasoning human into even more devastating disaster."[26]

Agrarian Virtues

When humans live close to the land, it is easier to see and learn self-control as well as other virtues. When humans disconnect from the created world around them, they lose a vital resource for moral instruction. The problem has been exacerbated over the past two centuries when more and more people have chosen to leave the rural countryside and relocate in urban settings. Still these virtues are a part of the earth's soil and readily available to those willing to learn.

As North Americans moved off the land and the farms during the nineteenth century they gravitated toward urban centers.[27] The cities provided more opportunities in the form of jobs, schools, entertainment, and conveniences. In so doing most Americans lost touch with the agricultural way of life and the virtues that were endemic to it. We do not want to idealize the agrarian past because it had its share of ethical problems, and the systematic mistreatment of the earth extends back in history far beyond the late nineteenth century when urbanization began in earnest in the United States. There was, however, a closer connection to the earth and with that connection, as we have already seen from wisdom's perspective, came a clearer awareness of certain character values and virtues.

Some secular philosophies have sprung up to address the disconnectedness between humans and the land. While they provide valuable insights, and though they align in a number of ways with the theology of biblical wisdom, in the end they can only take us so far. As we will see, when critiqued by the sages of Scripture they still come up short.

Elisabeth Graffy, in assessing a recent book by philosopher Paul Thompson,[28] describes the philosophy Thompson calls "agrarianism." Agrarianism is a virtue-based worldview and prior to the twentieth century

---

26. Youngblood, "Cosmic Boundaries," 148.

27. In the United States, the pace of urbanization in the seventy years between 1840–1910 was actually higher than the rate of urbanization in rest of the twentieth century.

28. Thompson, *Agrarian Vision*.

influenced even the way non-farmers lived.[29] As a philosophy, agrarianism is primarily concerned with teaching a specific type of moral character that included virtues like stewardship, self-reliance, and community solidarity.[30] An agrarian context naturally produced these virtues, even though anyone could and many did choose to ignore them. The loss of agrarian values as families moved into urban settings did not simply affect a small minority of the American population. It reached beyond agriculture and into a different worldview with different values.

As Americans continued to move off the farm and into the city during the twentieth century a more industrial mentality replaced them. Graffy uses the phrase "industrialism" to describe the urban worldview. The urban industrial paradigm became such a dominant force that even the practice of farming came to follow the industrial model. The industrial mentality "allows the pursuit of excesses that take the form of vice."[31]

In contrast to industrialism, agrarianism strengthens the connectedness between society and the natural world. Agrarianism tends to invest more in a shared sense of identity with others. Generally speaking the agrarian philosophy creates more of an awareness of the interconnectedness between the natural and social realm of life.

Central to an agrarian mindset is the development of a sense of place, a clear understanding of our identity as individuals. Even though a sense of place is often associated with a geographic location, it is better defined relationally primarily within and between social and natural spheres. Character is developed through this interrelationship and that character, that sense of identity, is not confined to a specific locale but is transferable. This is especially important in light of the mobility of Americans. One can, for example, develop the agrarian virtue of self-restraint and carry that virtue into different geographical locations.

Industrialism cultivates "competitive, self-interested, and largely atomistic individuals without a holistic grasp of sustainability or integration between social and natural spheres."[32] Industrialism does not so easily see interconnectedness. It invests more in the technical models and tends toward understanding agriculture from a technical perspective rather

29. "Agrarianism" is a term used by Paul Thompson as described in an article by Elisabeth Graffy. See Graffy, "Agrarian Ideals," 505.

30. Ibid.

31. Ibid.

32. Ibid.

than from a concern for efficiency. Agrarianism is more holistic whereas industrialism tends toward reductionism.

To tout agrarian virtues in an urban society is not a call to go back to the good old days of farming and rural life of the nineteenth and early twentieth centuries, because, as already mentioned, there were plenty of problems with that lifestyle. Rather it is an appeal to adapt and infuse the best of the agrarian ideal into the contemporary urban context. Graffy speaks of "urban agriculture" which seeks to accomplish four goals:

> (a) shape moral character by cultivating specific virtues: indus-triousness, stewardship, self-reliance, and good neighborliness or community solidarity; (b) inculcate an ethical sense of place; (c) support repetition of focal practices to reinforce habits that insure local integrity of natural and social patterns of interactions from one generation to the next; (d) connect many local communities characterized as above into a resilient democratic society.[33]

Graffy proposes that "urban gardens" may be one way of reshaping and activating agrarianism. She describes them as "self-styled vehicles for promoting a similar vision characterized by self-reliance, stewardship, and place-based and often deliberately multicultural and multi-generational communities that are simultaneously understood as both locally embedded and nationally related."[34] What she claims results from this is the develop-ment of a "moral character" that "once developed is tied to a person, not a place."[35]

Agrarianism has affinities with biblical wisdom. Both perspectives view certain virtues as innate to nature. Agrarianism confirms what we know from the sages, that certain virtues like discipline, stewardship, self-reliance, and community can be learned from living in rhythm with creation. But agrarianism can only takes us so far along the path to strength-ening character because it lacks the fundamental quality or relationship that enables humans to truly learn from creation. That is the fear of the Lord; the perspective that takes a God-centered view of life as opposed to a human-centered view. Without a God-centered view of creation our vision is myopic; we are limited in what we can learn about living in an orderly, responsible, and fulfilling way. From creation humans learn not so much

33. Ibid., 513–14.
34. Ibid., 514.
35. Ibid., 515.

what we are to do but what kind of people we ought to be. That in turn enables humans to responsibly care for creation.

What Humans Give to Creation: The Ecological Virtues

The virtues learned from creation not only enable humans to manage the social sphere productively but also the natural sphere. The solution to the environmental crisis is not the discovery of some new technology that will save the world but an ethic, a way of life that will respect and care for the world in which we live.[36] It is a set of ecological virtues that includes stewardship and community solidarity but also respect, sound judgment, and self-restraint.

From the book of Proverbs, Ellen Davis identifies two fundamental virtues that she claims are absolutely essential to the preservation of this planet: prudence and temperance.[37] These are the terms used in classical and medieval writing, but today the more familiar terms for these virtues might be good judgment and self-restraint. Davis maintains, and rightly so, that the book of Proverbs can be understood as an extended exposition of good judgment and self-restraint.[38] These are what she calls the "preserving virtues."[39] Neither one of these virtues is impressive by contemporary standards. It would be difficult to imagine, for example, a blockbuster film extolling prudence and temperance in the same way our culture valorizes virtues like courage, justice, love, and persistence. But these two virtues are absolutely essential in the preservation of our planet.

The Preserving Virtue of Prudence

Good judgment, or prudence, is of central concern to the sages in Proverbs. The prologue of Proverbs introduces it as one of the purposes of the book: "to teach . . . knowledge and prudence to the young" (1:4; see also 14:8;

---

36. This is not to suggest that pursuing green technologies—solar and wind power, electric and hydrogen cars—is not a worthwhile venture. The point is only that people cannot look to science for a silver bullet to "fix" creation. Apply new technologies with the same worn-out and destructive ethos will never produce the kind of significant and lasting change that our present times require.

37. Davis, "Preserving Virtues," 185.

38. Ibid., 185n7.

39. Ibid., 186.

15:21, 32). Prudence is learning to make wise decisions in the routine affairs of life. One who is prudent has a God-centered direction and purpose in life (Prov 14:8). Prudence begins by accepting our own limitations and realizing that there is much about life we do not understand (Prov 27:1; Eccl 11:1–6; Job 38–41). The prudent ones learn from their mistakes and grow (Prov 15:5; 12:1; 10:17).

To get a better grasp of prudence, a person can observe its antithetic quality. The opposite of prudence for the sages is the one who "lacks sense" or, as the NIV consistently translates, it "lacks judgment."[40] A lack of prudence manifests itself in multiple ways including the inability to see the consequences of one's actions (Prov 6:32; 7:7), the use of words that belittle another (11:12), short-sighted goals (Prov 12:11), and a lack of motivation (Prov 24:30).

Prudence takes a long-range view of how our actions affect creation. What will be the long-range consequences for making this choice and what kind of impact will it have on the immediate environment as well as the larger ecosystem? This is when prudence must rely on self-control in order to delay gratification of a desire when it is in the best interest of both humans and non-humans. Sometimes we cannot know the consequences of our actions so we proceed with caution.

In light of not always knowing the consequences, prudence incorporates the ecological virtue of humility, which understands our inability to always know the outcome of our decisions. In caring for creation we have the responsibility to "act cautiously," to "consider worst-case scenarios."[41] Humility is developed when we face the realization of the brevity and finitude of our lives, especially when compared to the permanence of our actions and their consequences. The writer of Ecclesiastes struggles with this dilemma of human finitude more than any other. Death comes to both the wise and the foolish, humans and animals (2:12–17; 3:19; 9:2–3; 12:1–7). Humility calls humans to understand their place and limitations in life and to see creation as a gift from God rather than an entitlement to use for self-gratification (Eccl 2:24–26; 9:7–10).

---

40. The literal translation is "needy of heart." See 6:32; 7:7; 9:4, 16; 10:13, 21; 11:12; 12:11; 15:21; 17:18; 24:30. On occasion the NRSV will translate the phrase "stupid person," (e.g., 24:30). *The Message* translates the phrase in several different ways including "shortsighted," empty-headed," "witless," "chatterbox," and "brainless."

41. Bouma-Prediger, *For the Beauty of the Earth*, 141.

The Preserving Virtue of Temperance

Temperance, or self-control, is another fundamental ecological virtue in wisdom's dictionary. We have seen how self-control is a virtue creation displays. But how is it displayed in humans for the benefit of creation? In wisdom's vocabulary temperance is about discipline and the control of desires. This virtue is put on display in many of the better-than sayings found throughout Wisdom Literature but especially in Proverbs. Many of these sayings speak of material wealth. Though the sages do not consider wealth bad in and of itself, sometimes it carries with it destructive vices. In addition, some things are more important than wealth. Here are a few examples:

> Better is a little with the fear of the LORD
> > than great treasure and trouble with it.
> Better is a dinner of vegetables where love is
> > than a fatted ox and hatred with it. (Prov 15:16–17)

> It is better to live in a corner of the housetop
> > than in a house shared with a contentious wife. (Prov 21:9)

> A good name is to be chosen rather than great riches,
> > and favor is better than silver or gold. (Prov 22:1)

Many similar examples could be given but these suffice to indicate that, whatever their feelings about wealth, the sages understood that relationships are more important than material goods. Character is more important than creature comforts. Wealth often brings with it unwanted baggage that destroys both relationships and creation.

The epitome of self-control is highlighted in the sage's prayer to God in Proverbs 30:7–9:

> Two things I ask of you;
> > do not deny them to me before I die:
> Remove far from me falsehood and lying;
> > give me neither poverty nor riches;
> > feed me with the food that I need,
> > or I shall be full, and deny you,
> > and say, "Who is the LORD?"
> > or I shall be poor, and steal,
> > and profane the name of my God.

The sage prays only for "the food that I need" just as Jesus taught the disciples to pray, "give us this day our daily bread" (Matt 6:11). It is a request for God to give us strength to restrain our appetites. Because this planet contains limited resources, temperance or restraint becomes a fundamental preservation virtue.

Davis concludes that temperance "means that one must want fewer material goods than we are generally disposed to want."[42] It is the human tendency to want more and more that has depleted the resources of this planet. This tendency is built into our culture which constantly persuades us to believe that what it has to offer is "not more than you need. It is more than you are used to."[43] The naturalist John Muir of the late nineteenth and early twentieth century once said, "Nothing dollarable is safe!"[44] Humans find creative ways to turn all of nature and its natural resources into economic profit. Using restraint and good judgment in the way we conduct our lives is fundamental to preserving our natural resources and to preserving our relationships with others. Again Davis puts it this way: "Using the classical terminology of the cardinal virtues, prudence means investing ourselves properly in creation, making decisions that demonstrate steady reflection on what God has done. Temperance denotes the practice of steadily limiting our 'take,' which is essential if the investment is to be healthy."[45] It is the discipline of living within our means and learning to control our appetites.

The Preserving Virtue of Simplicity

Expanding on Davis's virtues of prudence and self-restraint is another preservation virtue: simplicity. Embracing a simple lifestyle leads to consuming less of the limited resources our planet produces and less of the material resources our culture craves. Simplicity leads to uncluttering our lives and the potential to live more in keeping with God's design for creation. As the sage of Ecclesiastes concludes, "God made human beings straightforward, but they have devised many schemes" (Eccl 7:29). That is, God designed for both humans and non-humans to live simply but humans have concocted ways to complicate it. It is this lifestyle the Teacher of Ecclesiastes advocates in the summary statements made throughout the book:

42. Ibid., 194.

43. GMC advertising slogan of a previous decade.

44. See Burns, "Last Refuge."

45. Davis, "Preserving Virtues," 198.

> This is what I have seen to be good: it is fitting to eat and drink and find enjoyment in all the toil with which one toils under the sun the few days of the life God gives us; for this is our lot. Likewise all to whom God gives wealth and possessions and whom he enables to enjoy them, and to accept their lot and find enjoyment in their toil—this is the gift of God. (Eccl 5:18–19)

> So I commend enjoyment, for there is nothing better for people under the sun that to eat, and drink, and enjoy themselves, for this will go with them in their toil through the days of life that God gives them under the sun. (Eccl 8:15)

After the exploring and experimenting and indulging in all the material wealth life has to offer, the Teacher comes to the realization that it is the simple joys that bring the greatest satisfaction: eating and drinking with family and friends and accepting the work God gives us to do. All of this, the Teacher discovers, is a gift from God. It is not something we earn, it is not anything we are entitled to; rather it is a gift pure and simple. So we work hard and enjoy the simple pleasures that come along the way. Disciplining ourselves to live simply is a fundamental ecological virtue.

Conclusion

One of the basic differences between humans and animals is that only humans squander and pillage because of greed. Wendell Berry gets to the heart of the problem with this observation:

> One of the oldest human arguments is over the question of how much is necessary. How much must humans do in their own behalf in order to be fully human? The number and variety of the answers ought to notify us that we never have known for sure, and yet we have the disquieting suspicion that, almost always, the honest answer has been "less."[46]

It is neither necessity nor ignorance but greed which lies at the heart of human exploitation of the earth's natural resources.

God created the world by wisdom. Because God imbued creation with wisdom, creation possesses a dynamic quality that exhibits both stability and flexibility. Humans live with the tension between the predictable and the unpredictable facets of creation. Though creation does not or cannot

46. Berry, *Home Economics*, 148.

make deliberate moral choices, God embedded within its genes fundamental virtues. It is this natural quality of creation that gives creation the ability to teach humans how they are to live. Those individuals who live out a God-centered life and who have an awareness of their own character strengths and limitations are most capable of benefitting from creation's instructions. From creation humans learn not so much what they are to do but what kind of people they ought to be. Virtues such as respect, stewardship, self-control, simplicity, industriousness, and prudence that are learned from creation in turn enable humans to responsibly care for creation.

Chapter Four

Creation as Character

But ask the animals, and they will teach you;
the birds of the air, and they will tell you;
ask the plants of the earth, and they will teach you;
and the fish of the sea will declare to you.

—JOB 12:7–8

ONCE UPON A TIME, in a very distant land, a prosperous kingdom lay atop great fertile mountains overlooking the sea. The kingdom was happy and stable under the rule of powerful kings until one day rumors began to trickle in from the lands to the south that a great army was approaching. Every day, the king heard new stories of how a massive army toppled cities, pillaged fields, and slaughtered whole populations. As the fabled army drew closer, the stories grew more and more terrible, until finally the king heard that the ruler of the neighboring people had been killed, along with all his armies and all his sons so that no one survived. The kingdom had been forever erased from the world.

Fearing for himself and for his people, the king of the mountain nation sent for a great magician and soothsayer who might bless him and curse his enemy. Only then could the king be sure that no tragedy would befall him. To persuade him, the king first promised the soothsayer wealth beyond compare, but the soothsayer refused to come. Again the king sent for him, this time promising him not only gold and silver but glory beyond his wildest dreams. But a second time the soothsayer refused to come.

Finally, after receiving a vision, the soothsayer consented and made preparations to depart.

The great seer mounted his trusty steed, an old donkey that had served him faithfully for many years, and began on the road to meet the king and pronounce his fortunes. On the way, the donkey suddenly and inexplicably turned off the road and wandered into a nearby field. Furious, the soothsayer beat the donkey until it returned to the path. Again, when passing by a vineyard, the donkey wandered off the path and crushed the foot of the soothsayer against a vineyard wall. Angrier still, the soothsayer beat the donkey even more vigorously. Finally, when the soothsayer was passing through a narrow place and there was no space to wander from the road either to the right or the left, the donkey stopped suddenly and lay down on the ground. Flying into a rage, the soothsayer called for a sword to have the donkey killed. But no sooner had he issued the threat than the donkey opened its mouth and spoke.

"Many years have I served you, soothsayer, even since you were a boy. Have I ever behaved thus before?"

The soothsayer reluctantly admitted that the donkey had always been a faithful servant.

"Then hear my words. The God of the army from the south sent an invisible warrior to block your path and do you harm, so I turned into the field to avoid it. Again the God of the army of the south sent an armed warrior to slay you, so I crushed your foot to save your neck. Finally the God of the army of the South sent a fiery warrior to kill you, and having nowhere to turn, I lay down beneath you."

When the soothsayer looked up, his eyes were opened and he saw the terrible warrior standing in his path, poised to strike him down. The soothsayer immediately repented his cruel treatment of the donkey, for he understood that only by its loyalty had he been saved.

The story of Balaam and his donkey is familiar (though perhaps not in that form), but one of its key lessons may not be: animals are the unsung heroes of the Bible. While every human behaves with reckless foolishness in the narrative, the donkey alone displays sound judgment and virtue. The donkey is not alone; not only animals, but plants, forces of nature, and all of creation in its many manifestations embody the wisdom of God's creation. Everywhere in the sacred narrative, creation emerges as a critical actor in God's story, but more often than not these characters are overlooked.

True, as children, our first lessons in Scripture are about Noah's ark full of animals and Jonah inside the big fish, but as adults we quickly graduate to the spiritual meat of longwinded prophets and longsuffering apostles, forgetting all our felt board days spent learning about Daniel's sleepover with the lions or Elijah's dinner parties with ravens. The morals of these stories are morals for children, learned and then surpassed in our spiritual maturity. After all, the characters are straight out of a catalog of children's films: tamed and virtuous lions (Lion King), deceitful serpents (Jungle Book), giant fish who swallow people (Pinocchio), and, of course, wise, talking donkeys (Shrek). The media teaches, and our Sunday schools reinforce, the notion that narratives about an active creation are best suited to the active imaginations of children.

In spite of the enlightened outlook we embrace as adults—and, at least in part, specifically to counter it—a fair assessment of the nature of creation requires a significantly less facile engagement with the importance of non-human characters in the biblical narrative. In fact, the great cosmic timeline is punctuated with important acts by God's non-human creation, from the moment when the first couple was deceived by the serpent to the final eschatological renewal when the lion and the lamb[1] set aside their enmity and lay down together in peace. God's creation plays a critical role in the story of which we are all a part.

The failure to realize this is part of a much larger forgetting that has occurred in the last two centuries of human history. Across time and human cultures, there has been a tremendous intimacy between human and non-human creation that has led to a much readier recognition of the role of the latter in everyday life. This began to change a little over two hundred years ago, in very circumscribed ways at first—in a still emerging corner of the world among a very small group of intellectuals—but quickly spread so that it has now become the dominant mode of thinking. This intellectual revolution, the so-called "Enlightenment," came on the heels of generations of concentrated scientific discovery and philosophical inquiry, but not coincidentally it also began in a time when people became increasingly distant from agricultural production. As people moved away from the countryside and into the cities, away from the production of their food and into consumer modes of engaging with the land, they began to see nature

---

1. This is the popular pairing of predator and prey because of its alliteration. Isaiah, however, pairs the wolf with the lamb and the lion with the calf (Isa 11:6).

as something to be abstracted and analyzed, something static and comprehensible, something to learn about rather than to learn from.

This Enlightenment shift in thinking involved a complete reappraisal of creation, both its nature and its worth. It can be seen in the way we treat our natural resources (and even in the phrase "natural resources" which commodifies creation) or in the way that we imagine animal behavior (in ways very different than the Puritans, for example, who in the eighteenth century still prescribed human punishments, like hanging, for dogs who broke human laws).[2] Most critically for our purposes though, it comes through in the way we read stories about non-human actors in Scripture. The tendency is to read stories like Daniel's as if the lions were pliant props, no more characters in the story than the stone blocking the door. Just as, with a little force, the stone is rolled from in front of the door, with little effort God flips a biological switch inside the lions and turns off their natural instinct to prey on Daniel. In this mode of reading, the switch can be flipped the other direction as well, as when Elisha issues a curse in the name of God and two bears maul more than three dozen children. Like entering data into a computer, God codes the instincts of the animals to suit the needs of the current story and then runs the program.

Such a mechanical view of creation sits well with the modern mechanized mind, but it is entirely foreign to the biblical authors, an anachronism of the highest order. Consider the story from Numbers 22, retold at the start of the chapter as a Moabite fairy tale. When the donkey acts, it is not out of instinct or divine programming. In fact, the biblical authors portray the actions of the donkey as specifically thwarting the apparent will of God who sent the angels to kill Balaam. Neither does it seem that the donkey moves out of an instinct for self-preservation, because the angel tells Balaam that the donkey would have been spared regardless. What then, if not inborn instinct or divine puppetry, drove the donkey repeatedly off the road? Loyalty to a longtime master: "Am I not your donkey, which you have ridden all your life to this day?" (Num 22:29). When given its own voice, the donkey freely expresses its own rationale for behaving the way it has. Casually we smile and nod and dismiss this as a personification for rhetorical effect, a tool of narrative for the benefit of the reader.

Perhaps it is for effect. But even so, as readers we must come to terms with the fact that, throughout Scripture, this sort of personification, this casting of creation as an actor rather than a prop, is a key instructional

2. See Anderson, *Creatures of Empire*, 95.

mode. Regardless of what they may have believed about animals, plants, and forces of nature in their so-called primitive or prescientific modes of thinking, the biblical authors saw not only pedagogical utility but instructional necessity in depicting a fully-embodied creation that humanity must engage in ways more often reverent than imperious. Following their lead, we must—no matter our so-called modern or scientific modes of thinking—embrace the creation's agency, that is the ability of non-human creation to be genuinely active rather than merely reactive and especially to live and move apart from human desire, need, or stimulus.

This point returns us to the Wisdom Literature, in which this basic observation about the agency of creation forms a critical prerequisite to the lessons of the previous chapter, that creation has a message to teach us. To understand creation as a teacher—in contrast to creation as a subject of study, the whole tenor of science since the Enlightenment—Christians must first learn to recapture the biblical willingness to treat creation as something more than static backdrop to a human story. This worldview is everywhere evident in and central to the wisdom literature, in spite of the genre's general lack of narrative forms. There are no sustained story arcs like Jonah's or Balaam's from the sages, but in everything from psalms to proverbs, creation lives and breathes and acts in ways every bit as substantial as humans.

Understanding the agency of creation is the first step in understanding the sages. It is also critical for rediscovering the lost roots of a robust environmental ethic. For centuries and across continents, a basic appreciation of creation's agency was preserved and echoed in the form of folktales, even as now it is being creatively reimagined for the modern circumstance in an effort to combat the escalating environmental crisis. Understanding how the agency of creation operates scripturally and how this agency has functioned in human society historically allows Christians to evaluate how to adapt it to contemporary environmental ethics in ways that are ecologically responsible and biblically accountable.

The Agency of Creation in Wisdom Literature

That the sages expect their pupils to consider and to learn from creation is not, in itself, an especially novel argument. After all, it is impossible to miss the frequency of passages, especially in Proverbs, in which the content of the natural world provides a concrete example of wisdom. Proverbs 6:6–11 is but one exemplary instance of a broader trend in which humanity is directed to non-human creation and indicted because they lack the wisdom which seems self-evident to the rest of God's world:

> Go to the ant, you lazybones;
>> consider its ways, and be wise.
> Without having any chief
>> or officer or ruler,
>> it prepares its food in summer,
>> and gathers its sustenance in harvest.
> How long will you lie there, O lazybones?
> When will you rise from your sleep?
> A little sleep, a little slumber,
>> a little folding of the hands to rest,
>> and poverty will come upon you like a robber,
>> and want, like an armed warrior.

The ant has wisdom which many humans tragically lack. Though it has no ruler, the ant does what is necessary for its survival and even its prosperity. Many people, in contrast, are told what to do by their superiors, but neither these orders nor the prospect of their own poverty and demise is enough to overcome the inertia of foolishness.

Still, the injunction to "go to the ant" rings suspiciously in the ear of the modern reader like "consult this book" or "check out this website." Rather than "ask" the ant to "teach" us (the language of Job 12:7), our inclination is to look at the ant as part of a great natural canon which may be read alongside of and subordinate to Scriptures, a perspective which is born out of early modern philosophies in Europe. We too easily fall into the trap of believing that the ant's behavior has been prepared for our benefit to exemplify—rather than to embody—the wisdom of its Creator so that we may consider it an object lesson intended to illustrate divine principles revealed for our benefit in the Bible.

This is especially true for many American Protestants, who in the mid-nineteenth century became enamored with a way of reading Scripture which mixed the methods of Francis Bacon with the philosophy of the Scottish Realists to create what has been termed an inductive reading of the Bible.[3] According to this highly modern approach to Scripture, any

---

3. See Hughes, *Reviving the Ancient Faith*, 31.

problem—ethical, theological, doctrinal—may be solved by simply assembling the necessary facts from the text and then drawing whatever conclusion emerges logically and naturally from those facts. Even when admitting that nature has something to teach, Christians have largely adopted this method for approaching creation. The ant is reduced to a fact in an inductive chain of logic the point of which is to reach a conclusion utterly in abstraction from creation. In this mode, Proverbs 30:24–28, discussed in the previous chapter, reads rather dryly: given that four examples can be manifest from nature in which something without means or power can nevertheless achieve amazing feats through wisdom, it is evident that much is possible through the wisdom of God. Since this same basic conclusion appears as a straightforward declaration in Philippians 4:13, these animals can be seen as illustrations in a divine sermon, useful mnemonics offered by God so that we might remember this biblical truth.

Certainly the wisdom of God is greater than earthly power, and just as certainly this is the lesson which we can learn from Proverbs 30. Yet something important is lost when we read Wisdom Literature and creation this way. In ways very similar to Balaam's donkey, the sages' ant gathers food without being told not for the benefit of foolish human observers nor, in the sages' reckoning, out of mechanical instinct. The ant gathers because it is wise, because it has understood the way of the world, has discerned what is right, and has undertaken to do it. It is not wise so that humans may learn from it; humans may learn from it because it is wise. It acts in accordance with the divine wisdom whether humans observe it or not and must be accounted all the wiser for doing so. For Christians to think otherwise ultimately misses the point. If we return to creation and learn wisdom only to treat ants—and badgers, locusts, and lizards—in the same basically destructive and exploitative spirit with which we approach fossil fuels, air, and water, we have learned nothing at all.

The sages stress this independence and agency in nature precisely to combat this sort of hubris. Such is the case with Job, who is reminded in the midst of his grand tour of creation that all animals have been created free by God, even those that humans most often think exist primarily for their benefit. "Who has let the wild ass go free?" (39:5), asks God, before explaining that this servant of humans survives quite well in the steppes and the salt lands, eating well the green produce of the earth far away from human cities and human task masters. In the same way, the ox, on whom the agricultural livelihood of the entire people depended (Prov 14:4), had been made wild by God, free and independent:

> Is the wild ox willing to serve you?
> Will it spend the night at your crib?
> Can you tie it in the furrow with ropes,
>> or will it harrow the valleys after you?
> Will you depend on it because its strength is great,
>> and will you hand over your labor to it?
> Do you have faith in it that it will return,
>> and bring your grain to your threshing floor? (Job 39:9–12)

Far from human watchfulness and with no thought of human benefit, the wild ass and ox exist freely with God watching over them both. Job, who has claimed to know (and thus to judge) God, in truth cannot even grasp the fullness of creation. The world exists independently of him and human necessity, and his ignorance of it is jarring. Job would have been wise to remember, as the sages did, that God laid the foundations of the earth and created everything in it before creating humanity, and that ants and oxen both existed with wisdom and purpose before there were people to learn from them.

This recognition of agency in creation is important in part because it helps to account for the occasional and apparent lack of wisdom in creation. The sages recognize that just because God made everything in wisdom and through wisdom, not all of creation may be looked at as an example of how to be wise. The same passage in Job moves on from the noble and free ox to the anomalous ostrich whose "wings flap wildly" and who "leaves its eggs to the earth, forgetting that a foot may crush them" (Job 39:13–15). What lesson could humanity possibly learn from this creature? To aim to exceed our capacity (like a flightless bird flapping its wings) or to be careless with our children, an endorsement of free-range parenting? Either would be a reasonable conclusion if creation is approached as a manual for wisdom rather than a teacher of it. Job, for his part, learns that just as God made the ox free and the horse mighty, "God has made [the ostrich] forget wisdom and given it no share of understanding" (39:17). Just as Jesus can rebuke wind (Luke 8:22–25) and curse a fig tree (Mark 11:12–14), so God proves perfectly willing to deride the folly manifest in divine creation. Christians, if they are wise, will understand that non-human creation, like its human counterpart, displays the full spectrum of wisdom and folly.

The opening passage of Ecclesiastes suggests the same point. There, the Teacher begins his quest for wisdom quite logically by looking to creation. Yet it is not wisdom that he finds there. Instead, it is only meaninglessness. The sun rises and sets only to repeat the same behavior the next day. The wind blows one day to the north, the next day to the south, going round in endless circles. Water completes the image, flowing endlessly in streams to the sea only to return again to its headwaters. The Teacher no more suggests that the sun, wind, and water have been set up by God in foolishness than the author of Job means to imply that the ostrich was not created by God through wisdom. In fact, the meaninglessness of these cycles forms the basis of the Teacher's much larger observation, supremely wise in its conclusion, that life is fleeting and human striving is meaningless. This is not the discovery of a kernel of wisdom which God has embedded in creation for humans to seek out with scientific methodologies, but a dynamic encounter with a creation that "hurries" (1:5) around senselessly in precisely the way that humanity does. Looking to creation, the Teacher sees less divine wisdom than he does human folly, suggesting that all of God's creation, human and non-human, struggles with the same transience and futility.

More important than the wisdom or the folly about which creation may teach the wise observer, an embrace of agency in creation forces students of wisdom to understand that God's creation exists apart from their knowledge of it. It compels all of us to understand both our own limitedness and the vastness of creation. After all, "a generation goes, a generation comes, but the earth remains forever" (Eccl 1:4), and not exclusively or even primarily for the benefit of the generations to come. Consider this: even now, with more than seven billion people living on earth, the best estimates suggest that 95 percent of people live on only 10 percent of land. This statistic becomes even more dramatic when you realize that the earth is more than 70 percent water, which leaves most humans occupying only about 3 percent of the earth's total surface. Not so different from Job, all of us might easily be led on a grand tour of our own region or country or planet (not to mention the apparent infiniteness of intergalactic creation) and be fascinated by how little we know, admitting the judgment of the Teacher that we "do not know the work of God, who makes everything" (Eccl 11:5).

Out in this vast wilderness—a name we so humbly use for those spaces not graced by human development—creation lives and thrives not by mechanical instinct or in meaningless toil without humanity to observe it.

From the sages' perspective, non-human creation engages with its creator in much the same way that human creation ought to, even when humans are not around to witness it. All God's works praise him: the sky, the sun, the moon, the oceans, the storms, the fish, the birds, and the beasts (Pss 19, 148). All submit to God's will and, as humans ought, offer their Creator praise from and through their very being.

It is evident that, for the sages, creation is alive, and not in some strictly biological sense. Whether we consider the choice of language in the Wisdom Literature to be rhetorical, a personification of nature for the benefit of the reader, or accept that it reflects a robust, even quasi-animistic, view of the non-human creation, it is inescapable that wisdom approaches creation to learn not as a scientist approaches a subject but as a student approaches a teacher. Creation teaches wisdom not as book but as an interlocutor, complex and dynamic, that must be engaged with an attitude not only of critical analysis but of patient receptiveness as well.

Environmental Agency and Folk Culture

To embrace this stance and derive the full benefit of it, however, requires a sense of the agency of creation no less robust than the sages'. This sense has been lost in our culture at large, but the records of a past alive with respect for and wonder at a living world remains within our grasp. Cultures across the world for centuries embraced this disposition and, critically, embedded it in rich folklore traditions that continue to enthrall modern imaginations even if they rarely inform our environmental thinking. Talking trees and birds and rocks, like talking donkeys, populate our bedtime stories as children, often handed down through the centuries only to be discarded in our adulthood.

But the world's folklore contains an essential record of a forgotten wisdom and a key tool in inspiriting us again to look to a living and active creation. With remarkable clarity and consistency, folktales with no direct connection to biblical narratives or Jewish and Christian cultures nevertheless echo the wisdom of the biblical sages on the agency of creation. On this single but significant point, the folk cultures of ancient Japan, China, or India remain nearer to the biblical sages than modern Christians. A brief review of the way agency is manifest in the folktales of three different cultures suggests just how thoroughly our modern society has set aside the ancient, even primordial, recognition that our world is alive and active apart from human activity and beyond the scope of human benefit.

It is perhaps most fitting to begin with Jewish folklore, which preserves all the basic themes seen in the biblical text and amplifies them through its fantastic mode of storytelling. Throughout the full canon of traditional Jewish folk literature, animals and a variety of natural forces serve to instruct the wise in the basic features of righteous living. This is nowhere more true than in the case of the archetypal sage, Solomon, who in Jewish folklore is typically credited with the ability to speak with animals and tasked by God with settling disputes between them, much as he does between humans in the biblical narrative.[4] Thus, one story has Solomon judge the case of an otter whose children have been trampled by a weasel. Solomon resolves the case by interviewing a host of involved parties—a tortoise, a scorpion, a lobster, a woodpecker, and so on—before deciding wisely in favor of the weasel. In another, Solomon takes up the case of a boastful and duplicitous bird who is bragging to impress his wife, saying he could topple the great kingdom's of the world entirely without effort. In this case, the king's judgment goes so far as to include a punishment for both birds: he turns them into stone. As will be seen later, Solomon even settles disputes between animals and humans. In each case, Solomon has wisdom to offer non-human creation, which, like its human counterpart, needs divine wisdom in order to live fruitful lives. Yet more significant are the many stories in which Solomon is made to learn from the very natural world he has been tasked with judging.

Even with his legendary wisdom, imparted by God, Solomon still emerges in Jewish folk literature as having much to learn from creation. More startling still, Solomon proves himself to be something of a slow learner, giving hope to the rest of us who struggle to make sense of the wisdom God has embedded in creation. Though examples could be multiplied, a single story from the Midrashic literature serves to illustrate the point adequately. The created world, neither idle, static, nor reactive, has much to teach even the wisest man in history.

The tale begins with God giving Solomon, in addition to great wisdom and dominion over all the animals and creation more generally, a tremendous flying mantle, sixty miles wide and sixty miles long, on which Solomon carries his subjects, as well as the princes of humans, demons, beasts,

---

4. A brief introduction to the place of Solomon in Jewish folklore can be found in Ausubel, *Treasury of Jewish Folklore*, 448–49.

and birds respectively. Carried by the wind, Solomon rides this great treasure all over the known world quickly becoming bloated with pride at the thought of his own greatness. Overawed by his own wisdom and dominion of all of creation, Solomon declares, "Behold there is none like me in the world." But no sooner has he made this boast than the wind withdraws from him. Solomon's mantle, the source of his arrogance, will no longer fly. Outraged, Solomon demands that the wind return to him, but the wind answers, rebuking the king on behalf of God: "Return thou, O Solomon, to thy God . . . then I will return to thee."

Solomon, once chastised, repents his pride and resumes his transit across the face of the earth. One day, he is flying over a valley when he hears an ant queen warn her colony to return to their homes lest they be crushed by Solomon's armies. Solomon descends to inquire, and the ant explains that if her people had come out to see Solomon in all his splendor they would have paused wrongly from praising God. Solomon, deciding the ant is wise, tries to ask her a question, but the ant queen points out the impropriety that the one who asks should be seated higher than the one who is asked. So Solomon lifts her up in his hand and asks her his question, "Is there in the world one greater than I?" To which the ant responds that she is because, "If I were not greater than thou art, the Holy One would not have sent thee to me to take me into thy hand." Solomon once again repents his pride and is sent off with a final warning, "Go, but forget not the Lord, nor boast thyself exceedingly."

Twice rebuked, Solomon receives a final object lesson in humility. He flies on his mantle to a hidden city of great wealth, but he cannot find anyone living in the city. Instead he finds only great, ancient eagles whom he interrogates one after another about the nature of the city. Finally he is directed through a parade of wealth to a mysterious tablet guarded by a demon which offers the answer to the riddle of the magnificent city populated by birds. The city had been the capital of a great king, greater even than Solomon, who ruled over "a thousand thousand provinces" and "a thousand thousand kings" but "in the hour that the Angel of Death came . . . could not withstand him." The moral of the story of the city of birds was that Solomon should not "trouble himself greatly about this world, for the end of all men is to die, and nothing remains to man but a good name."[5]

In Jewish folklore, Solomon is both the wisest arbiter and the most troublesome student, but in either case nature emerges as a key agent in

---

5. Ibid., 488–90.

parables about wisdom, both as its recipient and as its teacher. In every case, it is clear that definite lessons must be learned, either by Solomon or by his pupils, and wisdom remains the common and explicit goal of all of God's creation. But as we move gradually away from Jewish culture, the clear moral purpose of the sages fades slowly into the background. What remains, however, is a definite sense of creation's agency and the role of that agency in the moral fabric of the world, however conceived.

In European fairy tales, the wisdom evident in creation is often significantly more ambiguous than the lessons learned from Solomon. Rather than simply learning or teaching, creation can often be seen competing with and challenging the extent of human wisdom. Such is the case in an often retold and reformulated tale about a man who finds a snake trapped under a rock.[6] Out of curiosity, the man lifts the rock to see the snake, thus releasing the serpent from its captivity. The snake proves grateful but only to an extent, as it had been trapped under the rock for days and, being very hungry, resolves to eat the man. The premise having been set, the snake and the man begin a life-and-death debate about the nature of justice and gratitude. The man argues that the snake must show its gratitude for being saved by sparing the man's life; the snake rebuts that the man has not saved its life if it ends up dying of hunger. So the arguments persist.

To resolve their impasse, the snake and the man make a pact to ask the first three creatures that pass by and to accept whatever their judgment should be. Surrendering their respective fates to the wisdom of a random sampling of creation, the man and the snake first encounter a horse. When asked whether gratitude should trump necessity, the horse sides with the snake: "Here have I been slaving for my master for the last fifteen years, till I am thoroughly worn out, and only this morning I heard him say. . . . 'I shall have to send him to the knacker's and get a few pence for his hide and his hoofs.' There's gratitude for you." The next passerby, an old and wearied hound offers a similar story and judgment, citing a cruel human master who, no longer having any use for the dog, has discarded it to fend for itself.

With that, the snake seems to have made its case and prepares to eat the man. But, insisting that the snake honor its deal, the man waits for a third judge. Along comes a fox. Proving itself very clever, as foxes are wont to do in fairy tales, the fox makes a deal with the man, that in exchange for a pair of chickens it will help the man escape the snake. Having struck the bargain, the fox tricks the snake into crawling back under the rock, thus

---

6. "Inside Again," in Jacobs, *Europa's Fairy Book*, 165–69.

rendering the judgment of the animals moot. The man returns to his farm with the fox, but he has learned his lesson from creation well. Instead of a sack of hens, he offers the fox a sack of hounds and so proves himself more clever than the cleverest of animals.

Incidentally, he also proves himself every bit as cruel as the other humans mentioned in the story. Like the owner of the horse and the hound, the man shows himself more than willing to treat God's creatures as disposable resources. Rather than learning from creation a lesson in further compassion, the man takes away a lesson in deceit and ruthlessness. Tellingly, Jewish folklore has a version of this same tale in which a man warms a snake that has frozen nearly to death. When the same complication arises, the disputants turn to an ox and an ass who offer the same indictment of human hypocrisy and cruelty. In this rendition, however, the final judge is not a fox, but a young Solomon, allowing for a just resolution to the case but omitting from the story the ultimate treachery.

Just as there are folktales are about enmity between human and nonhuman creation, there are tales in which the collaboration and mutual expression of virtue come to the fore. Such is the case in a Japanese folk story about a man and a wolf.[7] The story bears a marked resemblance to a more familiar European tale about a Roman and a lion and expresses many of the same motifs, teaches many of the same morals as Androcles. In the Japanese expression, a young man must traverse a mountain in order to do business in a nearby village. Night falls on him before he can finish his journey, and from the depths of the thicket he hears a horrible noise, at once like growling and like wheezing. Armed with nothing but a paper lantern, the man wanders into the thicket to investigate. When he reaches the source of the noise, he is shocked to find a massive wolf, its mouth yawning open to bear its monstrous teeth.

Terrifying though the scene is, the man does not run. Just as surprisingly, the wolf does not attack. Instead, the animal bows its head low, as if to make a request of the man. The man, leaning in, discovers a bone lodged in the wolf's throat. So moved by compassion as to set aside all fear, the man reaches his arm into the wolf's mouth, down its throat, and removes the bone. Before continuing on his way, the young man offers the wolf a good-natured scolding: "After this you must be more careful when you eat big bones like that."

---

7. "The Wolf's Reward," in Seki, *Folktales of Japan*, 20–22.

Many days later, after he had concluded his business and returned to his own village, the young man finds himself at a neighbor's home for the harvest celebration. The friends laugh and drink and feast together, only to have their revelry interrupted by the sound of growling at the front door. The entire party trembles with fear, but the young man, undaunted, goes to the door to investigate. On the other side stands the same great wolf, lurking menacingly in the night, blood dripping from its jaws. But again the man does not flee, and again the wolf does not attack. Instead the wolf drops a pheasant from its mouth onto the door step and wanders back into the darkness. The young man understands; the food was the wolf's way of expressing gratitude.

The plot of the story almost perfectly reverses the tale of the snake, who would have surely gobbled up the young man the moment he reached his hand into its mouth. European and American Christians are more accustomed to the wolf as a villain, in no small part because in northern Europe, predatory wolves posed a constant threat to livestock. In Japan the human relationship with wolves functioned in the opposite way, with wolves preying on the deer and wild boar that would otherwise destroy peasants' farms. As such, the wolf becomes in Japanese folklore a powerful and dangerous but ultimately virtuous figure.[8]

While the animals in the European fairy tale choose bitterness and self-interest—even the helpful fox—the Japanese wolf models duty and reciprocity, in short, wise behavior for the hearers of the folktale. Tales of this kind about wolves are relatively common in Japan, with another famous account telling of a wolf who is rescued from a pit by farmers, only to return a few days later to leave a deer in the pit for the farmers to eat.[9] In both stories humans must overcome their fear of the wolf and allow their more compassionate instincts to prevail (in marked contrast to the characters in the two accounts of the troubled snake who lack the good sense to be afraid). Their virtue is rewarded because, unlike humans, the wolf immediately understands and acts upon its duty. If the moral of the parable of the snake is Proverbs 14:16 ("the fool throws off restraint and is careless"), then the moral of the parable of the wolf is something like Proverbs 6:6. Look to the wolf and consider its ways; though it has no master, it still respects its duties and pays its debts.

8. Knight, "Extinction," 138–40.
9. Ibid., 142.

Yet, for our purposes here, the specific lessons are less significant than the process of learning, which always and essentially involves the independent actions of creation. In the minds of the generations who composed, rehearsed, and recited these folktales, the non-human world was part of a comprehensive moral society in which right and wrong must be daily negotiated and in which no party had a monopoly on virtue or wisdom. The wolf might as easily have consumed the young man, the snake as readily slithered away in fear, and the ant might have bitten Solomon on the hand only to be crushed under his foot. The possibility of choice is easily imagined for all the non-human actors in these stories because agency rather than instinct dominates how cultures across time and space have believed the world to operate. The stories work—they teach and we learn—precisely because these animals are characters and not scenery.

Examples might be fruitfully multiplied to include far more than three cultures and far more than only animals, which, after all, are the easiest to imagine as actors in their own right. For the Athapaskan and Tlingit people of northwestern North America, not animals but glaciers occupy the preeminent place among actors in their central folk narratives.[10] Even as globalization continues to level the cultural playing field and propel all people into an increasingly technological future, what may indeed be the last predominantly oral cultures in tropical Latin America, sub-Saharan Africa, and the Pacific Islands still preserve the richest and most timely folktales that may be considered. Yet, with confidence, we can be certain that no matter how many stories are explored, the final conclusion will appear very much the same: that people have intuitively understood that the world around them is alive, active, and dynamic in ways that both defy their understanding and demand their attention.

Recovering Agency for the Modern World

Specialists who study folktales are keen to point out that we will always have folk and thus we will always have folk stories, but the modern folktale rarely resembles its predecessors in its basic assumptions about nature and the human relationship to it. We have learned too much science and forgotten too much wisdom to read Numbers 22 the same way the sages might have. Even if we bemoan this, we cannot turn back time and reenter a world where this kind of folk wisdom predominates. The purpose in relating the

10. See Cruikshank, *Do Glaciers Listen?*

above folktales, or even in cataloging the free use of personification by the sages, is not to suggest that we try to lose ourselves in a blind acceptance of a literal reading of these tributes to environmental agency. Even if our fore-bearers had read these stories in this way, contemporary Christians can no more shrug off the accumulated weight of cultural and intellectual change from the last two centuries than we could discard our own DNA.

Moreover, it is safe to assume that even the most distant and ancient people did not accord these stories a status anything like modern scientific fact, empirically tested and reproducibly verified. When they heard wolves howling outside at night, Japanese peasants did not expect to open their doors and find pheasants anymore than Jews expected everyone who an-gered God to be swallowed by a fish or mauled by a bear. No one, placed in a life or death situation, referred the case to passing livestock for arbitration.

Instead, the sages offer—and the accumulated folk culture of the world's people reflect—a basic disposition toward the non-human world that accepts a measure of life and active independence for creation apart from human awareness or concern. This disposition can and must be re-covered as much for the spiritual well-being of modern Christians as for the biological well-being of the environment. Yet, knowing that we must recover the agency of creation does not in itself bring us any closer to knowing how to incorporate an ancient mindset into our modern context. Understanding the tremendous importance of the loss of sapiential or folk perspectives, various modern efforts have been made to reclaim the centrality of agency for environmental thinking. Pioneered primarily by secular actors and from principally secular motives, these efforts cannot simply or easily be transplanted onto Christian ethics. They neverthe-less, with varying degrees of applicability, can offer useful frameworks for meaningfully encountering the sages and, through them, the wisdom and agency of creation.

The first, and perhaps most obvious response, to the loss of a folkloric perspective on the non-human world is to attempt to recapture the legiti-macy of folklore—complete with all its magic and mystery and wonder—for the modern world. Pioneers in this area have been public folklorists who advocate on behalf of the "folk" and their traditions that are being marginalized and even wiped out by the encroachment of mass culture. To do this is not to endorse the scientific validity of folktales or even their basic truth claims. Instead, folklorists simply acknowledge the value of folk traditions, like the stories related above, as means of encountering the world around us. This is particularly true as folk traditions often represent a direct challenge to modern ways of thinking that have proved devastatingly destructive, especially to the non-human environment.

As such, folktales can offer, in the words of one folklorist, "a potent antidote to alienation" in the modern world, including and particularly the alienation of humanity from the non-human environment.[11] They can, in the language of the first chapter, provide humanity a sense of place. Famed activist and folklorist Alan Lomax puts the problem more dramatically, speaking of the advent of our modern world with its mechanistic view of nature and its mass reproduced culture as a

> profit-motivated society smashing and devouring and destroying complex cultural systems which have taken almost the entire effort of mankind over many thousands of years to create. We have watched the disappearance of languages, musical languages, the sign languages, and we've watched *whole ways of thinking and feeling in relating to nature* and relating to other people disappear. . . . I think we have all been revolted by this spectacle and in one way or another have taken up our cudgels in the defense of the weaker parties.[12]

The solution for Lomax and other public folklorists to a host of contemporary problems is to allow folk traditions to stand as a countervailing voice to dominant modern modes of thinking. These natural, practical ways of approaching the world are the product of thousands of years of careful maturation and must be juxtaposed to the authoritative knowledge of modern scientific expertise, not in an either-or ultimatum but as a check against the extremes of our modern cultural assumptions.

The reappropriation and reapplication of folktales has been a primary mechanism for achieving this, and this effort has been nowhere more evident than in the use of folktales in animated film. Unfortunately, as suggested earlier, folk stories as presented in the American film industry often lack the moral force that their predecessors had. The clear sense that creation has a wise truth to offer humanity gets lost in market-driven antics to appeal to a very young target audience, meaning that, even as technology allows for three dimensional visual effects, the agency of creation is still presented in decidedly two-dimensional terms. The facile environmentalism of Disney's

11. Baron, "All Power," 311.

12. Lomax, "Making Folklore Available," quoted in Baron, "All Power," 279. Emphasis added.

Pocahontas is one example. Here the nearly incalculable environmental destruction that resulted from colonialism is quarantined into a single song where the charge to "roll in all the riches all around you and for once never wonder what they're worth" is buried under empty but provocative-sounding Native American-esque platitudes encouraging people to "sing with all the voices of the mountains and paint with all the colors of the wind."[13] Otherwise, the abundant cast of non-human characters—dogs and trees, raccoons and hummingbirds—is reduced to the comic relief in a thoroughly human story about love, war, and greed.

For a more productive example of the reappropriation of folktales in film, it is necessary to move across the Pacific and consider a similar impulse in Japanese animated films to recapture the wisdom of traditional folk narratives. Though any number of films and studios might be highlighted, Studio Ghibli—founded in 1985 by directors Hayao Miyazaki and Isao Takahata—has received an unparalleled degree of international acclaim, from film critics, activists, and academics, for its socially conscious deployment of animation, a medium conventionally known in the United States and Europe as suitable primarily for children. Drawing extensively from the world of Japanese folktales, Miyazaki and Takahata produce visually stunning worlds populated both with the more fantastical animistic forces of Shinto (e.g., Totoro, the keeper of the forest, or Haku, the dragon spirit of the river) as well as more familiar folktales animals, like the majestic and terrible wolves of *Princess Mononoke*, who resemble very clearly the wolves in the folktales above.[14] Studio Ghibli has even recently and successfully moved beyond Japanese folktales to offer a creative reinterpretation of Hans Christian Andersen's "The Little Mermaid" with the 2008 film *Ponyo*.[15]

13. *Pocahontas*, dir. Gabriel and Golberg.

14. An even more direct appropriation of the wolf folktales above can be found in Mamoru Hosoda's 2012 film *Wolf Children*, in which a human mother is left to raise two wolf cubs as humans, dealing constantly with the stigma of failing to keep the appropriate boundaries between the "wildness" of nature and the "civilization" of human culture.

15. In fact, a constructive contrast might be drawn between the way *Ponyo* and Disney's *Little Mermaid* allow for the agency of nature to figure into their respective lessons. In *The Little Mermaid* the ultimate conclusion is that love—namely, the romantic love of the hero and heroine—conquers all, particularly the forces of nature, personified and controlled by the sea witch Ursula. Here the lesson is that humanity triumphs over nature and the human story is foregrounded. *Ponyo* adapts the same material but concludes with an ultimatum for the hero: could he love Ponyo even if she were to remain a fish. Here again love conquers all, but it is the willingness to love nature in its natural form rather than a willingness to destroy nature out of love that resolves the conflict.

Many of the Studio Ghibli films have an all-but-explicit environmentalist message, perhaps none more clearly than the Takahata's 1994 film *Pom Poko*. Known in Japanese as *Heisei Tanuki Gassen Ponpoko* (roughly, the Tanuki War of the Heisei Era), the title offers an immediate personification of nature that will be the mode of the entire film. Centering on a group of tanuki—a species of raccoon-like canids known in English as Japanese Racoon Dogs—the story follows their struggles against human encroachment into their natural habitat. When a new housing development threatens to level their entire forest, the tanuki must try to cope with their precarious new situation. Struggling to overcome their own instinctive laziness, gluttony, and disorganization, they first try to prevent the settlement from being completed. Figures of tremendous ingenuity and power (if not moral fortitude) in Japanese folklore, the tanuki use their traditional ability to shape-shift first to scare and then to harm humans in an effort to preserve their forest. But for all their abilities, the tanuki must eventually come to terms with their own powerlessness in the face of human encroachment. Some take the folkloric route and use their powers to pose as humans and integrate directly into human society; others integrate as animals, living off trash and hiding in storm drains. Both are haunted constantly by the tenuousness of their new existence in a world where the prevailing facts are human intrusion and apathy.

What Takahata offers in *Pom Poko* is not a flat morality tale in which nature is an object, personified in cartoonish ways to make a moral or political point.[16] Instead, *Pom Poko* offers, from a traditional folk perspective on the world, a tale in which we are forced to see human behavior from the perspective of an active, independent nature trying desperately to cope with environmental change. The tanuki are fully embodied characters in the way that Pocahontas's Grandmother Willow is not. They fall in love in season, they mourn the loss of their loved ones, and they struggle, often unsuccessfully, to overcome their own vices for the sake of their survival.[17] Only by recognizing them as such and treating their plight in this way can

---

16. Which is to say, it is not the Australian-American film *Fern Gully* (1992) in which, on behalf of an apathetic human population, magic and fairies will save the rainforest from quasi-demonic forces that are ultimately beyond human control.

17. In this sense, they as are much a mirror of humanity as a critique of it. Just as humanity can see but not overcome the greed and expansiveness that provokes environmental destruction, the tanuki can see but not overcome the laziness that is going to make them complicit in their own downfall.

humanity truly respond to Takahata's environmentalist message about un-checked human encroachment on the habitats of the non-human world.

Takahata, to be sure, makes no scientific claims about the actual lives and behaviors of tanuki and he certainly does not expect his audience to actually believe the film's contention that the spike in energy drink con-sumption in Japan is driven by transforming tanuki posing as humans. Yet the basic contours of the story are objectively real; animals sleep, mate, eat, relax, play, and even influence the market (whether or not they are secretly buying up Red Bull). By projecting human trappings on to these basically universal behaviors, Takahata forces viewers to imagine their own lives, families, and homes being threatened and to empathize with the responses of the animals who, after all, struggle with their own moral and material failures in ways that human seem especially keen to resist. The affective force of folklore is loosed on the audience and, in ways neither superficial nor incredible, the lines between the human and non-human worlds are allowed to blur.

The spirit which Takahata brings to traditional Japanese folk stories might usefully inform our own readings of the sapiential literature. After all, what Takahata accomplishes in his voyeuristic excursion into the world of the folkloric tanuki is not so very different from what the sages offer in Job's own sightseeing tour of creation. We may fruitfully imagine Job peer-ing into the unseen worlds of God's expansive and unknown creation and, by suspending our scientific disbelief, we can imagine the Leviathan whom only God can covenant with or the Behemoth wading into the flooded rap-ids of the Jordan river. What do the wild ass and oxen do with their free time? Does the wind still make the grass rustle and sing when there are no humans around to appreciate it? The sages, and the Scriptures at large, offer a wealth of stories and observations about non-human creation that strike us as fantastic, but if we allow them to they can also affect us at levels which challenge and critique our scientific notions of creation. Accepting the affective power of the sage's representation of an active and living na-ture can help to move Christians from the cartoonish environmental eth-ics of Disney—where supposed exaggerations of environmental agency in Scripture can be glossed over with arrogant modern amusement—to the deeper environmentalism of Studio Ghibli, in which we recapture the spirit of folklore and willingly suspend our disbelief in order to find the wisdom available in a robust biblical embrace of environmental agency.

Critically, however, not all nods to environmental agency in recent times have stressed a return to the power of folklore and a critique of scientific perspectives. In fact, whole academic disciplines have emerged in which the reality of environmental agency is pursued on rigorously scientific grounds by applying many of the basic observations of post-Darwinian science (viz., that humans are animals, different from other life in degree not in kind) to the humanities. Among the most notable of these has been the relatively new discipline of environmental history, which aims to demonstrate that not only humans but animals, oceans, rivers, and trees all have history that can and should be remembered and recorded.

Environmental historians' themes and subjects vary widely, but all share a basic presupposition that history told from a human perspective alone is profoundly lacking. William Cronon, a pioneer in the field, offers an example in *Changes in the Land*, his landmark treatment of the colonial encounter in New England. Like most historians, Cronon began his account with a brief introduction to the sources he used, but unlike most, his history derived not only from written records but from analysis of pollen trapped in the soil and from the information embedded in relict tree groves. He understood that all creation can keep a record of its past, not in the sentimental way a folktale might imagine a tree writing a diary but in the rigorously scientific way that allows him to draw logically conclusions defensible to even the most stubbornly modern mind.

The conclusions Cronon drew, however, were far from resonant with contemporary modes of thinking about nature. In fact, Cronon made two dramatic breaks with many scholars. First, he argued that contrary to the mythic Disney Pocahontas who swims with otters and sings with mountains, the indigenous population of the Americas profoundly shaped their environment in ways both deliberate and unintentional. Like all societies that have ever existed, the Native Americans entered into a give-and-take arrangement with the non-human world that left both parties changed. Perhaps more radical though, Cronon argued that even before and apart from human contact, nature was far from static. Defying conventional wisdom about a self-correcting, fundamentally stable ecosystem, Cronon followed his observations about environmental agency to their logical, even scientific conclusion: the non-human world lives, changes, and dies apart from human interaction with it. (A sagacious observation if ever there was one.) Unsurprisingly, this recognition of environmental agency, both before and after human contact, prompted explicitly environmentalist concerns for Cronon, who concludes his history with a strong indictment of the way modern modes of conceptualizing nature have produced devastating results.

Cronon is neither the first nor the last to make these kinds of observations in environmental history, and many have carried his project forward in time through American history and the history of other societies. Often, like Cronon, they adopt explicitly environmentalist ethical concerns—with several of these authors and their arguments to be taken up in the final chapter. But for the purposes of understanding environmental agency in the sapiential literature, Cronon's book is enough to consider an alternate framework for approaching the sages and their perspective on creation.

While the folklorist approach asks that we suspend scientific disbelief to recover the moral and affective power of a fully embodied nature, the approach of environmental history invites us to recognize the scientific confirmation of the sages' basic premise: that creation is active, independent, and in every sense alive.[18] In this view the rhetorical devices of personification and exaggeration are understood to be just that, rhetorical. Behind them, however, is not the premodern mind, enfeebled by a lack of science and in awe of a nature that it could not (but we can) understand. Instead, the creation which labors and praises in the sages' writing corresponds to a now confirmed scientific fact that creation lives and works and dies. Together, both suggest—and the sages point directly to—the underlying moral truth that God's creation has its own being apart from us. We might reasonably go one step further and suggest that when malfeasance or apathy destroys creation, the sin more nearly resembles killing a neighbor than to breaking a vase. The ant who labors, who teaches the lazy fool diligence, does so as part of an active life distinct from but intertwined with our own; it is a life which belongs only to God and not to us.

If the perspectives of folklorists and environmental historians suggest positive ways to return once again to the environmental wisdom of the sages, other efforts to recapture agency in nature provide critical warnings. If it is dangerous, even destructive, to reduce creation to a mechanistic manifestation of physical laws and biological instincts, there exists an equal and opposite error which accords creation a kind of absolute embodiment that not only is apart from human existence but transcends human value.

18. These approaches—recovering the magic and mystery of folklore and recognizing the science of environmental agency—are not necessarily mutually exclusive. They are better understood as complementary, operating on the rational and affective parts of our being respectively to keep always in view the reality of a living creation.

Some environmentalists, so eager to recapture a sense of a living nature, have made the environment the absolute life more important in its abstraction than any human life could ever be.

This tendency has been evident both among Christian and non-Christian environmentalists, and criticism of this inappropriate reverence for nature has been one of the principle weapons of Christians who would prefer to check or ignore efforts at environmental reform. The fear of a pantheistic environmentalism is legitimate, if overblown. Certainly many environmentalists believe that human life or property is rightly destroyed if it means the protection of non-human life. Eco-theologians have, for their part, often taken aim at the transcendence of God, subsuming not only human worth but divine reality into creation.[19] This final extreme, if nothing else, the sages speak very clearly on: creation reflects but does not constitute the greatness of God.

Other issues raised by eco-theologians and the radical fringes of environmentalism are more difficult to address with confidence. Whether or not non-human creation is in any ultimate sense of equal or greater value than humanity is mostly beyond the scope of this book. The belief that, ethically, the concerns of humanity should trump the concerns of the rest of the created world falls closer to the heart of the topic at hand. Certainly the dogmatic insistence on human superiority seems like a curious (maybe even foolish) place to begin in ethics for a people claiming to follow a Savior who conquered all by rejecting his rightful and inherent power and becoming weak, who demonstrated in his time as a man the sublime ethical principal that serving those who are immeasurably less than you glorifies the served, the servant, and God. But the purpose here is not to argue that humility and self-sacrifice should be the driving virtues in environmental ethics nor that John 13 has usefulness as an eco-text.

Instead, it is critical to remember that a recognition of environmental agency does not necessarily imply a kind of identical status for nature and humanity. Wherever any given person may happen to fall on arguments about a proposed hierarchy of worth in the created world (and such arguments about relative worth seem largely unproductive), the reality of agency in creation remains. This proposition must be accepted or rejected on its merits regardless of any anxiety about the slippery slope toward pantheism. Nevertheless, there are important distinctions to be made between

---

19. A summary of eco-theology and its stance on divine transcendence can be found in Fowler, *Greening of Protestant Thought*, 91–107.

the human exercise of free will and the agency that is evident in all of creation. Perhaps most critically, non-human creation does not sin—though it is not immune to sin effected profoundly as it is by the sins of humans, to devastating effect.[20] When God points Job to the foolishness of the ostrich, there is no accompanying call for the ostrich to repent and begin storing its eggs in a tree. While non-human creation functions as a way to call foolish humans to repentance, there is no reciprocal expectation for creation in Scripture, even if it emerges at times in folktales. For the sages, the distinction is clear.

This special status of humanity implies additional responsibility rather than additional worth, which is precisely the flaw in those forms of environmentalism that try to subordinate humans to nature. The Christian responsibility to develop sound, biblical environmental ethics (ones based on and incorporating the recognition of an active and living creation) arises from humanity's unique position in God's creation. A balance must be struck, however, between this uniqueness and the realization that creation is not merely the backdrop for a human story of sin and redemption—played out cosmically or individually. Our ethical duties include responsibility for a vibrant non-human community that is anything but inert and most certainly has not been created as a catalog of commodities to be disposed of for human benefit.

Conclusion

Creation is a teacher, and the metaphor is truly the most apt because it imagines an instructor who we may come to as a pupil to learn the wisdom that God has revealed and the folly that God has allowed to persist. Scripture embraces this vision by presenting creation not as a stage for human action but as characters in a drama that embraces all of creation, from fig trees to big fish.

The sages understood the non-human world in this way too, as being alive and active in ways that defy human control and understanding. As such, creation could teach the wise sage what it meant to be wise as well as what it meant to be foolish, often in equal measure. Most importantly, however, the sages understood that creation exists apart from human control

---

20. Made all the more devastating by the realization that the natural world becomes complicit in decidedly unnatural sins that are not, as we shall see in the final chapter, strictly environmental in nature.

and concern. It praises God, fears God, and covenants with God much as human creation does. And though the sages do not allude to it, the prophetic voices of both the New and the Old Testament assure us that, like humanity, creation will participate in the final salvation that God offers.

What the sapiential literature attests about environmental agency, cultures across the world have for centuries understood intuitively to varying degrees. An active non-human world figures prominently in world folklore, particularly a non-human world which acts as an instructor, intentional or otherwise, in wisdom. From the wind that teaches Solomon humility to a wolf that teaches Japanese villagers gratitude, the natural world has more to offer in folk literature than food, fuel, and shelter.

Yet, this is precisely how non-human creation has come to be understood. A series of profound intellectual changes beginning in Europe and being disseminated globally in the last two centuries have radically altered the way creation is approached. Gone is the teacher, replaced with, at best, a textbook, which people are encouraged to probe scientifically so as to uncover and to interpret the mechanistic workings of instinct and physics.

Too much is lost in this perspective, in both pragmatic and absolute terms. Creation disappears as a meaningful instructor in wisdom, leaving humanity that much farther from a wise Creator who created humans and non-humans alike with the same principles of life and, more critically, the same essential wisdom. On a more basic level, Christians can forget not only that creation can instruct but that creation is alive at all, existing and thriving before and beyond human need of it. This forgetfulness breeds the kind of exploitative attitudes that allow for the unthinking equation in our minds of cows with meat and trees with timber, as if creation had our wants embedded in the very fabric of its nature.

Efforts are being made, by Christians and non-Christians alike to reclaim a healthy sense of environmental agency. Some prefer, insofar as possible, to reclaim the magic and mystery embodied in folklore, so that our imaginative reconstruction and exaggeration of an embodied nature can serve to highlight just how reckless the present course of environmental degradation is. Others take the opposite tact, looking for the scientific fact of environmental agency in an effort to provide more stable ground for personal and political reform. Both provide useful frameworks for returning to the sages, through either a creative embrace of their personification of nature (in direct defiance of our strongly held modern preconceptions) or an exegetical route out of those personifications that preserves their basic message. As long as we avoid animistic readings of Scripture which forget the real limits of creation's autonomy, Christians can only benefit from a rediscovery and embrace of the sapiential literature's understanding of environmental agency.

Chapter Five

Creation, Justice, and Food

Introduction

ACCORDING TO TIMOTHY EGAN, former writer for the *New York Times*, American meteorologists rated the Dust Bowl of the 1930s the number one weather event of the twentieth century: "Historians say it was the nation's worst prolonged environmental disaster."[1] It began innocuously enough; no one set out to destroy the environment. In fact, they were attracted to the vast plains of the American heartland in droves because of the fertility of the land. Two hundred million acres were homesteaded on the Great Plains between 1880 and 1925, and "every man a landlord" was the cry of the day.[2] Subsistence farmers discovered that, if they plowed up their land and planted wheat, they could make big money. Converting millions of acres for the mass production of cereal grains, thousands of farmers became wealthy all but overnight in the 1920s. As a consequence, however, by 1931 thirty-three million acres of grassland had vanished. The decade that followed was one of the most widespread environmental crises this country has ever experienced. Land that had sustained thirty million bison at any one time and Native Americans for thousands of years was laid to waste in a mere decade. Plowing did what nothing else was able to do—not prairie fires, not tornadoes, not wind, not hail, not cold or heat. It destroyed the grass of the Great Plains. A craving for wealth and a gross misunderstanding of the relationship between humans and creation drove a gross exploitation of God's creation. Whatever the various social and environmental causes, at

1. Egan, *Worst Hard Time*, 10.
2. Ibid., 57.

its most fundamental level the Dust Bowl of the "dirty thirties" was caused by greed.

The Dust Bowl is but a particularly visible symptom of a much larger disease. The relationship between irresponsible, even sinful, human behavior and environmental consequences is undeniable. The evidence continues to unfold in all shapes and sizes, from the contamination of local water sources by fracking, to regional disasters like the Exxon Valdez or Deep Water Horizon spills, to the "smog" that envelopes so many Chinese cities and continues to drive up rates of lung disease there, to the much more hotly debated anthropogenic global warming. While the public service announcements of past decades urged us to clip bottle rings and turn off lights when we leave a room, humanity as a whole has apparently failed to internalize the intimate relationship between human behavior and environmental degradation. Only when these injustices force their way into our collective consciousness does outcry emerge—only when crude washes up on Gulf Coast beaches or when homeowners light their tap water on fire.

Yet, even if we can embrace the obvious, that human injustices against the environment have an effect on human lives, we have either not realized or not acknowledged that the question of justice has much broader implications than merely curbing pollution. Injustices committed against fellow human beings are enmeshed with the injustices committed against the non-human world. In vivid imagery, an African proverbs describes the convoluted relationship, "When two bulls fight, it's the grass that suffers." The same is true of human behavior: often when we sin against one another, the environment is a silent victim, just as when we sin against the environment we can fail to see the effect on fellow humans.

The final two chapters of this book explore the critical role of justice in environmental ethics, and particularly the relationship between social justice and environmental justice. When, as we have seen in the previous chapter, humans view creation only as scenery, as a stage on which human action is played out and not as an active dynamic agent embodying wisdom, injustices against the environment are inevitable.

The present chapter investigates the sapiential view of justice and its ramifications for both humans and non-humans. Building on a fuller explanation of the sages' understanding of justice and the role of creation in it, what follows is a case study on one specific realm of creation, food and the act of eating, which brings all humans into direct contact with creation every day whether or not they realize it. Understanding the role of justice in even the most quotidian aspects of our relationship to creation helps to lay bare the degree to which sin can move seamlessly between acts directed at others and acts directed at the environment. The final chapter will then examine the social justice dimensions of environmental degradation, specifically how injustices committed against the environment disproportionately affect the poor and disenfranchised.

Wisdom's Theology of Justice

Sometimes it is assumed that when it comes to a biblical theology of justice, the prophets—especially Amos, Hosea, and Micah—hold a monopoly on the subject. That is not the case. In reality the prophets and the sages are united in their concern that God's people live out a life that is founded on justice for all. These two guilds simply come at it from different perspectives.

The prophets ground the practice of justice in the mighty acts of God in history who brought the Israelites out of slavery, led them through the wilderness, guided them to the promised land, and provided them with competent leaders (Amos 2:9–11; Micah 6:3–5). The kind of justice and steadfast love God provided Israel is now expected of Israel to practice toward others, especially to the disenfranchised (Amos 5:24; Micah 6:8). In other words, Israel is expected to do unto others as the Lord has done unto them. Wisdom Literature in contrast makes hardly any reference to the mighty acts of God in history but instead bases the practice of justice on grounds rooted in a theology of creation. God is Creator who imbued creation with justice, even if that justice is not always evident to the sages or their pupils.

Job is among the baffled pupils, and discourses in the book of Job are in many ways disputes about the nature of God's justice. Job experiences a series of traumatic losses, which leads him to conclude that God's governance of the world is unjust and whimsical (Job 27:2). Job and his three friends believe, as the sages are often accused of believing, that the just will prosper and the unjust will suffer more or less automatically. In testifying to his character, Job claims "I put on righteousness, and it clothed me; my justice was like a robe and a turban" (Job 29:14). Job even understands the importance of creation in demonstrating his righteousness. In chapter 31, Job lists a series of negative oaths or confessions that are intended to prove his innocence and protect his integrity. In the process Job claims that he cared for the land.

If my land has cried out against me,

and its furrows have wept together;

if I have eaten its yield without payment,

and caused the death of its owners;

let thorns grow instead of wheat,

and foul weeds instead of barley. (Job 31:38–40)

Job vows that if he has violated the soil or any worker of the soil then may God curse him. The relationship between land and people—between Job's righteous conduct toward human and non-human creation—is inseparable. "In antiquity the land's integrity or lack thereof, reflected the community's conduct, moral or otherwise. When Israel sinned, the land mourned or reacted adversely"[3] (see Hos 4:3; Jer 12:4; 14:1–8; cf. Gen 3:18; 4:10–12). So when speaking of environmental justice one must also speak of social justice. As Steven Bouma-Prediger concludes, "Social justice and ecological health are bound together."[4]

From Job's perspective, however, God is not returning the favor. Job has lived righteously, including treating God's creation justly, but God had not been treating Job in a similarly just manner. Significantly, God will answer Job in much the same manner, demonstrating divine justice by reference to creation. In speaking the final word on the matter, God responds to Job's accusations by taking Job on a whirlwind tour of the wild kingdom. God's case, unsurprisingly, has a bit more oomph.

One of Job's friends, Elihu, had actually already prepared Job for God's environmental rationale in his final speech to Job in chapters 36 and 37. Elihu begins by instructing Job, "Remember to extol his work, of which mortals have sung" (36:24). Yet while the prophets might then have launched into a reprise of the Exodus, Elihu instead turns to creation. He describes for Job a storm, itself an act of creation in which the divine is intimately involved: God draws up water, distils mist, spreads clouds, scatters lightning, looses rain, breathes ice, and roars thunder. "Whether for correction, or for his land, or for love, he causes it to happen" (37:13). God creates the storm sometime out of divine love and sometimes out of divine wrath but always for just purposes. The animals, for their part, provide a silent rebuke to Job, neither questioning the storm's creator nor pretending

---

3. Brown, *Wisdom's Wonder*, 10.

4. Bouma-Prediger, *For the Beauty of the Earth*, 150.

to understand the motives for creation but simply retreating into their dens to wait on the Lord (37:8).

Not only the storm, but all of creation testifies to the inscrutability of God. Elihu reminds Job that not only do they not understand creation but there are parts of it on which they cannot even bear to look (37:21). Based on what the Almighty did in creation, Elihu pronounces that the main quality of God is justice and that those who, arrogant in their supposed wisdom, think they have determined otherwise only prove themselves foolish (37:23–24). God's later response to Job drives home the foolishness of Job's false perspective. As Peter Lockwood observes:

> Job is shown that though the Sea has been fenced off, it has not been eliminated, that God's best intentions notwithstanding criminals remain at large as an ever present threat to social stability and good order. . . . God has not designed nor does he oversee and administer the world as a risk-free "nanny state." He has not designed it in such a way that mechanically, piece by painstaking piece, the virtuous invariably prosper and the wicked invariably suffer, in the precise correspondence to their deeds. Karma is not part of the deal.[5]

God created a just world, one with natural boundaries and limits and principles and laws. Within those boundaries, however, Job learns that the forces of chaos still exist and suffering is a part of that realm. The justice of the Creator does not contradict the injustice of Job's experience; it gives it context and meaning.

The remainder of the Wisdom Literature bears out the intimate relationship between creation and justice outlined in Job. The Teacher in Ecclesiastes, for example, grapples with the ever-present realities of death and the brevity (or vanity) of life. Touching on the same basic complaint of Job, the Teacher notes that life does not seem fair: righteous people "are treated according to the conduct of the wicked," and wicked people "are treated according to the conduct of the righteous" (Eccl 8:14). He discovers that "the race is not to the swift, nor the battle to the strong, nor bread to the wise" (9:11). The Teacher observes life only to discover that "in the place of justice, wickedness was there, and in the place of righteousness, wickedness was there as well" (Eccl 3:16). Injustice seems to be an endemic part of the whole political system (Eccl 5:8–9). The Teacher looks around and sees "all the oppressions that are practiced under the sun. Look, the tears of the

---

5. Lockwood, "God's Speech," 176.

oppressed—with no one to comfort them. On the side of their oppressors there was power" (4:1). God's governing justice in the world does not make sense. As with Job, the Teacher's solution to the enigma drives him back to the fundamentals of God's created order, in this case to eat and drink, find enjoyment in work, and appreciate the basic gifts God gives to humans (5:18–19; 9:7–10).

Proverbs, as well, grapples with the concern for justice. The introductory poem sets the tone when it announces that its overall goal is "for gaining instruction in wise dealing, righteousness, justice, and equity" (Prov 1:3; cf. 2:9 and 8:20). The sentence literature in Proverbs is rich with references to justice. In keeping with the message of the prophets the sages announce that "to do righteousness and justice is more acceptable to the Lord than sacrifice" (21:3). Regardless of what the Teacher observed about the reality of politics in practice, the sages in Proverbs insist that the king, serving as God's representative on earth, ought to rule justly: "By justice a king gives stability to the land, but one who makes heavy exactions ruins it" (29:4; see also 16:12). King Lemuel's mother advises him likewise:

> Speak out for those who cannot speak,
>> for the rights of all the destitute.
> Speak out, judge righteously,
>> defend the rights of the poor and needy. (31:9–10)

But alas, the sages again recognize that many rulers ignore their God-ordained responsibility, directing petitioners to the true source of justice instead: "Many seek the favor of a ruler, but it is from the Lord that one gets justice" (29:26).

The same justice that the wise seek only from the Lord is also the basic component of the well-lived life. Ultimately, Proverbs proclaims, the virtue of a simple lifestyle is much more conducive to practicing justice than the possession of great wealth: "Better is a little with righteousness, than large income with injustice" (Prov 16:8). Understanding what justice truly involves comes only to those who practice it as a lifestyle and who seek the Lord: "When justice is done, it is a joy to the righteous, but dismay to evildoers" (21:15). "The evil do not understand justice, but those who seek the Lord understand it completely" (28:5).

Proverbs too roots this quest for justice in creation theology. Creation is the basis for the way humans are to treat each other because our common source unites all humans together in one community. The same God created all; the haves and the have-nots claim the same origin. A number of the proverbs reveal this perspective: "The rich and the poor have this in common: the LORD is the maker of them all" (22:2). The word for "maker" (עָשָׂה) is the same word used in Genesis and other places to describe God's work in creating the world (Gen 2:2; Job 14:15; Ps 8:4; 19:2; 104:24). Regardless of economic status, what everyone shares in common is that they are created by God. The rich must remember that the poor were created by God with no less love or purpose. They are equal in the sight of God, and the wealthy must therefore respond appropriately to their needs. On the other hand, the poor must remember that God created the wealthy as cherished creatures and not to revile them as villains. The poor are challenged to learn contentment and resist the dual urge to resent the wealthy and covet what they have. That the Lord is the Creator of all people means that all have an inherent right to justice and respect.

If respect is not shown, it is an affront to God as Creator. According to the warning of the sages, "Those who mock the poor insult their Maker; those who are glad at calamity will not go unpunished" (17:5; see also 14:31). The ground for reaching out to the poor, according to this proverb, is that the Lord is "their Maker" (עֹשֵׂהוּ). When the poor suffer injustice God is dishonored. Job echoes this perspective in his defense before God, acknowledging that in the act of creation God made all humans of equal value. In an oath Job vows to God,

> If I have rejected the cause of my male or female slaves,
>   when they brought a complaint against me;
>   what then shall I do when God rises up?
> When he makes inquiry, what shall I answer him?
> Did not he who made me in the womb make them?
> And did not one fashion us in the womb? (Job 31:13–15)

God created all—slave and free, rich and poor, male and female—a fact which conditions the practice of justice for Job, as it ought to for us. The sages essentially foreshadow the logic of Paul in Galatians 3:28. Yet while Paul stresses the leveling effect of salvation, the sages base their egalitarianism on creation.

God is not only the creator of the intricacies of the human body—and the sages do not hesitate to take their case down to the level of specific organs (see Prov 29:13)—but also the natural resources, so that the demand for justice extends even to the use of non-human creation. Thus the sages announce, "Honest balances and scales are the LORD'S; all the weights in the bag are his work" (16:11). The word for "work" (עָשָׂה) once again is the word used for God's act of creating. God creates just weights and measures. That is, justice is actually a part of the material resources of creation; it permeates the cosmos. God therefore desires all humans to live in rhythm with the order of the cosmos. When merchants misuse what God created to enhance their wealth at the expense of others, God's wrath is released, "A false balance is an abomination to the Lord" (11:1a; see also 20:10). The word for abomination (תּוֹעֵבָה) communicates the strongest expression of rebuke possible and is often used when subtle acts of injustice would easily go undetected by others enabling violators to get off scot-free.

The sages use this same strong reprimand to describe God's reaction to employing our mental faculties for personal gain, suggesting that the intimate link between justice and creation extends even to those features of the created world that we perceive as immaterial. God created the mind but when the mind is used to destroy others, for example, it repulses him, "Crooked minds are an abomination to the Lord" (11:20). The same is true for the organs of the mouth. When lips are used to lie, it is "an abomination to the Lord" (12:22). When humans use any part of their anatomy to hurt or destroy others—whether it be "haughty eyes," "a lying tongue," "a heart [read mind] that devises wicked plans," or "feet that hurry to run to evil"— it is an "abomination" to God (6:16–19). In contrast when God's creation is used with integrity it brings God joy. So "an accurate weight is his delight" (11:1b); "those of blameless ways are his delight" (11:20); "those who act faithfully are his delight" (12:22); "the prayer of the upright is his delight" (15:8); and "the thoughts of the righteous are just" (12:5).

Permeating the core books of Wisdom Literature, the willingness to root justice in creation finds its way as well into many of the psalms, none more so than Psalm 33. Here the psalmist extols the greatness of God, particularly the "word of the Lord" which is upright, faithful, righteous, and just (33:4–5). To demonstrate this, the psalmist looks, unsurprisingly, to creation:

> By the word of the Lord the heavens were made,
>   and all their host by the breath of his mouth.
> He gathered the waters of the sea as in a bottle;
>   he put the deeps in storehouses.
> Let all the earth fear the Lord;
>   let all the inhabitants of the world stand in awe of him.

For he spoke, and it came to be;
he commanded, and it stood firm. (33:6–9)

The justice of God is manifest in the creation of the world, and humanity's common source means that justice rather than human might will prevail. The psalmist reassures readers that they can appeal to "he who fashions the hearts of them all" (33:15) against the power of kings and the wealth of warriors.

For the sages, the foundation of justice is grounded in a theology of creation. While both Job and Ecclesiastes address conundrums of injustices that challenge the conventional wisdom of their day the book of Proverbs turns to a common Creator to inspire just behavior among the wise. Common to all is the realization that we must understand creation in order to understand and practice justice in our world.

Even though the terms "social" and "environmental" justice are foreign to the biblical sages, the concepts that lie behind them—treating humans and creation with respect—are not. The sages build a case for this kind of justice on the premise of God as Creator. God is the Maker of all people regardless of economic status, ethnicity, or gender. We were created, in all our particulars, to honor and respect both God and others. God created the natural resources for us to use in order to make an honest living and serve others. All that we have is from God and is to be used responsibly. God expects us to practice justice and righteousness because God is the Creator.

Creation, Food, and Justice

God's status as creator means that God is the source of all material blessings that sustain us. The sages acknowledge that this includes even the most basic sustenance of all, food (Eccl 5:18–19). There is no better place to see issues of justice or injustice at work than in the daily activity of eating. The production, distribution, and consumption of food are common sources of social as well as environmental injustices. At the same time our production and consumption of food serves as an example of how each day individuals can choose to act respectfully and responsibly toward others and toward the land. All creation, humans and non-humans alike, must have food to grow and live healthy productive lives. In a time when urbanization has separated humans from direct and daily contact with the natural world, the act of eating remains perhaps the only consistent link we have with creation, whether or not we are always aware of that link. Food plays a prominent, yet unexamined role in our lives.

Eating provides a unique way to look at the intermingling of environmental and social concerns because, while the production of food requires our conscious manipulation of the environment around us, the consumption of food often also brings us into communion with others. Eating is not just about providing fuel for our bodies; it is a way to participate in each other's lives. The holiday meal is a staple of most world cultures: turkey and stuffing for Thanksgiving in the United States, roast pig and dumplings for Noche Buena in the Philippines, buckwheat noodles on New Year's in Japan, the réveillon in France, the reunion dinners for Chinese New Year's. These celebratory feasts are exaggerations of a more basic human impulse that can be felt in moments as simple as two friends reminiscing over coffee or as significant as the meal at a wake. Something in our collective makeup transforms a biological necessity into a site of communal intimacy.

What we eat, with whom we eat, and how we eat, whether thoughtfully or thoughtlessly, reveals much about our character. Eating is a spiritual discipline through which we express gratitude to God, show hospitality to others, practice justice, and exercise good stewardship of the environment and our bodies. The act of eating reveals a whole world about us that most have not seriously assessed.

Strikingly, the one place where you are least likely to hear anyone talk about the ethics of eating is in church. The church has simply taken this daily activity for granted. Christians love to eat together; we enjoy potlucks and fellowship meals and feasting on the proverbial "Gospel Bird." Yet as much as we love to eat, we loathe talking about it. Seriously discussing food carries with it a lot of baggage, and for several reasons addressing it automatically creates defensiveness.

First, the feeling exists, whether verbalized or not, that talking about mundane matters such as food and eating is a waste of time when Christians need to grapple with heavier theological issues like the death, resurrection, and second coming of Christ, the love for God and love for neighbor, the role of the Holy Spirit, and the responsibility of the church to save the lost. The church cannot spend precious time dallying around with trivial matters like eating. Yet as we have said, eating is far from trivial. It is a locus for a host of critical issues at the heart of the Christian experience, including love for God and neighbor and care for creation.

Second, the ethics of food is often viewed as a part of a politically liberal agenda, one that is unfriendly to most churches. Discussions of food immediately conjure the specter of radical left-wing issues like animal rights, tree-hugging environmentalism, organic food, and veganism. Yet fears like this create a self-fulfilling prophecy. Precisely because mainline and conservative Christians fail to bring a serious and thoughtful voice to discussions of food ethics, these discussions are dominated by a single voice. Creation, and our relationship to it, is not a politically quarantined issue; it is a human issue.

The fear of the political agenda embedded in debates over food ethics becomes especially acute when people assume that all such discussion is a thinly veiled way to tout the benefits, moral or medical, of vegetarianism or veganism. Such anxiety is completely unwarranted. In the interest of full disclosure, one of the authors is a vegetarian and one is not. More importantly, neither is interested in binding vegetarianism on anyone. While arguments might reasonably be made from Scripture for either position, such arguments often serve as a distraction from more foundational issues in the ethics of eating. It is these points which we hope to address and, as such, prefer to leave to others debate about debatables.

There is also a tendency, related to the above, to consider reflection on what we eat as an implicit attack on farmers. Turning a critical eye toward food necessarily means turning that same eye onto how our food is produced. This potentially poses not only a threat to the livelihoods of real people but also, at least in the United States, a threat to one of the most cherished cultural images we have, that of the wholesome, salt-of-the-earth citizen-farmer.

Finally, because we implicitly realize that eating is a part of who we are, we balk at the prospect that anyone might challenge or change one of our most cherished and enjoyable activities. Matthew Halteman expands on this threatening feeling:

> Not only must we face the unwelcome prospect of subjecting our culinary identities to potentially life-changing scrutiny, but also if we discern that changes are requisite, then we risk estrangement from family and friends and invite the wider perception that we are too idealistic, sentimental, or judgmental of others. And putting aside all such self-interested aversions to reconsidering our diets, a sincere altruist might genuinely wonder whether food

ethics should be a priority for the church in a world facing so much brokenness and injustice.[6]

People have become increasingly covetous of privacy, particularly in recent years as so much of our lives have become unavoidably public. Therefore we strongly resist anyone invading what we consider to be our private space. We cannot, however, presume to quarantine any part of life, including our eating habits, from examination by God or the community of faith. The psalmist invited God to invade his privacy not as an act of ruthlessness but as an act of grace: "Search me, O God, and know my heart; test me and know my thoughts. See if there is any wicked way in me, and lead me in the way everlasting" (Ps 139:23–24). God remains sovereign over every thought and act no matter how routine or mundane that habit is. Nothing is exempt, not even the most cherished act of eating. It is a practice that must be engaged in thoughtfully and responsibly. In admonishing the Corinthian Christians Paul writes, "So, whether you eat or drink, or whatever you do, do everything for the glory of God" (1 Cor 10:31; see also Col 3:17).

We must then ask the hard questions: Do our dietary habits contribute to practices of justice or injustice? Do they promote spiritual maturity or detract from it? How do we eat: in a hurry, with others, or usually alone? How much do we eat? The food ethic we practice ought to contribute to strengthening Christian virtues like discipline, patience, good stewardship, love for neighbor, and hospitality to mention a few. We are tempted to practice a disembodied faith, content to spiritualize Christianity and conclude, at least in practice, that the physical realm is not what Christianity is about. As Ellen Davis observes, "Our need to eat presents us with our primary opportunity to work with the laws of creation."[7]

Food and the Sages in Proverbs

The sages writing the book of Proverbs provide important perspectives regarding food practices and eating habits, beginning immediately with the opening instruction poems in Proverbs (chs. 1–10). Here the sages use the analogy of food that entices youth to follow either the path of wisdom or the path of folly. The food offered possesses no moral value in itself but, because eating is both a necessary and a pleasurable experience, it serves as

---

6. Halteman, "Knowing the Standard American Diet," 384.

7. Davis, Scripture, 95.

a powerful metaphor to represent the appeal of two opposing choices: on the one hand, Woman Wisdom who persuades the naïve to follow the path of wisdom and, on the other, Woman Folly who tempts them to pursue folly (Prov 9). Nevertheless, important as food is as an analogy, the sages in Proverbs dedicate substantial attention to the real use and misuse of food as part of a moral life. Through their discussion of food, we can see not only the role of eating in personal morality but also how our most mundane acts can stretch beyond ourselves and into the realms of social and environmental justice or injustice.

Food and the Diligent

Throughout the book of Proverbs the sages speak to the obligations that surround the act of eating. To eat in a healthy and responsible way involves discipline and hard work. As youth prepare to embark on the responsibilities of adulthood, the sage advises them not to be too hasty and to establish the right priorities, making sure they have sufficient food before they begin raising their families. "Prepare your work outside, get everything ready for you in the field; and after that build your house" (Prov 24:27). Another proverb observes, "Those who till their land will have plenty of food" (Prov 12:11a). One of the instruction poems concludes that the farmer who responsibly cares for his land and livestock will have sufficient and nutritious food to eat:

> Know well the condition of your flocks,
> and give attention to your herds;
> for riches do not last forever,
> nor a crown for all generations.
> When the grass is gone, and new growth appears,
> and the herbage of the mountains is gathered,
> the lambs will provide your clothing,
> and the goats the price of a field;
> there will be enough goats' milk for your food,
> for the food of your household
> and nourishment for your servant girls. (Prov 27:23–27)

The woman described in Proverbs 31:10–31 "rises while it is still night and provides food for her household" (v. 15). "She considers a field and buys it; with the fruit of her hands she plants a vineyard" (v. 16). "She looks well to the ways of her household, and does not eat the bread of idleness" (v. 27). She is a hard working farmer, and her relationship to the land and particularly to food is a reflection not only of her personal virtue but of her social commitments as well. The expectation from sages is that for good food to be sufficient and available it comes as a result of planning, discipline, care for land and animals, love for family, and hard work.

Very few of us, though, still relate to the land the way the farmer in Proverbs 31 does. The relationship between her personal character, her family commitments, and her relationship to the land, therefore, seem obvious but obsolete. Yet today, no less than in ancient Israel, the choices we make concerning food must be made with the virtue of diligence in sight, stressing always the imperative to feed ourselves and our families all the while resisting the "bread of idleness" which allows convenience to trump conscientiousness in our food choices. In a world in which technological and bio-chemical shortcuts have all the tempting allure of Woman Folly, Christians must remember that they come with an equal amount of destruction, personal and environmental, physical and spiritual.

Food and the Lazy

A lack of this love and discipline often leads to insufficient food and poor nutrition. The sages call individuals who have not established priorities fools: "Those who till their land will have plenty of food but those who follow worthless pursuits have no sense" (Prov 12:11b). The lazy will harvest nothing but weeds and poverty:

> I passed by the field of one who was lazy,
>> by the vineyard of a stupid person;
>> and see, it was all overgrown with thorns;
>> the ground was covered with nettles,
>> and its stone wall was broken down.
> Then I saw and considered it;
> I looked and received instruction.
> A little sleep, a little slumber,
>> a little folding of the hands to rest,
>> and poverty will come upon you like a robber,
>> and want, like an armed warrior. (Prov 24:30–34)

It is significant the amount of emphasis the sage places on the relationship between sloth and food. The prudent constantly chide the lazy: "The appetite of the lazy craves, and gets nothing, while the appetite of the diligent is richly supplied" (13:4). "The lazy person does not plow in season; harvest comes, and there is nothing to be found" (20:4). Sometimes the image used to describe the slacker is bitingly sarcastic: "The lazy person buries a hand in the dish, and is too tired to bring it back to the mouth" (26:15).

The relationship between food and indolence, though, extends far beyond the level of the individual unable to make good food choices. Laziness can exist on a societal level, especially in an unwillingness to address key issues that threaten future generations. Ellen Davis identifies this type of neglect as a form of laziness maintaining that a lifestyle pursued without regard for the future health of the community is one that is ruled by indolence. This kind of sloth is all the more pernicious because it is socially acceptable.[8] Individuals may work hard, but they do so for the sole purpose of self-gratification and status with no regard for the sustainability of the environment for the next generation. Any work not motivated by a love for the well-being of the community, Davis claims, is a form of lethargy. Whole societies can be populated by eager, active workers, but the lack of social will to make the necessary changes to our collective lives represent a kind of culturally institutionalized laziness that has allowed many of our most environmentally destructive behaviors to continue.

Food and the Greedy

This sort of proactive laziness is typically driven by greed. While it is true that sometimes a lack of food comes from the result of irresponsible behavior, it is increasingly common for it to come from injustices. Food is often used by the wealthy in order to display power, to practice conspicuous consumption, to use for their pleasure, and to control others. The result is that while some work responsibly to provide food for themselves and their family, they have it taken away by those who want to hoard: "The field of the poor may yield much food, but it is swept away through injustice" (Prov 13:23).

The reality of greed and the sin of covetousness are ever-present, as the wise know all too well: "All day long the wicked covet, but the righteous give and do not hold back" (21:26). Greed sometimes flows out of a sense

8. Davis, *Scripture, Culture, and Agriculture*, 142.

of insecurity, sometimes out of a desire for more and more power; often the two are interrelated. These are probably among the reasons that drive the behavior of the gang described in the opening poem in Proverbs:

> Come with us, let us lie in wait for blood;
>> let us wantonly ambush the innocent;
>> like Sheol let us swallow them alive
>> and whole, like those who go down to the Pit.
> We shall find all kinds of costly things;
>> we shall fill our houses with booty. (1:11–13)

Yet in desiring more the sages conclude that the gang members "kill themselves! And set an ambush—for their own lives" (v. 18). The final line in the poem reiterates the devastating consequences: "Such is the end of all who are greedy for gain; it takes away the life of its possessors" (v. 19). It is no surprise then that the parents strictly forbid their son to eat with those who are greedy:

> Do not eat the bread of the stingy; do not desire their delicacies;
> for like a hair in the throat, so are they. "Eat and drink!" they say
> to you; but they do not mean it (23:6–7).

Eating and drinking with those who are stingy is like gagging on a hair you have swallowed. Such people give the appearance of generosity by their welcoming words, "Eat and drink!" but in reality they are greedy. The image in this proverb is just the opposite of an earlier one that affirms, "Those who are generous are blessed, for they share their bread with the poor" (22:9).

Greed leads to food shortage and starvation with desperate people crying out for relief. The sages depict a stark contrast between the greedy and the generous in this proverb: "People curse the man who hoards grain, but blessing crowns him who is willing to sell" (Prov 11:26). The pharaoh in Egypt practiced the hoarding of food upon hearing Joseph's dream of seven years of food scarcity (Gen 41:15–26). As a result he began to accumulate grain and build storehouses (Exod 1:11) that ultimately gave him a monopoly on the food supply resulting in the subjugation of a whole people.

The Teacher comes to much the same conclusion about the consequences of hoarding in Ecclesiastes 2:1–11 while describing his concerted effort to amass food and possessions. In trying to come to grips with the brevity of life (2:3), the Teacher occupies himself with accumulating everything under the sun he can get his hands on. He plants vineyards, gardens, and parks placing all kinds of fruit trees in them. He makes himself pools to water the forest of growing trees. Yet after all the planning and work and energy expended, the Teacher finds that riches hoarded by the possessors "were kept by their owners to their hurt" (Eccl 5:13). The result was that they would eat alone: "They eat in darkness, in much vexation and sickness and resentment" (Eccl 5:17). Eating alone is the punishment for hoarding, a natural consequence.

The problems working themselves out in local communities for the sages have now begun to play themselves out on a national and even global scale. The United States, for example, is faced with a curious and disturbing paradox. On the one hand, the Environmental Protection Agency reports that Americans discard 34.7 million tons of food every year. More than plastic, paper, glass, or rubber, food stands at the top of America's trash heap. This number has more than tripled since it began to rise in the 1980s. At the same time, however, food insecurity has been on the rise in dramatic fashion along much the same arc as food waste. The United States Department of Agriculture reports that, at some point in 2014, 14 percent of US households were food insecure, that is, they lacked the resources to guarantee regular and nutritious food for all family members. Beyond that, one in twenty US households additionally experienced what is called "very low food security," a worse category in which some or all family members were forced to reduce or do without food at some point during the year. Predictably, as we will see in the next chapter, single-parent households and households headed by racial minorities tended to experience food insecurity at dramatically higher levels.[9]

The dichotomy between the haves and the have-nots—or in this case the eats and the eat-nots—functions on a global scale, with the world's most wasteful countries sitting at a comfortable distance, geographically and economically, from the countries with the highest rates of starvation. But if all this seems as distant to us as the ancient world of the Teacher and his quest for absolute consumption, Laura Hartman brings the issue back to our dinner tables and shopping carts, "Eating food links us to the economy: money I spend and the demand I create encourages the practices that bring the food to my table. Unjust food practices are, often unwittingly, supported by consumer demand, as well as by public policy and social expectation. The blessing and delight of food is burdened with hidden injustice."[10] Our most

9. USDA, "Household Food."
10. Hartman, "Seeking Food Justice," 397.

quotidian behaviors embed us in broader systems of injustice. If we object that those behaviors are unconscious, driven by ignorance or routine rather than deliberate greed, then we reveal rather than excuse the sin: it is our failure to think critically, to pursue wisdom, that allows injustice to persist.

Food and the Glutton

Of all the ethical concerns about food, gluttony is the one most familiar, but gluttony is substantially more than overeating. It is often a manifestation of greed and more general self-indulgence, and, as such, the sages reserve some harsh words for gluttony. The sages describe the glutton as one of four types that cause the whole earth to quake:

> Under three things the earth trembles;
> under four it cannot bear up:
>> a slave when he becomes king,
>> and a fool when glutted with food;
>> an unloved woman when she gets a husband,
>> and a maid when she succeeds her mistress. (Prov 30:21–23)

Parents give a strong warning to their son to stay away from the gluttonous. Gluttony is viewed not as a single act but a lifestyle and one that leads to a dead end:

> Hear, my child, and be wise,
>> and direct your mind in the way.
> Do not be among winebibbers,
>> or among gluttonous eaters of meat;
>> for the drunkard and the glutton will come to poverty,
>> and drowsiness will clothe them with rags. (Prov 23:19–21)
> Those who keep the law are wise children,
>> but companions of gluttons shame their parents. (Prov 28:7)

Notice how gluttony is antithetic to keeping the law in the last proverb.[11] It is as though the sin of gluttony represents the antithesis of everything the law or sapiential instruction stands for. If wisdom, like the law, is about love

---

11. It is possible that *torah* here refers to the instruction of the father. But the message remains basically the same. Gluttony remains the antithesis of everything the parents have taught the son.

for God and love for neighbor gluttony is the full-throated embrace of love of self.

Unfortunately, gluttony can be difficult to detect in affluent societies. The abundance of wealth, manifest particularly in the ready availability of food, and our general cultural embrace of "self-esteem"—a regular gloss for self-love—make gluttony almost invisible. Even when we identify it, we too often reason that gluttony is just a mostly harmless overindulgence in something we desire.[12] Or, in our more callous moments, we stereotype the glutton in ways that safely exclude ourselves: gluttons are are overweight and unattractive. Gluttony, however, comes in all shapes and sizes and has more to do with a perspective on life than a body type. Gluttons can be dieters or health food addicts just as easily as couch potatoes or junk food addicts. Gluttons have an obsession with food even if all they eat is fruits and vegetables or they eat very little at all.

Gluttony also involves a kind of social perversion of food, a corruption of the community created at a shared meal. Often gluttony takes advantage of occasions where camaraderie is found—the holiday feasts described above, for example—but gluttons prove incapable of companionship be-cause they are too focused on the self and on the body. Gluttony makes us solitary, isolating us from our communities and alienating us from God's creation, even as we abuse the fruits of the earth. As Wirzba describes it, "Gluttony reflects an inordinate and inappropriate desire for food, a de-sire that is focused on self-satisfaction rather than sharing and communal celebration."[13]

Gluttony creates space for the columniation of the kind of social in-justices discussed with greed. Wirzba continues: "The sin of gluttony is not confined to individual persons. It is possible for a whole culture to become gluttonous in its aspirations and manners, and in so doing deprive many of the world's peoples of the food and nurture they need."[14] Amazingly there are as many people dying today from starvation as there are from obesity.[15] Gluttony emerges from a disrespect for food which reflects a broken rela-tionship with creation, together making possible the terrible reality we face now in which our personal eating habits are simultaneously starving others

---

12. Fairlie, *Seven Deadly Sins*, 170.

13. Wirzba, *Food and Faith*, 139.

14. Ibid.

15. Ibid., 140.

and killing ourselves. Like those who take the Lord's Supper unworthily, we eat and drink our own damnation.

The culture of greed, accumulation, sloth, and gluttony does not end with the avarice of the fool in the book of Proverbs or the indulgences of the Teacher in Ecclesiastes. It is the perennial problem of the human race that is always anxious about what we will eat and what we will drink and what we will wear. We refuse to learn from creation and how the birds of the air "neither sow nor reap nor gather into barns," and yet they are well taken care of by the Creator (Matt 6:26).

Food as Gift

The sages, for their part, reflect this disposition of gratitude much better than modern Christians often do. The rote gratitude expressed in pre-meal prayers often masks a lifestyle that looks more like the greedy or gluttonous fools of Proverbs than the humbler birds of the field. In the only prayer found in the book of Proverbs, the inquirer reveals a very different sort of gratitude. The prayer makes just two requests of God:

> Two things I ask of you;
>> do not deny them to me before I die:
> Remove far from me falsehood and lying;
>> give me neither poverty nor riches;
>> feed me with the food that I need,
>> or I shall be full, and deny you,
>> and say, "Who is the LORD?"
>> or I shall be poor, and steal,
>> and profane the name of my God. (Prov 30:7–9)

What this worshipper requests is a very modest lifestyle symbolized by having just enough food for each day; "feed me with the food that I need," no more and no less. If, on the one hand, he is too full he will be tempted to deny the Lord. The enticing power of riches that would provide an overabundance of food could lead him to forget God, which was precisely the temptation Israel faced as they entered the promised land (Deut 8:11–17). If, on the other hand, the worshipper is in a state of desperate hunger he will be tempted to steal from others harming them and violating a fundamental command of God. The prayer of the worshipper in Proverbs 30 acknowledges not only that food is a gift from God, but that the simplicity and mere adequacy of that food is itself a gift.

The problem with trying to live out this disposition is that we are enticed by the good life, which is now more accessible than it ever was in ancient Israel. With our abundant resources, we are less like the simple everyday Israelite and more like the Teacher in Ecclesiastes who himself struggled with this temptation. The Teacher wanted to experiment with finding what was good for mortals to do during the few days of their life so he amasses food and material goods:

> I made great works; I built houses and planted vineyards for myself; I made myself gardens and parks, and planted in them all kinds of fruit trees. I made myself pools from which to water the forest of growing trees. I bought male and female slaves, and had slaves who were born in my house; I also had great possessions of herds and flocks, more than any who had been before me in Jerusalem. I also gathered for myself silver and gold and the treasure of kings and of the provinces; I got singers, both men and women, and delights of the flesh, and many concubines. So I became great and surpassed all who were before me in Jerusalem; also my wisdom remained with me. Whatever my eyes desired I did not keep from them; I kept my heart from no pleasure, for my heart found pleasure in all my toil, and this was my reward for all my toil. Then I considered all that my hands had done and the toil I had spent in doing it, and again, all was vanity and a chasing after wind, and there was nothing to be gained under the sun. (Eccl 2:1–11)

Much of the imagery in this section reflects the imagery of Genesis 1–2 with vineyards and gardens, fruit trees and pools of water, cattle and sheep. It appears that the Teacher's experiment in seeking out a meaningful existence is an attempt to recreate the garden of Eden. Yet there are noticeable differences between these two gardens. For one, in this garden only the Teacher is present; God is completely absent. In Hebrew the prepositional phrase "for me" occurs eleven times in the passage and the word "pleasure" occurs four times. Clearly this is all about the owner of the garden and a display of power. The Teacher is trying to play God for a day. Another difference also surfaces, after God finishes creating the garden in Eden God reflects on it and proclaims it "very good" (Gen 1:31). But after this owner reflects on his garden he proclaims it useless; nothing was gained from it (Eccl 2:11). Greed and gluttony were the driving forces behind his garden and they destroyed its beauty.

After all the experimenting, indulging, and hoarding, the Teacher realizes it is all in vain and comes to a new conclusion:

> There is nothing better for mortals than to eat and drink, and find enjoyment in their toil. This also, I saw, is from the hand of God; for apart from him who can eat or who can have enjoyment? For to the one who pleases him God gives wisdom and knowledge and joy; but to the sinner he gives the work of gathering and heaping, only to give to one who pleases God. This also is vanity and a chasing after wind. (Eccl 2:24–26)

At this point in his quest for meaning, the Teacher steps back to take a fresh look at life. All along he has announced that life is *hebel*[16] but now, as this part of his experiment comes to an end, he reflects on what he discovered. At first glance there seems little difference between his attempt to recreate the garden of Eden (2:1–11) and what he concludes in 2:24–26. Formerly, however, he *sought* after "pleasure;" now he *finds* "enjoyment." There is a major distinction between his *pursuit* of pleasure and his *reception* of enjoyment. The Teacher no longer speaks of the task of *pursuing* pleasure as he has in 2:1–11. There is no obsessive attitude about enjoyment at this point. Rather than *pursuing* enjoyment, the Teacher now *accepts* it as a gift from God (see also 5:18–19). Now he discovers joy *in* work and not just joy in the *results* of work as in his former pursuits (the pleasure of which only lasted temporarily). His work now becomes a vocation that applies his talents to a task that provides a service for others (see also 9:7–10).

The Teacher realizes that the true gifts of life are neither earned or planned or produced or achieved but *received* as gifts from God. Enjoying the activities of eating and working and being, especially when these activities are done in community, brings us into contact with God. God is distant (Eccl 5:2; 7:13–14). Nevertheless God spans this distance when humans receive and enjoy God's earthly gifts (see also 3:12–13 and 9:7–10). To put it in the words of James Limburg, "The gulf between God and humans is

---

16. This word is translated differently in various English versions. In all thirty-eight times the word appears in Ecclesiastes, the NIV unfortunately consistently translates it as "meaningless." The NRSV, KJV, and JB favor the translation "vanity." Other translations prefer "absurdity" or "emptiness" or "useless." The translation favored here stays with its fundamental meaning of "vapor" or "breath" and thus much of the time it refers to the brevity of life. In many cases in Ecclesiastes this is the translation that make the most sense in the context. The Tanak, a Jewish translation, favors this interpretation in several places (see e.g., 6:12; 7:15; 9:9; 11:10).

bridged from God's side by God's giving of everyday good gifts."[17] Even though God is remote, we can see "the hand of God" in the everyday gifts of food and drink and work (Eccl 2:24).

The Teacher repeats the conclusion he reaches in 2:24–26 several more times throughout the book.[18] He does not make these statements about enjoying eating, drinking, work, friends, and family as a hedonist because he is not pursuing enjoyment while striving to accumulate more. He does not see enjoyment as an entitlement but as a gift. As William Brown concludes, Ecclesiastes warns against the uselessness of "striving for luxury and legacy and commends a life of grateful simplicity, of acceptance and sufficiency, a life of settling for less while living for joy." The one who seeks simplicity "replaces greed with gratitude, enslavement with freedom, despair with joy.[19]

Herein lies the wise disposition toward food. When we treat the bounty of creation—whether in the fields, on the grocery store shelves, or at our tables—as something to be earned, acquired, accumulated, or consumed we invite all the folly of the sages' most dire warnings into our hearts and into our bellies. Yet we can learn from the mistakes of the Teacher and internalize his conclusions: food is a gift. God, not bounded by natural law or the limits of human imagination, might rightly and easily have made humanity photosynthetic, making questions of gluttony and food insecurity moot from the beginning of time. Instead the Creator crafted a world in which basic survival behaviors carried with them pleasure, personal enrichment, and communal significance. We squander that gift when we indulge in it thoughtlessly. God chose, thoughtfully and deliberately, to create a world with food; when we receive that food as a gift, we are called to thoughtfully and deliberately evaluate how we produce it and how we eat it.

Conclusion

The wisdom tradition is quite concerned about issues of justice, both social and environmental. Even though the sages were not experiencing anything like the global environmental crisis of the present, they nevertheless understood justice was rooted in God's role as creator and that sins against

17. Limburg, *Encountering Ecclesiastes*, 34.

18. These summary conclusions are sometimes referred to as the joy passages or the *Carpe Diem* passages. There are seven of them: 2:24–26; 3:12–13; 3:22; 5:17–19; 8:14–15; 9:7–10; 11:9–10.

19. Brown, *Seven Pillars*, 237.

God's creation were intimately linked to social injustices. Those avaricious practices and gluttonous lifestyles led to crimes committed against other human beings, and these same lifestyles today remain the root cause of injustice. Embedded in the entanglement of concern for creation and community, and what we seem to have forgotten, is the implicit recognition that crimes against humanity invariably result in crimes against the environment and vice versa.

As such, neither historical distance nor the difference in ecological circumstance can silence the sages' voices. Wisdom Literature provides an essential perspective on our current dilemma. Its fundamental message is that God is the creator of all, the wealthy and the poor, men and women, human faculties to see, hear, and think, and the natural resources humans use to make weights, measures, houses, and computers. God is creator of land and water, flora and fauna. God is sovereign Creator. It is out of this premise that the practice of justice flows.

God's act of creation is no less an act of giving, and it is in the recognition of this that we can check many of our unconscious tendencies toward injustice. From God all blessings flow, spiritual and material. Daily the Lord comes into relationship with us in providing food, family, friends, and work. We must express gratitude in ways more substantial than habitual prayers. Instead we *live* our gratitude by becoming good stewards of these gifts, disciplining our desires, curbing our appetites, and recognizing the virtue of not wanting more than we need. If we respect all of God's creation, humans and non-humans, rich and poor alike and show generosity, practice hospitality, and open our hands to the poor and needy (Prov 31:20), we will find, perhaps to our surprise, that the environment we live in is blessed. Environmental justice requires a lifestyle of environmental gratitude.

Chapter Six

Justice for All Creation

A generous person will be enriched;
And one who gives water will get water.

—PROVERBS 11:25

IN 1999, HURRICANE FLOYD buffeted the east coast of the United States causing widespread flooding and, at the time, unprecedented economic and human loss. It struck North Carolina on September 16, then having downgraded from a category 4 to a category 2 hurricane. It brought with it ten-foot storm surges and dumped almost twenty inches of rain on coastal North Carolina, which only added to the waters left by Tropical Storm Dennis only two weeks earlier. Floyd killed fifty people, thirty-five in North Carolina alone, mostly by drowning in the devastating floods that followed. Parts of ten states were declared disaster areas, and in North Carolina 7,000 homes were destroyed and 150,000 people were left without electricity. Understandably, the North Carolina Secretary of Health and Human Services remarked, "Nothing since the Civil War has been as destructive to families here."[1]

But hurricanes happen. Whether we believe that God always intended them as part of the natural order of things or that they are the result of sin being introduced into the world, hurricanes, tornadoes, blizzards, tsunamis, earthquakes, and volcanoes are a part of the world we live in, no matter what humans do in it. Even if we choose to accept—and not having the least scientific aptitude, we will not presume to rule on it either way—that

1. National Weather Service, "Hurricane Floyd."

manmade global warming has caused a marked increase in the number and intensity of devastating weather events, Floyd is not typically placed at the center of these debates with the likes of Hurricane Ike and Superstorm Sandy, unnatural manifestations of nature at its most brutal. Hurricane Floyd, in contrast, was a manifestation of extreme but usual weather patterns recurrent as far back as human records exist in the region.

If that is the case, what does Hurricane Floyd have to do with environmental ethics? Tragically, the destruction in the wake of the hurricane cannot be blamed on the storm alone; Floyd had accomplices. The decisions made by certain communities, those with the power and means to make those decisions, shaped the nature of Floyd's destruction. They created a specific geography of loss that was decidedly uneven and, more importantly, unjust. Who died, who lost homes, who was displaced, none of it was random, none of it accidental. The truth of this is manifest nowhere more vividly than in the memories of North Carolina residents. Take for example Elberta Pugh-Hudson and Thomas Samuel Hudson—an assistant pastor and a member respectively in the African Methodist Episcopal Zion Church in White Stocking, NC—who together provide a window into just how thoroughly human interaction with the environment serves to exacerbate social inequalities in our society.[2]

The Hudsons lost everything in Hurricane Floyd—with the exception of the family truck that they drove to safety, a miracle that Mr. Hudson attributes to having the Lord's Prayer painted on the back—but they blamed neither God nor the storm. In fact, by their recollection, the hurricane had not been all that bad. Mrs. Hudson remembered,

> When the flood came, I mean the day before, like when the hurricane came itself, you know, it just was a lot of wind. Strong winds. You could feel the roof and stuff rattling and all. I woke up and we just seen branches and trees, you know, knocked down. I was just like, thank you Lord, because we didn't get a lot of damage. It was just limbs. And my neighbor, she was gone; she was gone for about two weeks. And so I went over to next door and I was cleaning all the leaves and limbs and stuff out of her yard and stacking it in the back. And then that next morning . . .

That next morning the flooding began. The sky had opened up and let loose up to ten inches during Dennis and another twenty during Floyd, but only

---

2. Thomas Samuel Hudson and Elberta Pugh-Hudson, interview by Rob Amberg and Charles Thompson, Southern Oral History Program Collection.

once those storms had passed did the Hudsons first experience loss. Mr. Hudson believed he knew the reason why.

> My feeling about the flood is that they sent the water down here, all of it at one time, by the Lord. It's the Lord's water, but man controlled it and then released it. So it wasn't by the Lord for being what's called no disaster or flood. It was flood, man made flood in my belief. We went through the storms—the wind, the rain and blowing trees down and all that. But it was these dams that hold this water back. And, for some particular reason they didn't release the water at the time that they was supposed to. They hold it back, and it got too much on them. Instead of destroying them, they just released it on someone else.

Somewhere upstream, more affluent communities had built a reservoir and enjoyed waterfront homes and lake sports while the sun was shining. Yet suddenly they found that their environmental action could have dire consequences; the hurricane threatened to flood their manmade lake. As is tragically too often the case, those with the wealth and power to control their own destiny decided to shift the burden onto the powerless, the poor, the marginalized. Fortunately, the Hudsons' story has a happy ending: a combination of faith and a strong church community in White Stocking helped them get back on their feet. Unfortunately, the human complicity in environmental injustices the Hudsons recalled is neither exceptional nor rare.

In the popular imagination, environmentalism is, at its most benign, concerned with the preservation of pristine mountain streams or dense secluded forests; at its worst, it is linked to the divisive politics of culture wars in the form of debates about global warming and whether or not such-and-such endangered amphibian should prevent such-and-such economic development project. In truth, however, neither global climate change nor untouched wilderness is the primary concern. The environment plays a crucial role in the daily lives of everyone in ways that are just as often local as they are global. Because of this, we have argued throughout this book that environmental ethics must be deeply embedded in the broader moral consciousness of people in general and Christians in particular, in everything from the way we eat to how we read fairy tales to what we do in our free time. It must, as argued in the previous chapter, also condition our notions of justice.

It was precisely this desire to more fully integrate concrete social issues into the discourse of environmentalism that gave rise, beginning in the late 1970s, to the environmental justice movement.[3] Environmental justice, broadly defined, involves the recognition that environmental disasters—like Hurricane Floyd—and environmental degradation disproportionately affect poor and minority communities and that, as a result, concern for the environment and concern for social justice are inseparably linked. Though arising slowly and independently in various locations, nothing spurred the environmental justice movement more than events in Warren County, North Carolina, the location of a landfill for dumping tens of thousands of tons of toxic soil that had been deliberately and illegally contaminated to circumvent EPA regulations. Heated protests erupted when the deceit was discovered resulting in more than five hundred arrests and, more importantly, a study by the federal government that revealed that pollution was not indiscriminate and its effects not random. The study showed that three out of every four toxic waste dumps in the region were located in close proximity to predominantly African American communities (even though, in the area surveyed, the total population was only 20 percent African American). Later studies followed, showing that the greatest indicator of where a waste facility would be located was the race of nearby inhabitants. The cat was out of the bag: the dumping of toxic waste was not only ecologically unsound, it was socially unjust.

A combination of intense grassroots efforts in the effected communities and critical political action have served to push forward the environmental justice movement. In 1994, President Bill Clinton issued Executive Order 12898, "Federal Actions to Address Environmental Justice in Minority Populations and Low-Income Populations," which ordered that "to the greatest extent practicable . . . each Federal agency shall make achieving environmental justice part of its mission by identifying and addressing, as appropriate, disproportionately high and adverse human health or environmental effects of its programs . . . on minority populations and low-income populations."[4] In 2007, the United States Senate held its first hearing on environmental justice. Yet, for all its gains, the cause of environmental justice continues to linger beneath the consciousness of most people for

---

3. Countless quality histories exist of the environmental justice movement. The material here will be drawn largely from Johnson, "Environmental Justice," 17–45, and Fowler, *Greening of Protestant Thought.*

4. Executive Order 12898, "Federal Actions."

whom the environmental concerns of the socially marginalized would be uncomfortable to think about.

In this, Christians are lamentably no less guilty than politicians and media outlets. Protestant environmentalism began to flourish not long after secular environmentalism, and, unsurprisingly, a Christian recognition of the entanglement of social and environmental justice known as "eco-justice theology" came into being at roughly the same time as the secular environmental justice movement. Like the environmental justice movement, eco-justice theology has, in its finest moments, clarified the call for "building a just and loving social order, now expanded to embrace the whole community of creation."[5] Yet eco-justice theology has remained substantially more circumscribed than its secular counterpart, being largely restricted to the most liberal wings of mainline American Protestant denominations. For once, this is not primarily the result of apathy on the part of conservatives and evangelicals. The articulation of eco-justice theology in the past thirty years has created among the majority of Protestant Christians a real and legitimate aversion to the political and social agenda of the most radical Christian environmentalists. This is in large part the result of a particular ethical vision in which social justice must necessarily mean economic equality. There can be, for many eco-justice theologians no other truly just vision of society. As such, the way to solve the simultaneous problems of environmental destruction and social inequality is to erase the latter. If everyone has the same amount to lose and if everyone has the same social and economic power, then the Hudsons would never have had to worry about wealthy reservoir communities flooding their poorer downstream communities. This vision of an economically and socially reordered world is at once too radical for the mainstream of Christianity and too mild for the most vociferous advocates of eco-justice. Consider environmental sociologist Albert Bergesen's critique of redistribution from within the logic of environmental justice:

> There are studies of what society does to nature, or how different classes, races, ethnicities, genders and whole zones of the world system are exposed to hazardous wastes, acid rain, or have "their" natural resources exploited for the benefit of other zones of the world-system. But note. The idea that the rainforest belongs to the South, or to Brazilians, perpetuates the narrow human centricity of supposedly totalistic and radical social thought. It is indeed

5. Engel, "Post-World War II Eco-Justice Movement," 10.

radical for humans, but not for other living things, for it may be human justice to turn the rainforest over to Brazilians, or even more just and radical to turn it over to native peoples, but it is still one class of living things owning/controlling other classes of the eco-system. Human justice, therefore, is not, per se, eco-justice, and human equality is not eco equality.[6]

In this face of this kind of thinking, it is equally easy to assume that eco-justice is not biblical justice. The bewildering specter of the redistribution of wealth or, more radically, the erasure of all conceptions of property has driven the mass of Christians away from environmental justice, even from any of the positive observations that arise from the movement.

This has begun to change. It has become increasingly difficult in recent years to ignore the degree to which poor and minority communities around the world assume an unequal share of the burden for environmental degradation. Hurricane Katrina, the 2010 earthquake in Haiti, the Fukushima disaster, and the rising sea levels that threaten to swallow the tiny Christian nation of Tuvalu have all made their way into the world press highlighting the way in which human interaction with the environment has devastating effects for the poor. When a magnitude 7 earthquake can kill only four in wealthy Japan (e.g., the 2011 Miyagi earthquake) and 100,000 in Haiti, it very quickly becomes uncomfortable *not* to think about how environmental disasters—natural and unnatural—seem to target society's most vulnerable groups.

Just as importantly, a more vigorous debate has taken hold among Christians about the meaning of justice. The definition of justice by traditional eco-justice theologians cannot be regarded as self-evident, and many are now beginning to realize that alternative visions of justice can bring the marriage of social and environmental ethics to the center of Christian moral thought without necessarily implying a radical political and social outlook. While Christian debates have centered around conventional sources for environmental ethics (like Genesis) and social justice ethics (like Leviticus and the minor prophets), Wisdom Literature has something powerful to contribute to any discussion of the way wealth relates both to society and to the environment. What follows are three examples of the way the wisdom of the sages, drawn particularly in this case from Proverbs, complements or modifies the observations of environmental justice advocates. The sages offer a vision of justice that echoes many of the concerns of

6. Bergeson, "Eco-Alienation," 115.

environmental justice without in any way being consonant with the typical definition of justice offered by eco-justice theology. Through this vision of justice, for all of creation, Christians can construct a biblically-rooted ethic that is engaged critically with the latest environmental thinking.

Good Intentions and Ill Effects in Industrial Agriculture

One of the critical issues for social justice, both in Scripture and in modern thought, is the ability of the poor to access food. Perhaps the oldest and most universal way that people have shaped non-human nature for their purposes is agriculture. While the previous chapter discussed the ethical importance of eating for the sages, the ability of the poor to access food on a much larger scale has been one of the primary focuses for advocates of environmental justice. Biblical perspectives on access to food, particularly the effects of agricultural practices on the poor, have similarly provided one of the key avenues for linking social and environmental justice in recent discussions among Christian scholars. In fact, one of the hallmarks of the biblical vision of social justice is the practice of gleaning (Lev 19:9–10, 23:22; Deut 24:19) which involved Israelite farmers leaving fallen grain and the grain at the edges of fields to benefit the poor, widows, orphans, and aliens. Some of the earliest laws of God clearly connect for humans their relationship to nature and their relationship to fellow humans: a portion, the first fruits, must be set aside for God and a portion must be set aside for the poor. The sages reflect this ethical tradition in which the fruits of the earth cannot be seen simply as the personal fruits of one's labor. They command, "Honor the LORD with your substance and the first fruits of all your produce; then your barns will be filled with plenty, and your vats will be bursting with wine" (Prov 3:9–10). At the same time, they laud the person who gives freely, turning explicitly to agricultural production: "A generous person will be enriched, and one who gives water will get water. The people curse those who hold back grain, but a blessing is on those who sell it" (Prov 11:25–26). In a society constantly at risk of drought, disaster, war, and, as a result of any of the above, famine, the generous agricultural practices of farmers proved a key part of maintaining justice.

In the intervening millennia, however, food production has changed dramatically as have the ways in which society ensures access for the poor to affordable food. Advances in agricultural technology have always arrived hand-in-hand with massive increases in population, from the very first concentrated human attempts at agriculture to the development of better systems of crop rotation all the way into the present system in which an ever precarious balance of chemistry and engineering do an increasing amount of the agricultural labor. The fortunate blend of ample arable land and high levels of industrialization have allowed the United States in particular to produce tremendous amounts of food all while employing only about 1 percent of the US population in agriculture. In fact, the United States produces so much surplus food that it alone accounts for approximately half of the world's grain exports. All of that food, as a rule, means lower prices that benefit everyone, particularly the poor. A trip to the supermarket in an industrialized country *without* abundant agricultural land—such as Japan or the United Kingdom, both of which must import roughly half of their food annually—provides a vivid picture of just how fortunate Americans are to live in the midst of a veritable cornucopia.

Yet, as environmental justice advocates are quick to remind, the historically recent access of the poor to abundant and inexpensive food has not simply or uniformly meant justice for the poor. In fact, new methods of agricultural production have created new, largely unintentional, forms of injustice. These problems evoke once again biblical themes about the way people relate to the land and to the poor. Though examples abound, here it will be profitable to look at the phenomenon of pesticide drift which is generally thought of as an environmental disaster—the kind which usually concern traditional environmentalists—but which must also be understood as a grave social injustice. Like most environmental disasters, pesticide drift disproportionately effects the poor and minorities who have little role in shaping the behaviors that have the potential to destroy their lives and their livelihoods.

Pesticide drift describes what happens when, all too frequently, toxic chemical intended to kill off agricultural pests float out of their target area into residential neighborhoods or settle in natural areas and water sources.[7] The problem is global, with millions of cases of illness reported every year through either direct exposure or consumption of contaminated food or water. Yet in spite of the public perception that pesticide drift represents a series of uncommon and largely isolated disaster "events," pesticide drift is a persistent problem and one that does not affect all communities equally. Instead, those who bear the brunt of the poison are migrant workers—who are inevitably stationed near farmlands that are being sprayed—and the

---

7. This account of pesticide drift relies heavily on Harrison, *Pesticide Drift*.

residents of low income rural communities. The biochemical solution to food scarcity has created new and devastating problems for marginalized members of society, and environmentally questionable behaviors are having real human impact.

A recent study of the problem of pesticide drift suggests that in California alone, hundreds of thousands of residents are exposed to a buffet of harmful, often carcinogenic compounds: metam sodium/MITC, methy bromide, 1,3-dichloropropene, chlorpyrifos, methidathion, and molinate. The effects range from temporary and acute to chronic or terminal conditions including, but not limited to, asthma, migraines, rashes, bronchitis, reduced eyesight, miscarriages, heart attacks, and cancer. Areas with high rates of pesticide use also disturbingly (though not definitively) correlate to higher incidences of infant mortality, birth defects, autism spectrum disorders, and Parkinson's. Wealthy and middle-class communities are rarely located in these areas and, even if they were, these people generally have the means to relocate when faced with the above litany of maladies. Migrant workers, however, generally lack the political and social clout to argue for changes to established pesticide practices or for greater protections for workers. Faced with a choice between their lives and the livelihoods, many are pressured to keep quiet in order to keep their jobs. Adjacent rural communities are often just as powerless. One affected California resident reported:

> We live in a trailer park in a mobile home, surrounded by orange groves. At night during the spraying season we get sick, with symptoms that wake us up. We have asked the owner of the trailer park to do something about this problem, at least let us known when spraying is going to happen, but the owner always tells us we can leave if we don't like the situation, that we should look for another place to live. But we can't afford to rent a lot in another park.[8]

Without any viable alternatives, these communities are forced to sit and wait, knowing that they will be the primary victims of the next predictable, preventable environmental disaster.

The problem of pesticide drift does not emerge out of any extraordinary malice on the part of any of the involved parties. In fact, modern industrial-scale agriculture cannot survive without the extensive use of pesticides.[9] Farmers have centuries of precedent and engrained practice

8. Quoted in Harrison, *Pesticide Drift*, 126.

9. An excellent and accessible account of the role of pesticides in the development

prompting them to make liberal use of pesticides—with over-spraying actually being cheaper than the potential loss of a crop from disease or infestation. Pesticide companies respond to the real and legitimate demand for the new and constantly stronger pesticide formulae necessary to keep farmers, not to mention grocery store consumers, happy. These are not "the wicked" who "covet the proceeds of wickedness" (Prov 12:15) who the sages condemn. (They will make their entrance later in the chapter.)

Even so, the perils of pesticide use have been widely recognized and steps have been taken to try to spur agricultural practices which do not risk poisoning laborers and local residents most dramatically effected by pesticides. The most obvious of these is the birth of the organic food movement, which, among its other arguments, follows the very simple and logical train of thought that if toxic pesticides are the problem the solution is to stop using them altogether. Only "organic" means of pest control are used and, as a result, the threat of pesticide drift is rendered null and void.

Unfortunately, from the perspective of the poor, the unassailable logic of the organic food movement is of little comfort. Industrial agriculture solved the problem of food scarcity by inventing the problem of pesticide drift. The organic food movement represents a simple reversal of that process. Walk into the nearest grocery store and you can buy a wealth of organic produce secure in the knowledge that your kumquat is not tainted by a migrant worker's asthma or Parkinson's or cancer, but that same migrant worker almost certainly could not walk into the store and buy that produce as well. With organic products often costing as much as double that of non-organic foods, the problem of pesticide drift seems to have been solved by reintroducing food insecurity.

When faced with paradoxes like these, advocates of environmental justice begin to debate about contradictory perceptions of what environmental and social justice truly looks like, what sorts of risks are permissible in the face of what sorts of gains on behalf of the poor and of the environment. Here too the wisdom of the sages can function as a key point for critical reflection. As already noted, the sages do not understand farmers to merely be producing for their own benefit. In fact, the ethical expectations of farmers are unique, in large part because, unlike artisans, what they produce is essential to life. As such, the work of farmers has both sacramental significance in the form of the first fruits offering (Deut 26:1–11) and social

---

of modern agriculture can be found in Mann, *1493*, particularly ch. 6, "Agro-Industrial Complex."

significance in the form of leaving crops for gleaning. This exalted view of the farmer corresponds well with the archetypal American image of the small farmer living in the country's heartland and embodying its most sacred values. Americans, like ancient Israelites, imagine the farmer as a site of tremendous moral significance.

The tensions which characterize debates about pesticide drift exist in the Proverbs as well. As seen in the last chapter, the imperative to produce, to work diligently, is a key feature of wisdom, and understandably so. The observation that "those who till their land will have plenty of food, but those who follow worthless pursuits have no sense" (Prov 12:11) is wise on a number of levels, the most obvious of which is stated explicitly: the only way to get food is to till the land. The implication of the succeeding verse also suggests that wisdom understands the importance of positive efforts which yield fruits in keeping people from negative ones which yield nothing but trouble. The need to be productive has even greater significance though for Israelite society—the majority of which were engaged in agricultural production—because it represents both a key feature of their worship of God and of their duty to society as a whole.

Precisely for this reason the imperative to produce is not absolute. Agricultural production has limits for the sages. The well-being of the individual matters, certainly, and the sages advise "do not wear yourself out to get rich; be wise enough to desist" (Prov 23:4), but more crucial than this is concern for the poor. Agricultural practices which take production as their ultimate ethical value and forget the important role that they are meant to play in ensuring social justice risk invoking divine wrath. Consider this warning to those who have forgotten this duty in the pursuit of higher yields: "Do not remove an ancient landmark or encroach on the fields of orphans, for their redeemer is strong; he will plead their cause against you" (Prov 23:2). Farmers are tasked with balancing the wisdom of diligently working their fields so that they yield fruit and attending to the needs of those who exist, in this case literally, at the margins of their world.

Whatever the solution to the problem of pesticide drift—and predictably the sages give no clear answers—it must be remembered that solutions to problems of injustice, particularly environmental injustice, must have the specific situation of the poor in view. Clearly the current situation does not. Without any malice, those who can least afford it are being subjected to a perpetual environmental disaster in the form of toxic fallout wafting in their communities, and the most attractive solutions create as many new problems as they solve. Neither the blind pursuit of lower cost or cleaner production sufficiently accounts for needs of the poor or for the ethical imperatives placed on farmers responsible for providing societies most basic human needs. A wise solution will balance the right of the poor to life—both in the form of basic sustenance and a non-toxic environment to live and work in—and the ultimately good efforts of farmers to make a living in partnership with the land.

Hurricanes and the Geography of Social Injustice

Pesticide drift is a problem of human creation, incontestably. Manmade chemicals put to work by humans in the process of transforming creation to meet human needs negatively affect human lives. Whatever the motives and however innocent the perpetrators, it is impossible to shift the blame for the spread of toxins from people onto creation. The same is not the case with extreme weather, which is regularly portrayed as totally impersonal in its behavior and unpredictable in its results. To an extent, that must be true. Yet even the most cursory survey of extreme weather events show that it is the poor and the marginalized who bear the brunt of the devastation whenever hurricanes, earthquakes, floods, and tornadoes interrupt our orderly, well-planned lives. Just as it is no coincidence that the socially marginal suffer the most from problems generated by human interaction with nature, there is a powerful if silent logic at work in the way nature seems to take out its wrath first and foremost on the poor.

Even more than Hurricane Floyd, Hurricane Katrina exposed the way extreme weather events seem to target the poor and minorities. The image of thousands of poor African Americans packed into the convention center and the Louisiana Superdome made it impossible to ignore, because, in the infamous words of Jesse Jackson, it looked suspiciously "like the hull of a slave ship."[10] Of course, storms do not actually target any one socioeconomic group or ethnicity. The reason for this meteorological optical illusion is a combination of ignorance and lack of foresight in human society rather than any malfeasance in God's non-human creation. So-called "natural" disasters are anything but natural in their concrete and predictable impact on marginalized communities. As Christians become increasingly aware of how issues of social justice collide with the most violent forces of

10. Broder, "Amid Criticism."

nature, it becomes necessary for thinking about our responsibility to the poor to take on a distinctively environmental flavor.

In the aftermath of Hurricane Katrina, President George W. Bush addressed the nation to describe the monumental efforts being undertaken to house displaced communities and rebuild the Gulf Coast. Before recovery could begin, however, the disaster itself needed to be explained. "In the aftermath, we have seen fellow citizens left stunned and uprooted, searching for loved ones, and grieving for the dead, and looking for meaning in a tragedy that seems so *blind and random*."[11] This rhetoric about the blindness and randomness of hurricanes was echoed by key figures in the Bush administration and then parroted by the mass media which largely took upon itself the task of interpreting the event for Americans. Yet this language obscures just how predictable Katrina was.[12] Scientists, journalists, sociologists, and even politicians warned over and over in the decade leading up to Katrina that a hurricane was set to devastate New Orleans and particularly its poorest residents. As hurricanes Georges (1998) and Ivan (2004) threatened, the warnings only got louder and more accurate until finally, with more than sixty hours of advanced notice, Hurricane Katrina made good on the most dire predictions. The one thing New Orleans did have ready, and had waiting in stockpile for years, was 10,000 body bags set aside for just such a catastrophe.

The lack of foresight, however, actually begins much earlier in New Orleans's history. In 1719, the Mississippi River flooded. This was not in itself unusual, except that in response—flush with the confidence in human ability that characterized their Enlightened era—engineers suggested extensive augmentation of the natural levee of the river. The artificial levee project had been completed, at least in its first iteration, by 1727, yet it was never truly finished. New Orleans continued to flood and residents continued to augment the levee system so that, by the time the United States purchased the land New Orleans sat on, the artificial system extended from Baton Rouge to south of New Orleans. (Incidentally, these projects brought suffering and exploitation to poor and minority communities long before and for very different reasons than Katrina, as they were undertaken on

11. George W. Bush, "Hurricane Relief Address to the Nation" September 15, 2005, emphasis added.

12 Information about ignorance in the immediate lead up to Katrina is drawn from Steinberg, *Acts of God*. Steinberg's work includes a series of historical examples of the principle being illustrated here with Katrina. Deeper history is drawn from Kelman, "Boundary Issues," 695–703.

behalf of rich merchants through the use of slave labor. But that is a different story.) In 1849, the artificial levee broke, two hundred blocks of New Orleans flooded, and ten thousand people were displaced, a small foretaste of disasters to come.

Even in 1850, informed citizens knew that the levees brought short-term relief and long-term disaster to New Orleans. Early surveys of the lower Mississippi River drew conclusions about the effects of humans on their environment that prefigured environmentalist thought by centuries. Yet with the federal government taking control of the Mississippi flooding problem and the Army Corps of Engineers tasked with solving it, New Orleans was left to rely on more and larger levees to protect against "natural" disaster. In 1894, torrential rain pounded the city, and, as promised, the new, greater levees held the river at bay. They also served to create an artificial basin with the high levee on one side and the Louisiana backswamp on the other. More flooding ensued.

The problem now was not the river, which had been dealt with adequately through human ingenuity. Instead it was the extensive Louisiana backswamp that posed a continuing flood risk. The solution was to drain the swamps and create a system of gutters and canals to keep the city dry and safe. This new drive to pump existing water out of the New Orleans area had the dual benefit of promising security for New Orleans residents and freeing up new lands for commercial development. When Hurricane Betsy (1965) once again flooded New Orleans—particularly the predominantly African American Ninth Ward that would become all too familiar to those who followed the aftermath of Katrina—the Army responded by more extensive draining of surrounding wetlands and the construction of more and more canals, which now stretch as far as Shreveport north on the Red River.

Yet, as keen observers predicted in the nineteenth century, neither more and more magnificent levees nor more and more sophisticated systems of drainage could save New Orleans. In fact, just the opposite was true. The levees which restricted runoff actually increased the high water marks for the Mississippi throughout the twentieth century, even in years where the river actually carried less water and had lower flood seasons in general. Disaster was being cultivated even as the levees kept it at bay temporarily. Similarly, the swamplands that had been drained to prevent flood had actually been mitigating flood damage naturally for centuries, acting to absorb runoff from the river. The wetlands no longer took in seasonal rain and run off and instead, these natural receptacles for floods filled with people. When floods came, as they did in 1927 when the municipal drainage system failed, they were worse both in their intensity and their impact because of the swamps had been drained. In the words of historian Ari Kelman, "Across the twentieth century, New Orleanians, surrounded by levees, beholden to drainage technologies, lived in a prison of their own making. . . . The levee hid the river. And the urban wetlands were gone. Only during catastrophes were New Orleanians forced to reckon with the peril."[13]

When disaster did come, arguably the worst in the history of New Orleans, not all New Orleanians were forced to reckon with it equally. It seems, at first blush, that the folly of trying to prevent natural disaster by controlling nature would effect all citizens of the city equally. However, just as with pesticide drift, those with means were able to protect themselves—even when it is not necessarily clear that is what they are doing—while the poor were not. The swamplands that had been drained for the benefit of the many came to be inhabited by the few. Sitting lower than the surrounding areas and being firmly situated within the urban limits of New Orleans, these areas became places where low income and minority groups congregated out of necessity, while those who could afford to drove on elevated highways out to well-connected suburbs on better, and better protected, land. When flooding happened, as inevitably it did on a regular basis, poor neighborhoods were the first to succumb.

With all the warning issued in the immediate lead up to Katrina, as well as the long history of recurring disaster in New Orleans, it would have been logical and expected for the city to have an evacuation plan in place. Unfortunately, centuries of projecting an image of New Orleans as a well-constructed city that had saved itself from nature through its technological prowess and foresight would have made such planning seem deeply hypocritical. Thus, with only sixty hours notice, the best the city could hope to do is provide "shelters of last resort" for those who could not escape the city. This, for the most part, was not wealthy residents of far off suburbs or even the well off urban residents. Those least able to escape were the nearly one quarter of New Orleans residents who could not afford and therefore lacked access to private transportation of any kind. With no way to escape and with their homes directly in the most likely path of destruction—not

---

13. Kelman, "Boundary Issues," 702.

by accident but by a foolish human design—the poor and defenseless were herded into impromptu shelters while their world devolved into chaos.

So, in truth, Hurricane Katrina was a perfect storm, though not in a strictly meteorological sense. Instead, it was a perfect storm of human ignorance and hubris in which an abominable lack of foresight turned a powerful but predictable weather event into an unprecedented disaster. Ironically, the damage of the hurricane winds actually failed to live up to the catastrophic predictions of weather forecasters, and most buildings stood up well to the initial storm.[14] The disaster in New Orleans was, as it always had been, flooding. Storm surge proved more than the levee system could handle. Levees breached, canals overflowed, the pumping system failed (though it never would have been able to drain the city anyway), and the mass of the city that had been constructed on former swamps sitting well below sea level rapidly filled with water. A report by the American Society of Civil Engineers (ASCE) describes the compounding human failures:

> Within a few hours of the initial breach observed at the Industrial Canal, rising water in the canal overtopped and eroded levees. Torrents of water rushed into city streets. Multiple levee failures inundated some neighborhoods from several sides with such speed that houses filled to their rooftops in minutes. . . . Another large floodwall breach on the east side of the Industrial Canal quickly flooded the Lower Ninth Ward in what witnesses describe as a "wall of water." . . . By 8:30am the breach at the London Avenue Canal created a rush of water and sand into the already-flooded Gentilly area. . . .
>
> By the time the most significant I-wall failures had occurred, the peak of the surge levels was over. Though surge levels in the Gulf and in Lake Pontchartrain dropped, water continued to pour through the many damaged levees and floodwalls. This flooding continued until water in the city's bowl-shaped landscape equalized with the water level in Lake Pontchartrain. By September 1, over 80 percent of the New Orleans metropolitan area was flooded with approximately two-thirds of the flooding attributed to water flowing through breaches.[15]

The storm may have been the trigger, but humans caused this disaster and the poor and marginalized were its primary victims.

---

14. A good scientific perspective on Hurricane Katrina can be found in McCallum and Heming, "Hurricane Katrina," 2099–115.

15. American Society of Civil Engineers, "New Orleans Hurricane," 28–31.

The extent to which ignorance and lack of foresight compounded the disaster in the hurricane's aftermath only serves to demonstrate this point. The failures of the presidential administration then in office continue to be hotly debated and, as a result, are much too contentious to be of use here. Instead, there are less politically charged incidents from the aftermath of the hurricane that illustrate the degree to which people fail to learn and, in doing so, continue to perpetrate injustice on the poor in society. The flooding that had caused so much of the initial damage had secondary impacts as well. Toxic waste from Superfund sites—locations where hazardous waste had so contaminated nature that the federal government felt compelled to intervene to clean out the pollutants—mingled with the storm surge and washed into the streets and homes of New Orleans. Dangerously high levels of arsenic coated walls and floors of the homes that people were finally, after weeks, beginning to return to in order to assess damage and salvage lost possessions. Unfortunately, no one told these families these dangers at first, and, when they did, failed initially to provide protective gear to poorer families who could neither drive the hundred miles to the nearest store to buy these products nor afford them if they could. All the while, wealthy families hired others to clean the debris from their home, mirroring the government contractors who hired migrant workers to clean public spaces (again, initially without any protective gear).[16] As the historical distance between the present and Katrina increases, more of these stories continue to surface, stories that highlight the ways in which human ignorance and shortsightedness in interacting with the workings of non-human creation perpetuate the kind of injustice that Christians are called to oppose and correct.

The ASCE report on Katrina concludes that "the residents of New Orleans could not have known the actual risks with which they were living,"[17] but a simple glance at the history of the city suggests that someone somewhere should have known and acted on behalf of the city's most vulnerable. In fact, preparedness is a quality of wisdom extolled by the sages. As already noted in the discussion of creation as a teacher of character, the sages point to the ant as one who, without any external prompting, takes special care to be prepared for what it knows lies ahead (Prov 6:6–8; cf. Prov 24:27). The example of the ant reminds people to be diligent in times of plenty with the knowledge that times of want will inevitably arrive, and certainly hurricane

16. This problem is documented in Allen, "Environmental Justice," 103–10.

17. American Society of Civil Engineers, "New Orleans Hurricane," 62.

seasons are in some respect as predictable in their arrival as the season for planting and for harvest. Yet ignorance, in this case willful ignorance, rather than laziness is the folly which plagues New Orleans, and the sages have been no less clear on that.[18] "The clever see danger and hide; but the simple go on, and suffer for it" (Prov 22:3). The same logic had been highlighted for Job by Elihu, who implicitly contrasts the animals who, in the face of a storm, "go into their lairs and remain in their dens" (37:8) with Job who would rather curse the weather. New Orleans had been flooding since the eighteenth century; human ingenuity had been failing since the eighteenth century. Yet in New Orleans, as in countless other examples that might be offered, the philosophy for centuries had simply been to "go on" in the face of crisis after crisis, manifesting on a corporate level the kind of foolishness that the sages describe for individuals.

Unfortunately in modern society, some people seem to be able to afford the luxury of principled ignorance, in no small part because they are not typically the ones who suffer when they decide on behalf of society to plunge headlong into danger. Yet, just as the sages commend a vision of wisdom that includes preparedness, they also offer a vision of justice that requires that those who make decisions must be wise on behalf of the poor who are structurally prevented from deciding for themselves. In this, ignorance is no excuse and, for the sages, is actually a marker of human wickedness. To have wisdom and, as a consequence, to be righteous is to know. "The righteous know the rights of the poor; the wicked have no such understanding" (Prov 29:7). It is insufficient to lament natural disasters like Hurricane Katrina without acknowledging that they are not natural, that they are not "blind and random," that they effect the poor in ways more devastating than they affect everyone else, and that much of this is preventable in a society that embraces rather than flees from knowledge or that flees rather than courts danger.

It is easier, in some ways more comforting, to think that the weather is something governed only by immutable scientific processes or, in cases of exceptional divine operation, by the specific will of God. Yet for centuries people have been able to observe the way that humans have manipulated

18. In truth, the distance between willful ignorance and laziness may not be so great. Davis argues that the sages saw sloth as "work inadequately done" and therefore "destructive of both the individual and the community." Her summary of Karl Barth's position on laziness as "foolishly assertive action" describes the history of New Orleans (and too many other communities) with chilling precision. Davis, *Scripture, Culture, and Agriculture*, 140.

their environment in ways that produce rather than prevent weather disasters. Again, there is no need to decide on hot button issues like anthropogenic global warming to accept this as true. Humans created the disaster in New Orleans through more obvious and direct interactions with the environment: building levees, draining swamps, securing the city through pumps and canals, and, most importantly, opening up particularly dangerous regions to habitation by the poorest in their community. The result has proved both environmentally disastrous and socially appalling, demonstrating still more complex and devastating ways that the marked absence of wisdom destroys human and non-human creation indiscriminately.

Greed and the Destruction of Ducktown

Not all environmental injustice can be rationalized as arising from ostensibly pure motives or resulting from ignorance, willful or otherwise. All too frequently, social and environmental injustice, oppression of the poor and destruction of non-human creation, march brazenly hand-in-hand in full view of an unconcerned public. The apathy of Christians to these outrages has gradually been replaced by a heightened awareness of injustice and a correspondingly outspoken concern, yet nothing to match the divine wrath described in Wisdom Literature when the Creator sees creation under assault and promises retribution both in this life and beyond.

Consider Ducktown, Tennessee, where in 1849 John Caldwell discovered copper. This moment sparked a chain of deliberate and foreseeable events culminating, by 1965, in an ecological disaster zone known as the Ducktown Badlands. The manmade desert in the middle of a rainforest was until recently one of only two manmade objects large enough to be visible from space, at least that is the tale you are likely to be told, with a barely veiled tone of pride, by the attendant at the Ducktown Museum on the site of the now defunct Burra Burra copper mine. The century-long story of the Ducktown Badlands is a case study in the way injustice, fueled by greed, destroys the environment at the expense of the poor and the powerless to the benefit of the wealthy and powerful. Like the Great Wall of China to which it is compared, the Ducktown Badlands were commissioned by great leaders of men and constructed with the sweat and blood of everyday people. The result is a picture of how social and environmental injustice not only coincide but reinforce one another.[19]

19. The following account of the history of the Ducktown Basin is drawn in large part

The story of injustice in the Ducktown Basin actually begins long before Caldwell first appreciated the wealth to be carved out of the earth in the form of copper because, as is the case with so many "discoveries" by settlers in the Americas, European colonists were neither the first people to inhabit the Ducktown Basin nor the first to make use of its copper deposits. In the early part of the nineteenth century the Cherokee nation sprawled across the southern Appalachians and crossed the artificially drawn borders of Tennessee, North Carolina, and Alabama. Nestled in the protected heart of this territory since long before recorded history—with the earliest records dating from 1799—in a basin surrounded by tall mountains sat a small village known to the Cherokee as Kawa'na. "Duck" in English. There a small community, even by Cherokee standards, practiced subsistence agriculture, growing beans and squash, and hunting the slopes of the surrounding mountains which had deliberately been left wooded to preserve fertile hunting grounds. They used the copper in the basin, which was unusually close to the surface, to craft a variety of ceremonial and decorative objects.

The story of how the Ducktown Cherokee community would be driven from their lands is familiar enough, though the US Indian Removal policy is typically cast as a political tale in which the State of Georgia, the Supreme Court of the United States, and President Andrew Jackson struggle for power at the expense of helpless native communities. True as that all may be, it neglects the profound role that non-human creation played in this narrative, a fact which recalls the previous discussion of nature as an agent in the history of God's world. Initially the Cherokee in Ducktown had been spared any incursion by the forbidding presence of the mountains which impeded commerce and by the colder, highland climate which made Ducktown unsuitable for growing plantation cash crops like cotton. Yet as they began to run out of cheap, legally available agricultural land, Georgians began to push east into any Cherokee territory they could. Coupled with the discovery of small gold deposits in northern Georgia, the overwhelming desire to exploit the natural resources of the land took precedence over the well-being of fellow humans. The Ducktown Basin was carved up and sold off for a penny an acre to a flood of farmers who took possession of Cherokee lands, at times even before the army had arrived to forcibly remove the previous residents. A toxic mixture of avarice and racism paved the way for the immoral seizure of countless property, the deaths of tens of thousands, and the wholesale destruction of an entire ecosystem.

from Maysilles, *Ducktown Smoke.*

The farmers who bought land in Ducktown were not the glorious cotton royalty of the antebellum South. The climate was still no better suited to plantations and cash crops than it had been when the Cherokee lived there. These small farmers found themselves as part of a new marginalized poor, scraping together a living in an Appalachian backwater. Prospectors continued to comb the Georgia mountains hoping to duplicate the earlier gold rush with a fresh new find. Some came to Ducktown but, finding only copper and failing to imagine its potential value, left disappointed. John Caldwell's formal "discovery" of copper forever changed the social and environmental dynamics in the Ducktown Basin. Just as the Cherokee had seen farmers exercise their power unjustly for profit, those same farmers would soon find themselves the victims of an injustice they had inadvertently set in motion. Co-victims, that is, with their forested mountain home.

The commercialization of copper in the Ducktown Basin had immediate and widespread ecological impact, even before it would begin to negatively influence the lives of the people there. Before he could mine, smelt, and sell the copper, Caldwell knew he must first be able to transport labor and supplies in and out of the basin, a feat achieved by blasting a twenty-five mile path through the mountains, ironically over the objections of the new white residents and sourcing his labor from the few Cherokee remaining in their ancestral homelands. With the basic problem of transportation solved, copper miners began to extract and then smelt incredible amounts of ore. Miners accomplished this through an open roasting technique in which the ore was cooked over large piles of wood to burn away the sulfur content. The process obviously required a tremendous amount of wood to fuel these constant smelting fires—each smelter requiring roughly seventy-five acres of forest every year—and the readiest source was the mountain slopes of the basin that the Cherokee had kept wooded as hunting grounds and farmers had employed sparingly as wood lots. So miners stripped the mountains of their trees, all the while sending the sulfur content of the copper ore into the atmosphere. Trapped by the surrounding mountains, Ducktown became a microcosm for the effects of acid rain as the sulfur poured continuously back down into the basin. Whatever had not been cut down for the roasting fires withered under the burning rain. Between 1853 when Caldwell finished his road and 1863 when the Civil War brought a halt to the mine, hundreds of acres had been deforested and still more had been laid to waste by the rain. The respite allowed by the Civil War—when humans became much more deliberate about destroying one another and much less deliberate about destroying creation—was relatively brief. In the decade after the Civil War, the copper companies would cut down another thirty thousand acres and begin to smelt even more sulfurous copper drawn from deeper in the ground. The smoke would continue to issue from the smelters until 1907.

More than half a century of reckless pursuit of profits came at the expense not only of the environment but also the poorest members of society: the Cherokee already mentioned, the resident farmers, and the laborers brought in by the company to work in the mines. Not unlike the farmers responsible for pesticide drift, copper mining in Ducktown employed the most vulnerable members of society for labor, those who lacked the kinds of social and legal protection that would afford them even the most basic level of justice. In the case of the Reconstruction South, however, this labor force included a heavy contingent of convict labor. Of these, a disturbing number were always recently freed slaves who had been falsely imprisoned so that their unpaid labor could continue to be exploited. These laborers were leased by the state of Georgia for roughly one tenth the fee normally paid to free labor. Georgia thus freed itself of an "undesirable" segment of the population, took no financial responsibility for housing them, and profited from the leased labor. When the new source of labor completed the first railroad into Ducktown, an influx of new technologies and the new economical transport dramatically accelerated the mining operation. The exploitation of disenfranchised people fueled the exploitation of the land, and vice versa.

But the local farmers suffered most immediately and continued to suffer long after convict labor fell out of favor. Generations after Georgia's subsistence farming communities had forced out Cherokee ones, farmers found that they could no longer eek their meager survival out of the land any longer. The sulfurous smoke hung so thick in the air when the smelters ran at peak that it blocked out the sun. Even when the smoke itself had cleared, it left behind a residue of sulfur that withered plants and rusted tools. Then there were the rains, which, in the temperate rainforest of the southern Appalachians, came often. Ducktown had become the wettest "desert" in the world in which nothing grew because the very water that God ordained to nourish the earth had been turned into poison. Farmers tried to file lawsuits against the copper companies, but they did so at their own expense and on their own time. Corporations, then as now, had the resources and technical knowledge to defer litigation interminably. Meanwhile, farmers who would not have had the resources in normal circumstances to hold their own in court had the extra burden of trying to survive on dead land. In an impossible situation, many ended up making their living entirely in the mines of the companies that they were futilely trying to hold accountable in court. It would take protest from the heads powerful logging corporations whose forests were being damaged by spill over from the basin and, in the ultimate irony, the state of Georgia which—after seizing the land from the Cherokees and supplying the labor to open up the basin for greater mining—had become concerned about smoke pouring out of Tennessee and destroying Georgia's natural resources that some measure of relief would be found. Even so, well into the twentieth century, miners would find that every time it rained, their cars quickly began to rust and rot.

The story is familiar, in many of its themes if not in all the particulars of an admittedly extreme case. The rich get richer; the poor get poorer. Fortunes were made for a select few in the Ducktown Basin, though very little of that money remained in the community. For most people, however, the legacy of the copper mining in Ducktown is, at best, the meager benefits of labor as a miner. At worst, Ducktown's halcyon days of economic profitability are remembered as a time of dispossession and deprivation, for Cherokee inhabitants and for the settlers who forcibly replaced them. Yet what is critical in this story is that the rich were enriched and the poor impoverished precisely in proportion to the degree to which human action destroyed God's creation. The injustice in Ducktown was neither entirely that the rich cared nothing for the plight of the poor nor that people cared nothing for the integrity of nature because the two cannot be separated. Both the poor and nature represent in Ducktown an aggrieved party without an advocate, and those in power destroyed both, not in ignorance or with misinformed good intentions but out of unadulterated greed. Those in control pursued their folly with their eyes wide open, and the Teacher might have just as easily looked at the basin or its inhabitants and lamented, "Again I saw all the oppressions that are practiced under the sun. Look, the tears of the oppressed—with no one to comfort them! On the side of their oppressors there was power" (Eccl 4:1).

The sages understood that the fact of divine origin, the fact that God is the creator of all, erases all other boundaries. This is nowhere more evident than between the rich and the poor who share their creator's divine image. "The rich and the poor have this in common: the LORD is the maker of them all" (Prov 22:2). All the wisdom of the sages, already discussed, regarding the duties of the rich and the plight of the poor proceeds from this premise. The distinctions that arise from wealth cannot stand against the unity that arises from a common creator. For this reason, "those who oppress the poor insult their Maker, but those who are kind to the needy honor him" (Prov 14:31). God has made the poor no less than the rich, and so to act with utter disregard for their needs is to insult God as their creator.

The sages do not extend this argument to include non-human creation, nor should we expect them to. After all, the technologies necessary to systematically oppress the poor are old and comparatively simple. The ability, not to mention the will, to simultaneously deprive both the poor and the earth are comparatively recent and still much too complex for most of us to confidently grasp. Yet it is worth wondering if, over the course of fifty years, the ancient Israelites had created an artificial wasteland visible from space, the sages might have drawn their arguments to their logical conclusion. Speculative though that may be, it must be noted that the motive for moral behavior, the charge for the wealthy to show prudence and concern is not based on a common humanity but on a common source in the divine creation. The fact that God is the originator of all is sufficient for the sages to demand justice on behalf of creation. It should be evident to Christians now that not only the rich and poor but humans and non-humans have this in common, that God is the maker of them all. Consequently, it stands to reason that those who oppress any of God's creations insult their maker.

The poor and the earth share another characteristic that the sages recognize makes them prone to the injustices of those who hold society's wealth and power. As already mentioned, the Ducktown disaster persisted as long as it did because those most directly and profoundly affected lacked the power to have their complaints heard. Strictly speaking, of course, neither the poor nor the earth is voiceless. The farmers in Ducktown took their cases before the courts. The earth spoke in an arguably louder voice as vegetation died, rain corroded, and the ground dried up. Yet in both cases, no one listened. Tragically, when people finally began to speak against the continued destruction of the Ducktown Basin it was not out of a sense of moral outrage, not a crusade for justice. When loggers and the state of Georgia took the copper companies to court it was a collision of competing greeds. No one heeded the advice of the sages: "Speak out for those who cannot speak, for the rights of all the destitute. Speak out, judge righteously, defend the rights of the poor and needy" (31:8–9; cf. Eccl 5:8–9). The wise recognize that God demands justice for the entire created world and that it is their duty to advocate for that justice. Only fools believe that simply because no one hears about the plight of the needy that they are not in need.

Even if it is difficult—though, we would argue, very reasonable—to extend the thinking of the sages to include non-human creation in their concern for the poor, it is not possible to ignore that what at first seems like "victimless" crimes only against trees and grass and the air quickly become crimes against the very poor and needy that the sages reference. The human victims of the environmentally unsound practices in Ducktown were Cherokee villagers, convict labor, and subsistence farmers. The owners of the Tennessee Copper Company did not have to breath the toxic air, live under a shroud of sulfuric smoke, and try to grow the food necessary to survive in earth watered by acid rain. The reason was simple: the Tennessee Copper Company was headquartered in New Jersey, a fact that insulated owners not only from the consequences of their pollution but also from litigation in Tennessee courts which, after all, had no jurisdiction over the New Jersey company. The rich did not need to oppress the poor directly to pursue their greed; they destroyed the poor by destroying the environment which had sustained them. Yet it turns out that "oppressing the poor in order to enrich oneself and giving to the rich, will lead only to loss" (Prov 22:16). The sages' wisdom proved prescient, even if most of the victims of exploitation never lived to see the successor to the Tennessee Copper Company file for bankruptcy in 1989. As a long-term strategy, there was no wisdom in the destruction for which the company was eventually held to account.

The destruction of the Ducktown Basin is neither exceptional nor exceptionally bad. Incidents have been well documented throughout history persisting into the present where the wealthy and powerful prosecute their folly at the expense of both the poor and non-human creation, not to mention at the expense of the poor through their exploitation of non-human creation. (One saving grace in Ducktown was that, unlike in many copper mines in the western United States that practiced open roasting smelting, the copper in the Ducktown Basin did not contain arsenic.) In these situations, the sages offer readers very simple advice: the Creator takes assaults on creation personally.

Conclusion

It is no longer ethically justifiable, if it ever was to begin with, to ignore the basic premises of the environmental justice movement. Decades of focus by activists, journalists, and politicians have brought to light the very real inequalities and injustices visited on the poor and minorities through foolish human interaction with the environment. Whether it is the unintended consequences of new technologies, the failures precipitated by human ignorance and shortsightedness, or the very deliberate and craven actions of a wealthy few to profit at the expense of the many, society has clearly shifted the burden of costly environmental behaviors onto those least able to bear the weight. Justice must prevail, a justice which is simultaneously ecological and social, but precisely what justice means in these situations remains a contested issue.

Justice is a ubiquitous concern in Scripture, in no small part because it reflects a vision of a just God who created a world which thrives on justice and withers in its absence. After love, it is arguably the central ethical imperative for Christians, illustrated in the oft quoted command in Micah to "do justice, and to love kindness, and to walk humbly with your God" (6:8) and paralleled by the sages in the Proverbs who state in the prologue that their teachings are "for gaining instruction in wise dealing, righteousness, justice, and equity" (1:3). But it is much easier to identify justice as a necessary feature, even the core feature, of Christian ethics, than it is to sort out what exactly it is to "do justice." Answers to this question have rightly focused on the more benign features of the Law or the pronouncements of the prophets, for whom the lack of justice is a key reason that God visits wrath on Israel. Yet, the sages have a vision of justice as well, one that fits into the greater biblical vision of justice and most decidedly does not resonate with older Christian advocates of eco-justice for whom wealth is unequivocally evil and a just society is an economically uniform society.

It is important, however, not to demonize these Christian pioneers of eco-justice. After all, the inclination is certainly understandable. Given the stories retold in this chapter about how the ignorance, paternalism, and outright greed of the wealthy have subjected the entirety of creation to a broad spectrum of increasingly appalling deprivations, the simplest path would be to condemn wealth as patently immoral—as the root of all rather than merely many kinds of evil—and in extreme political cases advocate for its forcible redistribution. Thankfully, the jump to judgment of a small sector of theologians can be corrected by returning to consider what the sages say and do not say about justice in God's world.

For their part, the sages are ambivalent about wealth, as is the case throughout Scripture. In Proverbs alone, riches are both the enduring product of diligence and true wisdom (8:18; 10:4; 22:4) and a dangerously poor substitute for righteousness (11:4; 18:11; cf. 18:23). Solomon, the archetypal sage, gains global renown for his treasury as much as his wisdom; on the other hand Balshazzar had Solomon's wealth (quite literally, see Dan 5:1–4) yet none of his wisdom. Satan makes the curious argument in Job that it is easy for Job to be righteous because he is so wealthy; Jesus famously makes precisely the opposite argument using some of the Bible's most vivid imagery (Matt 19:24). Whatever else may be said, biblical wisdom does not allow Christians to condemn wealth, as such, outright.

Yet, if the sages refuse to make wealth an absolute moral issue, the same is not the case when it comes to the duties of society to the poor. As already noted, the socially marginalized are entitled to special privileges in society and those with wealth and power have special responsibilities to speak out for their rights and to defend their interests (31:8–9). To do otherwise is to commit a grave sin against not only one's neighbor (14:21) but also against God (14:31; 17:5) because God is the creator of all. When wealth does result from wisdom, it is not an end in itself. The riches of the wealthy exist for the benefit of society and to fail to use them to this end is to forsake the very wisdom that enriches. This is not redistribution, where ethics are reduced to balancing an economic ledger, or even really the New Testament notion of charity, which is as much about perfecting the individual giving as it is about wealth changing hands (see Matt 6:1–4). Instead, this is wise justice in which the wealthy (29:7) and the politically powerful (31:5) know the rights of the poor and employ their wealth and power to secure them.

Critically, this vision of justice is not secondary to wisdom but an essential component of it. When the purpose of the Proverbs is introduced, justice makes its first appearance alongside righteousness and equity in the key features of wisdom (1:1–6). Later, when the sages give wisdom its own voice to speak, justice emerges once again: "Riches and honor are with me, enduring wealth and prosperity. My fruit is better than gold, even fine gold, and my yield than choice silver. I walk in the way of righteousness, along the paths of justice, endowing with wealth those who love me, and filling their treasuries" (8:18–20). The presence of wealth in this passage is critical

for understanding the way the sages view the core tenet of justice in rela-
tion to material goods. First, wisdom is greater than wealth, as many of
the better-than proverbs proclaim (15:17; 16:16; 17:1), even though wealth
is promised to the wise. This creates a clear set of priorities in which the
imperative to act wisely outweighs the imperative to act in ways that are
economically beneficial. Sadly, in each of the above examples of injustice, someone employed precisely the opposite calculus. That something
is economically unsavory must never be an excuse for failing to do justice. Second, and related, justice is the path of wisdom and there can be
no wisdom which strays from justice. If wisdom is the highest goal and
wisdom can never be removed from justice, then the wise are bound to
pursue justice with all the vigor that they pursue any of the other features
of wisdom. Wealth which comes from wisdom is wealth which is employed
toward doing justice. If wealth is ever to be condemned, it is when it exists
in the absence of righteousness (14:1) and when it is employed in ways that
subvert rather than preserve justice. The tendency throughout history and
across cultures has been for the wealthy to profit from the deprivation of
the poor. This was the situation even in ancient Israel: "The field of the poor
may yield much food, but it is swept away through injustice" (13:23). Yet
the sages suggest the opposite should be the case. Wealth can and should
exist precisely so the poor can profit from the wealthy.

This includes those in power pursuing environmental justice on
behalf of the poor even when it seems costly to do so. In the 1960s, the
Ducktown Badlands could be seen from space. Today, you could drive in to
Ducktown, Tennessee, and never know that an environmental catastrophe
had ever taken place. A combination of federal and corporate effort (not all
of it voluntary) slowly began to restore Ducktown to roughly the state it had
been in when God created it—or at least when the Cherokee had inhabited
it. Over time, regulated emissions and concentrated reforestation began to
re-cover the denuded landscape with green slopes of grass and trees. The
economy of the basin no longer relies on logging or copper mining and
smelting. Instead, most people make their living off of tourism, fueled by
the natural beauty of the scenery and the world class white water rapids
on the Ocoee River—no longer diverted for industrial use—which played
host to the canoe slalom at the 1996 Summer Olympics. Only the museum
on the site of the old mine stands as a testimony to what transpired for
centuries in Ducktown. The citizens had voted to preserve a small piece of
the badlands for the sake of history, but without the toxic rain and chemical

smoke to keep it at bay, vegetation has begun to overwhelm even this memorial. Justice has prevailed in Ducktown for God's creation, human and non-human, just as the sages promised it would.

Conclusion

The sayings of the wise are like goads.

—ECCLESIASTES 12:11

So what now? In view of everything above, what are Christians to do with regard to contemporary environmentalism? Readers expecting to find simple answers in the foregoing pages may arrive here disappointed. Are we ethically obligated to drive smaller, more fuel-efficient cars? Do we need to vote creation theology as a political imperative? Do we support carbon credits or solar energy, hydrogen fuel or non-GMO foods? Is it enough to switch to reusable shopping bags and recycled paper? Is the greatest environmental threat of our time pesticide drift or Japanese whale hunts, deforestation in the Amazon or low fertility rates among pandas? Who or what is causing global warming, and do the sages prefer the Kyoto Protocol or the 2015 Paris resolution of the UN Climate Change Conference?

Those questions have all been left unanswered, and for the most part unasked, very much on purpose. This is not because those policy discussions are not important but because what to do about the contentious environmental questions of our time arises first and foremost out of why, as Christians, we care and act at all. We suggested from the outset that the method of engaging both Scripture and contemporary environmentalism are of just as much importance as the conclusions drawn from those engagements. Thus, rather than proposing a litany of debatable behavioral environmental imperatives, we have strived to cling closely to the dual purpose outlined in the introduction: to highlight the under-utilized creation theology of Wisdom Literature and to invite ways for that theology to engage, critique, or appropriate a variety of outside traditions. The sages give Christians a great deal to say within our own faith community and to our global community at large.

But it would be presumptuous to pretend that it is sufficient to simply point to the sages and hope we all draw the same conclusions. The answer to most of the above questions is that we simply do not know. The sages offer no more definite answers than can be found looking anywhere else in the Bible. Using the wisdom found in Job, Psalms, Proverbs, Ecclesiastes, and Song of Solomon, we have been able to critique with equal certainty industrialism and agrarianism, Enlightenment rationalism and free-wheeling mysticism, the agro-industrial complex and organic farming. Farmers, miners, industrialists, city planners, engineers, scientists, clerics, and kings have appeared no less often as examples of fools than as students of wisdom.

Frankly, a thorough engagement with the wisdom of the sages only seems to complicate the issue. Creation has lessons to teach us, but they are neither as accessible as science would have us believe nor as uniform as many older, superficial readings of the sages suggest; the world is not an open book and it certainly does not reflect a system in which righteousness is rewarded by immutable natural law. No wonder that the most vivid characters in Wisdom Literature are depicted as wandering more or less hopelessly through a fog of conflicting answers waiting on God to point the way. The collective intellectual powers of Job and his friends cannot seem to divine the answers that God—we might imagine with some exasperation—must show Job in the very creation that has been in front of him all along. The Teacher, with more wisdom than Job and infinitely more resources, struggles with equal futility to find satisfying answers to life's most probing quandaries. If the sages wrote their own shortcomings into the biblical books, we can at least sympathize with their confusion.

If, however, the matter has been complicated, it does not reflect any defect in the wisdom of the sages, always incomplete and in progress though they admit it is. The problem lies instead with our own environmental thinking which has been too narrow, too one-dimensional for too long. Christian environmentalism began in earnest on the defensive, trying to explain why the primordial command to "subdue" creation was not to blame for the wholesale destruction of the planet. In the mystery of global environmental degradation, Genesis 1:28 was the smoking gun, and Christians felt guilty until proven innocent. Christian environmental thinking has moved away from Adam and Eve only in fits and spurts and often only when some new challenge made such moves necessary.

Christians require a more deliberate and comprehensive expansion of our response to the ecological concerns of our time. Environmental thinking must become infinitely more complex to match both a rich and varied Scripture and an infinitely complex creation that we cannot and never will fully understand. So if the sages lack clear answers to all our questions, it is because they speak neither alone nor from a place of omniscience. The sages are as much the students of the Creator, not to mention creation, and they are our teachers, and we must hear their voices as part of a chorus of biblical wisdom all of which has God as creator and the world that God created intimately and inextricably tangled into its message. Thus, we read the creation theology of Wisdom Literature in light of Genesis 1, just as we read the command to humble ourselves and serve in John 13 through the creation-tinged justice of Wisdom Literature. They are all "eco-texts" and make sense only in light of each other because ours is an eco-God, which is to say a God that thought this world—from mountains to mayflies—important enough to divine purposes to make, through wisdom, precisely how it is. Keeping this always in mind, Christians are then tasked with sorting through the maddening complexity of these biblical voices to find the wisdom that has ordered it all and us with it.

As we try to find the harmony in the apparent cacophony of biblical environmental thought, it is nevertheless important to realize that the sages sing certain distinctive notes that we have tried to highlight in the above text. First and foremost, the sages stress that a proper relationship with creation must be above all a matter of character rather than a plan of action. None is more important than the divine character by which creation was made and which must be the human model for interacting with the world. Following Job on a grand tour of God's creatures—from the mundane to the magnificent—we learn, among other things, that God neither micromanages nor dominates creation. The Creator made the world a wilderness rather than a zoo, presumably on purpose. Without glorifying the absence of cultivation or the hardship of nature at its most wild, the Israelites understood the role this feature of creation played in God's work. As Holmes Rolston notes,

> Wilderness is often a locale for intense experiences: stark need for food and water (manna and quails in Exod 16), isolation (Elijah and the still small voice in 1 Kgs 19), danger and divine deliverance (Hagar and Ishmael in Gen 21:8–19), encounter with God (Moses, the burning bush and the revelation of the divine name

[Exod 3], and the giving of the law at Mount Sinai [Exod 19–20]). There is a psychology as well as a geography of wilderness. There is theology gained in the wilderness.[1]

While the preeminent human concern has been for millennia to control and conform creation to human needs and to mitigate the inherent risk of a wild nature, God remains content to leave creation a beautiful, awesome chaos. While biblical scholars can debate the meaning of the Hebrew in Genesis 1 or the textual relationship between the apparently conflicting commands to "subdue" earth and to "keep" the garden in the two creation accounts, the sages point toward more self-evident solutions: God does not dominate the world, so humans should not presume.

If the character of God is the ultimate litmus in testing our environmental behaviors, our own character has an important role to play as well. The sages concern themselves constantly with the cultivation of character, a fact announced at the outset of Proverbs and pursued relentlessly wherever wisdom took the sages. Though all the many virtues promoted by the sages—prudence, diligence, patience, self-control, service—all have appropriate environmental applications, the most evident eco-virtue is attentiveness. If we are to mirror the divine willingness to step back and allow creation to manage itself, if we are to know when it is appropriate to step in on our own behalf or on behalf of the world, Christians must cultivate a kind of watchfulness toward creation. Job's grand tour highlights this well, as God demonstrates in dramatic fashion that a greater awareness of the world provides Job with more wisdom than all the elaborate disputations with his friends. Though it lacks the divine flair, we can continue to ward off the environmental forgetfulness of Job by attending regularly and deliberately to creation. Whether on farms or in science classrooms, in neighborhood parks and bike paths or on grand excursions into national forests, keeping in regular, intimate contact with what God has made becomes a spiritual discipline, a way to cultivate in ourselves the right attitudes towards the magnificent, unmanageable, incomprehensible work of the divine Maker.

Unsurprisingly, this intimacy with creation produces some attitudes more readily than others, and none is more basic to the human relationship to creation than wonder. Though we have become quite comfortable with a worldview that has, for at least the last two centuries, understood the world to be fundamentally knowable and malleable—parsed into elaborate taxonomies, manipulated in ever more sophisticated laboratories, and

1. Rolston, "Loving Nature," 40.

confidently subjugated to human ingenuity—the sages model a very different outlook. It is wonder which provokes Job, after seeing the Behemoth and Leviathan, to repent of his hubris and humble himself before the Creator of all. It is wonder which fuels the passionate rhapsody of the lover and the beloved who can find no greater parallel for their ecstasy and aesthetic rapture than in the everyday features of God's natural world. It is wonder that has prompted Christian mystics for centuries, all the way down to the present, to contemplate the unknowable and incomparable Creator through unknowable and incomparable creation. These mystics offer a conduit through which to recapture and reinvigorate what has been lost from the sages' wisdom, though the mystical perspective must always be tempered by biblical orthodoxy. Christians must understand that wonder, like watchfulness and principled inaction, is an unrecognized prerequisite for action. In other words, before we can decide on proper forest management techniques, we must learn proper forest appreciation techniques. Otherwise, we only treat the symptoms of our environmental crisis rather than the spiritual disease which has provoked them.

And the environmental crisis must be seen, above all, as a spiritual crisis for Christians, because creation is one of the principal teachers of virtue. If, as above, the sages note how who we are governs how we relate to creation, they also insist that our relationship with creation molds who we are. The tried-and-true standby objection of many Christians to modern environmentalism is that Christianity is about saving souls, not saving planets, a religion of transcendentally spiritual concerns rather than immediate material ones. Nevertheless, because God has made the natural world a teacher of wisdom, environmental recklessness or apathy not only imperils the natural world but manifests and exacerbates a kind of spiritual anemia. The sages make very clear that part of spiritual growth and maturity is a willingness to come humbly before God's creation and learn something about ourselves, our world, and our Creator.

The role of the natural world as a teacher is inescapable for the sages because, in creating the world, God breathed into it wisdom. Not surprising then, the sages return constantly to that creation in order to seek out the nature and the roots of that wisdom. One of the most basic character qualities we learn from creation is the virtue of discipline or self-control, learning to pursue our own constructive tasks with the kind of foresight and deliberation that God evinced in creation. We learn duty from ants, to resist temptation from the gazelle, and surrender from the birds. Prudence, temperance, and simplicity form a triumvirate of ecological virtues that strikes us with their greatest force and immediacy when we turn to creation. We deprive ourselves of a great moral resource when we treat creation as a consumable commodity. Thus, we preserve streams, forests, oceans, skies, and animals, out of more than self-preservation or material self-interest; we do so out of spiritual self-interest, personal and collective.

Admittedly, the sages see creation neither as a sole nor a total teacher of wisdom. What can and cannot be learned has firm limits, just as how we learn from creation has specific boundaries. The tendency has been to look for moral nuggets in creation the way we might look up words in a dictionary or as though wisdom in creation ran like a computer operating system: plug in a command or query, generate an answer. The sages depict wisdom as much more like DNA, an infinitely complex basic material that can produce innumerable results in differing situations. This is why no metaphor for wisdom is more prevalent than personification: wisdom is a woman who has, with God, made the world and who, if we will listen, is prepared to teach us virtue. The sages approach creation, which manifests wisdom, the same way: in personal rather than mechanical terms, as a teacher rather than a reference work. Learning from creation involves attentive dialogue and patient growth; we are pupils learning from a mentor not scientists learning from a specimen. A willingness to learn in this way, to wait patiently on the lessons God's world has to teach us, has long been enshrined in the folk wisdom of the world's cultures. Yet today, rather than allowing folk stories to color our interactions with the environment, we have allowed our scientific approach to nature to sap our folk stories of their moral force. Remembering how and why our ancestors read fairy tales may yet serve to help us recapture a willingness to learn wisdom from God's wise creation.

As important as creation is in our holistic moral well-being, our environmental behaviors are also tied to specific sins that imperil our spiritual life. This is nowhere more evident than in questions of justice, which is a preeminent concern of all biblical writers, including the sages. Yet, while the Law and the Prophets root the human practice of justice in the divine justice manifest in the mighty acts of God, the sages find the roots of justice in the primordial act of creation. The creative act supersedes and thus makes irrelevant all human distinctions: rich and poor, man and woman, Jew and Gentile, black and white. God is the creator of all. Nothing must govern human behavior and particularly the pursuit of justice more than the realization that we all have a common source in God.

This creation-based theology of justice has at least two critical implications. The first is that, as a common feature of creation, the non-human world is also entitled to a measure of justice. The above list might just as easily have included plant and animal, field and stream, fish and fowl as those distinctions which do not nullify the most basic command to do justice. Just as importantly, however, the creation based theology of justice forces Christians to be aware of how their relationship with the non-human world has implications for more typical social justice concerns. This includes even our most mundane interactions with the created world: food. Though justice is rarely a concern at every evening meal, the sages suggest that it ought to be. The dinner table has become a site for the quiet reinforcement of greed, gluttony, sloth, and folly, all born not primarily from malice but from a lack of self-awareness and careful reflection, two virtues that a right relationship with creation is supposed to teach us.

The entanglement of environmental and social injustices goes even further, however, reaching societal and even global proportions. While our secular counterparts have for decades realized that environmental disasters and degradation disproportionately affect the poor and the socially marginalized, Christians have largely turned a blind eye out of fear that to embrace the observations of the environmental justice movement required us to accept the radical political and theological arguments of eco-justice theology. The sages' vision of justice offers a powerful alternative. Stressing neither the end of wealth nor the demotion of humans from their unique place in the created order, the sages nevertheless insist that the wealthy and the powerful must relate to the land in such a way that justice prevails for the poor. With many of their greatest heroes among the rich and powerful, the sages have no interest in suggesting that prosperity must somehow imply sin. Instead, wealth implies special responsibility—as does humanity.

These matters demand our attention, as uncomfortable as they may make us feel. In describing the lessons of the Teacher, the author of Ecclesiastes rightly observes that "the sayings of the wise are like goads" (Eccl 12:11). Does how I eat reflect an inordinate concern with the needs or desires of my body? Am I disconnected from the environment? Does my environmental apathy imperil the lives or livelihoods of the poor? Do I act as though God's creation is a machine rather than a living, breathing reality? When, if ever, was the last time I looked at a fly and thought "what can I learn" rather than "where is the swatter"? If the sages give us more questions than answers, we can take some comfort in the fact that learning to ask the right questions is a victory in itself.

As we seek the answers, hopefully we understand better now the importance of pursuing them in as comprehensive a way as possible. Creation is not merely the backdrop for our human story, including the story of salvation; it is an active and inescapable player on the cosmic stage. To learn how to engage it properly, the sages invite us to find our answers in community, by looking to the full ancient community of biblical authors—a kind of, to borrow from G. K. Chesterton, democracy of the dead—rather than a select few eco-verses; by inviting rather than avoiding the sometimes contentious discussions in our church communities; by engaging, appropriating, or critiquing as necessary the secular environmental movement; and, most importantly of all, by remaining attentive to the voices and the lessons of the non-human world together with which we make up a single community of creation.

Bibliography

Allen, Barbara L. "Environmental Justice and Expert Knowledge in the Wake of the Disaster." *Social Studies of Science* 37 (2007) 103–10.

Ambrose, Stephen. *Undaunted Courage: Meriwether Lewis, Thomas Jefferson, and the Opening of the American West*. New York: Simon & Schuster, 1996.

American Society of Civil Engineers. "The New Orleans Hurricane Protection System: What Went Wrong and Why." Reston, VA: American Society of Civil Engineers, 2007.

Anderson, Virginia DeJohn. *Creatures of Empire: How Domesticated Animals Transformed Early America*. New York: Oxford University Press, 2006.

Ausubel, Nathan. *A Treasury of Jewish Folklore: Stories Traditions, Legends, Humor, Wisdom and Folk Songs of the Jewish People*. New York: American Book-Stratford, 1967.

Baron, Robert. "All Power to the Periphery: The Public Folklore Thought of Alan Lomax." *Journal of Folklore Research* 49 (2012) 275–317.

Beisner, E. Calvin. *Where Garden Meets Wilderness: Evangelical Entry into the Environmental Debate*. Grand Rapids: Eerdmans, 1997.

Bergeson, Albert. "Eco-Alienation." *Humboldt Journal of Social Relations* 21 (1995) 110–26.

Berry, Wendell. *The Gift of the Good Land*. Berkley: Counterpoint, 1981.

———. *Home Economics*. Berkeley: Counterpoint, 1987.

———. *The Way of Ignorance*. Berkley: Counterpoint, 2005.

Bland, Dave. *Proverbs and the Formation of Character*. Eugene, OR: Cascade, 2015.

———. *Proverbs, Ecclesiastes, Song of Songs*. College Press NIV Commentary. Joplin, MO: College Press, 2002.

Bouma-Prediger, Steven. *For the Beauty of the Earth: A Christian Vision for Creation Care*. 2nd ed. Grand Rapids: Baker Academic. 2010.

Bratton, Susan Power. "Christian Ecotheology and the Old Testament." In *Religion and Environmental Crisis*, edited by Eugene C. Hargrove, 53–75. Athens: University of Georgia Press, 1986.

Bretzke, James T. "Natural Law." In *Dictionary of Scripture and Ethics*, edited by Joel B. Green, 542–44. Grand Rapids: Baker Academic, 2011.

Broder, John M. "Amid Criticism of Federal Efforts, Charges of Racism Are Lodged." *New York Times*, September 5, 2005.

Brown, William P. "The Moral Cosmologies of Creation." In *Character Ethics and the Old Testament: Moral Dimensions of Scripture*, edited by M. Daniel Caroll R. and Jacqueline E. Lapsley, 11–26. Louisville: Westminster John Knox, 2007.

———. *The Seven Pillars of Creation: The Bible, Science, and the Ecology of Wonder*. New York: Oxford University Press, 2010.

———. *Wisdom's Wonder: Character, Creation, and Crisis in the Bible's Wisdom Literature*. Grand Rapids: Eerdmans, 2014.

———. "The Wonder of It All: Faith, Creation, and Wisdom." *Journal for Preachers* 34 (2011) 33–38.

Brueggemann, Walter. "The Creatures Know!" In *Wisdom of Creation*, edited by Foley Edward and Robert Schreiter, 1–12. Collegeville: Liturgical, 2004.

———. *Texts Under Negotiation: The Bible and Postmodern Imagination*. Minneapolis: Fortress, 1993.

———. "What You Eat Is What You Get: Proverbs 15:17." In *The Threat of Life*, edited by Charles L. Campbell, 116–21. Minneapolis: Fortress, 1996.

Buck. Directed by Cindy Meehl. Documentary, 1h 28min. Back Allie Productions, Cedar Creek Productions, Motto Pictures, 2011.

Burns, Ken, dir. "The Last Refuge: 1890–1915." Documentary, 2h 11min. National Parks: America's Best Idea. PBS, 2009.

Classen, Albrecht. "Meister Eckhart's Philosophy in the Twenty-First Century." *Mystics Quarterly* 29 (2003) 6–23.

Clines, David J. A. *Job 21–37*. Word Biblical Commentary. Nashville: Nelson, 2006.

Cooke, Alistair. "Letter from America." Audio recording. December 26, 1980. http://downloads.bbc.co.uk/podcasts/radio4/lfanixoncarter/lfanixoncarter_19801226-1732a.mp3.

Crenshaw, James L. "The Acquisition of Knowledge in Israelite Wisdom Literature." *Word & World* 7 (1987) 245–52.

———. *Education in Ancient Israel: Across the Deadening Silence*. New York: Doubleday, 1998.

Cruikshank, Julie. *Do Glaciers Listen? Local Knowledge, Colonial Encounters, and Social Imagination*. Vancouver: University of British Columbia Press, 2005.

Davis, Ellen F. "Preserving Virtues: Renewing the Tradition of the Sages." In *Character & Scripture: Moral Formation, Community, and Biblical Interpretation*, edited by William P. Brown, 183–201. Grand Rapids: Eerdmans, 2002.

———. *Scripture, Culture, and Agriculture: An Agrarian Reading of the Bible*. Cambridge: Cambridge University Press, 2009.

Dawkins, Richard. *The God Delusion*. Kindle ed. New York: Houghton Mifflin, 2008.

———. *The Selfish Gene*. New York: Oxford University Press, 1989.

Duclow, Donald F. *Masters of Learned Ignorance: Eriugena, Eckhart, Cusanus*. Burlington, VT: Ashgate, 2006.

Dumitriu, Petru. *To the Unknown God*. Translated by James Kirkup. London: Collins, 1982.

Duncan, David James. *God Laughs & Plays: Churchless Sermons in Response to the Preachments of the Fundamentalist Right*. Great Barrington, MA: Triad, 2006.

Egan, Timothy. *The Worst Hard Time: The Untold Story of Those Who Survived the Great American Dust Bowl*. New York: Houghton Mifflin, 2006.

Engel, J. Ronald. "The Post-World War II Eco-Justice Movement in Christian Theology: Patterns and Issues." *American Journal of Theology and Philosophy* 18 (1997) 9–19.

Fairlie, Henry. *The Seven Deadly Sins Today*. Notre Dame: University of Notre Dame Press, 1979.

Fowler, Robert Booth. *The Greening of Protestant Thought*. Chapel Hill: University of North Carolina Press, 1995.

Fox, Matthew. *Passion for Creation: The Earth-Honoring Spirituality of Meister Eckhart*. Rochester, VT: Inner Traditions, 2000.

Fox, Michael V. *Proverbs 10–31*. Anchor Yale Bible. New Haven: Yale University Press, 2009.

Fretheim, Terence E. *God and the World in the Old Testament*. Nashville: Abingdon, 2005.

Graffy, Elisabeth. "Agrarian Ideals, Sustainability Ethics, and US Policy: A Critique for Practitioners." *Journal of Agricultural and Environmental Ethics* 25 (2012) 503–28.

Gregory Palamas. *Capita 150*. In *Saint Gregory Palamas: The One Hundred and Fifty Chapters*, 82–257. Toronto: Pontifical Institute of Mediaeval Studies, 1988.

———. *The Triads*. Edited by John Meyendorff. Translated by Nicholas Gendle. Mahwah, NJ: Paulist, 1983.

Gregory of Sinai. *On Commandments and Doctrines, Warnings, and Promises; on Thoughts, Passions and Virtues, and also on Stillness and Prayer. . . .* In *The Philokalia*, edited and translated by G. E. H. Palmer et al., 4:212–52. London: Faber & Faber, 1995.

———. *On Prayer: Seven Texts*. In *The Philokalia*, edited and translated by G. E. H. Palmer et al., 4:275–86. London: Faber & Faber, 1995.

———. *On Stillness: Fifteen Texts*. In *The Philokalia*, edited and translated by G. E. H. Palmer et al., 4:263–74. London: Faber & Faber, 1995.

Gushee, David. "Environmental Ethics: Bringing Creation Care Down to Earth." In *Keeping God's Earth: The Global Environment in Biblical Perspective*, edited by Noah J. Toly and Daniel I. Block, 245–65. Downers Grove: IVP Academic, 2010.

Habel, Norman C. "Geophany: The Earth Story in Genesis 1." In *The Earth Story in Genesis*, edited by Norman Habel and Shirley Wurst, 25–37. Sheffield: Sheffield Academic, 2000.

Habel, Norman C., et al., eds. *The Season of Creation: A Preaching Commentary*. Minneapolis: Fortress, 2011.

Halteman, Matthew C. "Knowing the Standard American Diet by Its Fruits: Is Unrestrained Omnivorism Spiritually Beneficial?" *Interpretation* 67 (2013) 383–95.

Harrison, Jill Lindsey. *Pesticide Drift and the Pursuit of Environmental Justice*. Cambridge: MIT Press, 2011.

Hartman, Laura M. "Seeking Food Justice." *Interpretation* 67 (2013) 396–409.

Hollywood, Amy. "Preaching as Social Practice." In *Mysticism & Social Transformation*, edited by Janet K. Ruffing, 76–90. Syracuse, NY: Syracuse University Press, 2001.

Hudson, Thomas Samuel, and Elberta Pugh-Hudson. Interview by Rob Amberg and Charles Thompson. Southern Oral History Program Collection. White Stocking, NC, December 18, 1999. http://docsouth.unc.edu/sohp/K-0283/K-0283.html.

Hughes, Richard T. *Reviving the Ancient Faith: The Story of Churches of Christ in America*. Grand Rapids: Eerdmans, 1996.

Iyer, Pico. "Where Is Home?" TED Talk, 14:01. Edinburgh, Scotland, June 2013. http://www.ted.com/talks/pico_iyer_where_is_home.

Jacobs, Joseph. *Europa's Fairy Book*. New York: Knickerbocker, 1916.

Johnson, Glenn S. "Environmental Justice: A Brief History and Overview." In *Environmental Justice in the New Millennium: Global Perspectives on Race, Ethnicity, and Human Rights*, edited by Filomina Chioma Steady, 17–46. New York: Palgrave MacMillon, 2009.

Kelman, Ari. "Boundary Issues: Clarifying New Orleans's Murky Edges." *Journal of American History* 94 (2007) 695–703.

Knight, John. "On the Extinction of the Japanese Wolf." *Asian Folklore Studies* 56 (1997) 129–59.

Levinovitz, Alan. *The Gluten Lie: And Other Myths about What You Eat.* New York: Regan Arts, 2015.

Limburg, James. *Encountering Ecclesiastes: A Book for Our Time.* Grand Rapids: Eerdmans, 2006.

Linge, David E. "Mysticism, Poverty, and Reason in the Thought of Meister Eckhart." *Journal of the American Academy of Religion* 46 (1978) 465–88.

Lloyd, Michael. "Harry R. Truman, Folk Hero of Mount St. Helens." Video, 6:15. *Oregonian*, May 14, 2010. http://projects.oregonlive.com/photos/2010/05/14/harry-r-truman-folk-hero-of-mount-saint-helens-plus-photos-from-the-oregonians-archive.

Lockwood, Peter. "God's Speech from the Whirlwind: The Transformation of Job through the Renewal of His Mind (Job 38–42)." *Lutheran Theological Journal* 45 (2011) 167–82.

Lossky, Vladimir. *The Mystical Theology of the Eastern Church.* Crestwood, NY: St. Vladimir's Seminary Press, 1976.

Louth, Andrew. *The Origins of the Christian Mystical Tradition from Plato to Denys.* New York: Oxford University Press, 1981.

Mann, Charles. *1493: Uncovering the World Columbus Created.* New York: Knopf, 2011.

Maughm, Somerset. *Of Human Bondage.* New York: Sun Dial, 1915.

Maysilles, Duncan. *Ducktown Smoke: The Fight over One of the South's Greatest Environmental Disasters.* Chapel Hill, NC: University of North Carolina Press, 2011.

McCallum, Ewen, and Julian Heming. "Hurricane Katrina: An Environmental Perspective." *Philosophical Transactions: Mathematical, Physical and Engineering Sciences* 364 (2006) 2099–115.

McClure, Cynthia Rowland. *The Courage to Go On: Life after Addiction.* Grand Rapids: Baker, 1990.

McKenzie, Alyce. *Novel Preaching: Tips from Top Writers on Crafting Creative Sermons.* Louisville: Westminster John Knox, 2010.

Merton, Thomas. *New Seeds of Contemplation.* Norfolk, CT: New Directions, 2007.

Meyendorff, John. *A Study of Gregory Palamas.* Translated by George Lawrence. London: Faith, 1964.

Mockenhaupt, Brian. "Fire on the Mountain" *Atlantic*, June 2014.

Muir, John. *John Muir in His Own Words.* Edited by Peter Browning. Lafayette, CA: Great West, 1988.

Murphy, Roland. *Proverbs.* Word Biblical Commentary 22. Nashville: Nelson, 1998.

National Weather Service. "Hurricane Floyd, September 1999." Event Summary. http://www4.ncsu.edu/~nwsfo/storage/cases/19990915.

Nicholas Cabasilas. *Commentary on the Divine Liturgy.* Translated by J. M. Hussey and P. A. McNulty. London: Society for Promoting Christian Knowledge, 1966.

——. *Life in Christ.* Translated by Carmino J. deCatanzaro. Crestwood, NY: St. Vladimir's Seminary Press, 1974.

O'Connor, Siobhan. "The Gluten Wars." *Time*, June 2015.

Patton, Michael Quinn. *Qualitative Evaluation and Research Methods.* 2nd ed. London: Sage, 1990.

PBS. "The Big Burn." Documentary, 51:46. February 3, 2015.

Pelikan, Jaroslav. *The Spirit of Eastern Christendom (600 –1700)*. Chicago: University of Chicago Press, 1974.

Philipsen, Gerry. "Speaking 'Like a Man' in Teamsterville: Culture Patterns of Role Enactment in an Urban Neighborhood." *Quarterly Journal of Speech* 61 (1975) 13–22.

Pidcock-Lester, Karen. "Earth Has No Sorrow That Earth Cannot Heal: Job 38–41." In *God Who Creates: Essays in Honor of W. Sibley Towner*, edited by William P. Brown and S. Dean McBride Jr., 125–32. Grand Rapids: Eerdmans, 2000.

Pope, Marvin. *Job*. 3rd ed. Anchor Bible 15. Doubleday: New York, 1983.

Preston, Christopher J. *Saving Creation: Nature and Faith in the Life of Holmes Rolston III*. San Antonio: Trinity University Press, 2009.

Rolston, Holmes. "Caring for Nature: From Fact to Value, from Respect to Reverence." *Zygon* 39 (2004) 277–302.

———. "Kenosis and Nature." In *Work of Love*, edited by John Polkinghorne, 43–65. Grand Rapids: Eerdmans, 2001.

———. "Loving Nature: Past, Present, and Future." *Interpretation* 70 (2016) 34–47.

———. *A New Environmental Ethics: The Next Millennium for Life on Earth*. New York: Routledge, 2012.

Sanford, Whitney. "Ethics, Narrative and Agriculture: Transforming Agricultural Practice through Ecological Imagination." *Journal of Agricultural Environmental Ethics* 24 (2011) 283–303.

Seki, Keigo, ed. *Folktales of Japan*. Chicago: University of Chicago Press, 1936.

Sides, Hampton. *In the Kingdom of Ice: The Grand and Terrible Polar Voyage of the USS Jeannette*. New York: Doubleday, 2014.

Sinkewicz, Robert E. *Saint Gregory Palamas: The One Hundred and Fifty Chapters*. Toronto: Pontifical Institute of Mediaeval Studies, 1988.

Steinberg, Ted. *Acts of God: The Unnatural History of Natural Disaster in America*. 2nd ed. New York: Oxford University Press, 2006.

Stoll, Mark. *Protestantism, Capitalism, and Nature in America*. Albuquerque: University of New Mexico Press, 1997.

Taylor, Steven J., and Bogdan Robert. *Introduction to Qualitative Research Methods*. New York: Wiley-Interscience, 1984.

Thompson, Paul B. *The Agrarian Vision: Sustainability and Environmental Ethics*. Lexington: University Press of Kentucky, 2010.

Tobin, Frank. *Meister Eckhart: Thought and Language*. Philadelphia: University of Pennsylvania Press, 1986.

———. "Mysticism and Meister Eckhart." *Mystics Quarterly* 10 (1984) 17–24.

VanDrunen, David. "Wisdom and the Natural Moral Order: The Contribution of Proverbs to a Christian Theology of Natural Law." *Journal of the Society of Christian Ethics* 33 (2013) 153–68.

Wirzba, Norman. *Food and Faith: A Theology of Eating*. Cambridge: Cambridge University Press, 2011.

White, Lynn, Jr. "The Historical Roots of Our Ecological Crisis." *Science* 155 (1967) 1203–7.

Wright, N. T. *After You Believe: Why Christian Character Matters*. Kindle ed. New York: HarperCollins e-books, 2010.

Youngblood, Kevin J. "Cosmic Boundaries and Self-Control in Proverbs." *Restoration Quarterly* 51 (2009) 139–50.